YARON MATRAS

I Met Lucky People
The Story of the Romani Gypsies

PENGUIN BOOKS

PENGUIN BOOKS

UK | USA | Canada | Ireland | Australia
India | New Zealand | South Africa

Penguin Books is part of the Penguin Random House group of companies
whose addresses can be found at global.penguinrandomhouse.com.

First published by Allen Lane 2014
Published in Penguin Books 2015
001

Copyright © Yaron Matras, 2014

The moral right of the author has been asserted

Set in Sabon LT Std
Printed in Great Britain by Clays Ltd, St Ives plc

A CIP catalogue record for this book is available from the British Library

978-0-241-95470-6

www.greenpenguin.co.uk

MIX
Paper from
responsible sources
FSC® C018179

Penguin Random House is committed to a
sustainable future for our business, our readers
and our planet. This book is made from Forest
Stewardship Council® certified paper.

Contents

Who are the Romani People?

THE 'GYPSY' BRAND: MASKS AND MISREPRESENTATIONS

It's a bright, sunny day in San Francisco, and a cool breeze is blowing from the bay onto Fisherman's Wharf. The pier is busy, a bustling and buzzing tourist attraction, with its stalls of deep-fried seafood to the right and a line of shops selling bargain merchandise, from clothing to electronics and of course souvenirs, to the left. Three young girls, probably not older than fifteen or sixteen, are standing in the middle of the pavement. They wear their dark hair long and decorate it with a ribbon. They look slightly Hispanic, but they stand out because of their long skirts in bright colours – not the typical fashion you'd expect from Californian teenagers out to catch the vibe of the big city. As we approach, the girls turn their attention to us. In perfect American English – they're certainly not foreign – they offer to tell us our fortune. Their base is a small folding table they have erected on the pavement. It's a makeshift stall, covered by a big, light-blue cloth, and it can be folded and hidden away in a matter of seconds. Unaware that the potential customer whom they've approached is a linguistics professor who specializes in the Romani language, they exchange a few remarks between them in an idiom they know to be unintelligible to most outsiders. They are careful to downplay the casual switch of tongues, lowering their lips and turning their heads at an angle away from the tourists whose custom they are seeking. Nonetheless, their speech has given them away, if nothing else has. 'What language are you talking?' we ask just to get confirmation and steer the conversation away from the offer of divination. 'Greek,' they say. But they are not Greek. They are Romani, timid to admit their true identity. They know that the word 'Rom' or 'Romani', which they use to refer to their people in their own language, is meaningless to most outsiders. They could say that they are 'Gypsies', but that might scare the strangers away.

Across the Bay, at the University of California in Berkeley, I have just been attending a seminar at the Department of East European Studies. I leave the building accompanied by a colleague, a distinguished linguist who has spent years of her career exploring the dialects of small tribes in remote locations around the world. We head towards the bus stop on Shattuck Avenue. On the way, just around the corner from the university campus, I notice a sign in front of one of the shops. It carries the illustration of a hand, ornamented with stars and various other symbols. A woman in her fifties stands in the doorway, talking to a young girl who has positioned herself outside. From afar, their clothes, their overall appearance and their gestures remind me of the Romani people I know in central and southeastern Europe. They have long, dark hair, fastened with a ribbon behind their head. They are wearing long skirts, holding burning cigarettes in their fingers and gesticulating exuberantly. They notice my stare, and as we come closer my greeting in Romani no longer takes them completely by surprise. They are fluent in the language, throwing in the occasional English 'all right' only as they pause before articulating long sentences in their native tongue. Their men sell used cars, they say, while the women use the store premises to tell fortunes. Their families number several dozen in Berkeley alone. In reply to my question they state that their ancestors have been in the country for 'one hundred years', implying that there is no direct recollection in the family of immigrant grandparents. Generations born in the United States, and yet they remain unknown to their surroundings. Alongside the German-speaking Amish of Pennsylvania and the Yiddish-speaking Orthodox Jews of Brooklyn, they are among the few groups of Americans who have preserved their old language four or five generations after they made the journey across the ocean and began to call this country their home. My colleague admitted walking by this very shop on her way home every day over the past eighteen years, but to her all this was new and astonishing. An invisible minority in the middle of Berkeley.

A number of Californian cemeteries contain entire sections with plots owned by Romani Gypsies. The gravestones go back almost a century, sometimes more. They tell an historical narrative that the fortune-tellers pretending to be Greek are quite possibly not even aware of. The oldest names on the graves are often Serbian – Nikolić, Marković, Jovanović – but in the next generation, the same family plots already show the English versions of these names: Nicholas, Marks, Johns. Like others pursuing the American dream, they valued the appearance of blending into the melting pot. But they remained the people they had been for centuries, with their particular dress, their own language, intact family and clan structures, and a preference for a certain portfolio of trades, which, however exotic, caters to the demands of those around them.

The ancestors of these Romani people began arriving in America in the 1880s as part of a wave of eastern European immigrants. They joined the population of Romnichals – Romani families from England and Wales who had crossed the ocean already in the first decades of the nineteenth century. Some people estimate that the American Roms number around 200,000 today, perhaps even more. Their distinct sub-groups or 'nations' include the Romnichals, the Kelderasha, the Rusurya or 'Russians' and the Machwaya. The latter, quite possibly the largest Romani group in the western United States, derive their name from the region in which they lived just before leaving Europe – Mačva in Serbia. This explains the Serbian names on the gravestones. But the people are not Serbian, nor Greek. The Romani dialect they speak contains many Romanian and Hungarian words, and their customs are shared with Romani Gypsies who still live in Transylvania and with others who left that region in the middle of the nineteenth century. On the rare occasions when Romani Gypsies meet south Asians from India or Pakistan, they are astonished to discover that they can understand many of the words these people use in their own languages, such as Hindi, Urdu and Punjabi. There is thus a connection not just with eastern Europe – Romania and Hungary – but also with far-away India. A cosmopolitan identity, with a history of travels and a disguised appearance: who are the 'Gypsies'?

In Berkeley, you can buy clothes in a shop called Gypsy Streetwear and have your hair done at the Gypsy Rose Hair Salon. Back in San

Francisco you can pay a visit to Gypsy Jeans or, for more specific requirements, turn to Gypsy Rosalie's Wigs and Vintage. The artistic can explore Trailer Gypsy Crafts or Gypsy Moon Design. Places to eat out include Gastro Gypsy and to find your way you might draw on the services of Trippin' Gypsy Maps. Altogether there are over 350 outlets in the San Francisco Bay area that carry the word 'Gypsy' in their title. The great majority, if not indeed all, are not managed by Romani Gypsies nor do they cater specifically for Romani customers. They just exploit the image.

We have come to associate a range of attributes with the label 'Gypsy', which make it a puller-brand for fashion and design, exotic gourmet cuisine, exploration and adventure, music and dance, passion and soul-searching, and the Bay area is not the only region to embrace these images. But given its history, it is almost predestined to do so. An assembly point for immigrants, a cradle of jazz, the bastion of the hippie movement and a hub for software developers, it is constantly on the look out for the unusual, the passionate, the creative, the liberating, the spicy and often norm-breaking and defiant aspects of life. When popular music started to promote values of peace, love, fraternity and liberation in the 1960s and early 70s, numerous artists adopted the image of 'Gypsies' into their songs. Cher's track 'Gypsies, Tramps and Thieves' is one of the most famous. It tells the story of a young girl born on the road, whose parents make a living through healing and dancing. A video clip featuring the track, first broadcast on *The Sonny & Cher Comedy Hour* in 1971, depicts the singer against the background of a wooden caravan and a tall campfire on a starlit night. The performance captures the romance of travelling and outdoor life, but also the complexity of relations with outsiders, who are curious and turn to the Gypsies for inspiration and comfort, but are at the same time suspicious and hostile towards them. Joan Baez writes and sings about 'A Young Gypsy' (1973), hinting at the upbringing of Romani infants, which is portrayed as being free of restrictions on adventurous outdoor activities and lenient on participation in adult celebrations. Jimi Hendrix sings of travelling, outdoor life by the open fire and a rebellious soul in 'Gypsy Eyes' (1968), and Carlos Santana hardly leaves out a cliché when he describes the caravan, the dance, the magic, the passion and seductiveness of the 'Gypsy Queen' (1970).

Other artists and bands who have recorded tracks on 'Gypsies' include Duke Ellington, Tina Turner, the Grateful Dead, Lynyrd Skynyrd, Elton John, Deep Purple, Black Sabbath, the Moody Blues and Fleetwood Mac – in fact, the University of Toledo's Library Exhibits Catalogue lists over 160 song titles, released between 1928 and 2004, which depict 'Gypsies'. They include such tracks as 'Gypsy Princess' and 'Gypsy Queen'; 'Gypsy Soul' and 'Gypsy Feet'; 'Gypsy Fiddle', 'Gypsy Forest', 'Gypsy Lullaby' and countless more.

Most Americans, as well as the majority of people in many European countries, know more about Gypsies from such portrayal in songs, stories and films than from real-life encounters. So entrenched is our fictional image of Gypsies that we often brush aside real-world experiences as a mirage when they contradict the picture that we have absorbed and internalized. When I was a student at a university in northern Germany in the early 1990s, I had a part-time job as media relations officer with a Romani civil rights organization. I had met the president of this society at a public event and was impressed by his speech. Curious about his group's work, I visited their office on a couple of occasions and heard about their campaign to prevent the expulsion of Romani refugees who had arrived from eastern Europe. I wrote up my impressions in a local political magazine and was then invited by the president to work with him on a regular basis.

Several months into the job I received a phone call from a journalist working for the regional broadcasting station Radio Bremen. He told me about an experiment he had conducted. It was the summer of 1990 and the aftermath of the democratic revolutions that had over-thrown the communist regimes in central and eastern Europe. The borders were now open and several thousand Romani Gypsies left their countries of residence, many of them trying to escape the rise in racist violence against their ethnic minority and growing discrimination in the competitive labour market of the new post-communist economy. Most applied for political asylum in order to obtain an entry permit to Germany. Some made a living by playing music on street corners, others by begging. The local press in Hamburg, the largest metropolitan area in northern Germany, reported an old 'remedy against Gypsies' that was adopted by shopkeepers in the surrounding small towns: they placed brooms outside their shopfronts, assuring customers and onlookers that these would scare away the Gypsies. The reporter from Radio Bremen decided to test the effectiveness of the remedy. He set off to a municipal residence that was occupied largely by Romani asylum seekers. When they came out to greet him, he showed them a broom he had brought along with him. To his surprise, the Gypsies didn't run away in fear, but enquired instead whether he was there to offer them a cleaning job. Why, the puzzled journalist asked me, as an expert, did the Gypsies not behave in the way he had expected them to?

My boss at that time, the president of the Romani association, told of an experience that shows another way in which popular images of Gypsies colour our ability to digest facts and reality. As a political activist working to raise public sensitivity towards his people and their needs and interests he spent many years lecturing to various audiences about the life, culture, history and aspirations of the Romani nation. He always went to great lengths to describe the discrimination his people had faced through the ages, the suspicion they encountered, the persecution they suffered under various regimes from medieval times to the Second World War and the prohibitions and exclusions placed on them under communism and even in some western democracies. His narrative often startled and moved his audiences and left them ashamed of society's present and historical misdeeds. At times he was challenged to respond to allegations of Gypsy criminality, of his people's reluctance to send their children to school or of their lack of respect towards the norms and rules imposed by state authorities and institutions. His answers invariably showed both patience and eloquence. But on one occasion he was lost for words. 'If it's all as bad as you describe,' asked an inconspicuous young man at the end of one of the lectures, 'then why did you choose to become a Gypsy?' His image of Gypsies had marked them as a mere lifestyle, a fashion, a brand.

In San Francisco, the 'Gypsy' brand stands for bondless individuality and excitement. But the hippie fascination with Gypsies has its roots in the Old World. European society has been cultivating a fantasy image of Gypsies since the Middle Ages. When they began to disperse across the European continent in the late fourteenth century, the Romani people impressed settled populations with their alien appearance. They stood out through the fact that they lacked the day-to-day obligations and constraints perceived by the majority as essential components of 'work', 'discipline' and 'morality'. Yet at the same time they appeared to possess their own code of loyalty and honour, their own aesthetics such as open displays of colour and jewellery, and a passion for music, song and dance. They had an unintelligible speech that was perceived as secretive. They showed a tight-knit manner of achieving goals in a collective, which appeared to outsiders as a propensity to conspiracy, and a seemingly shameless admission to be needy and dependent on aid but also to possess supernatural, magical powers. These depictions have become fixed in a tradition of literature, theatre, poems, art and journalism as well as in social and political treatises of European societies, and have made their way from there to the New World. There is, quite possibly, no bigger paradox in our contemporary multi-ethnic societies than the fact that Gypsies are so close and so present, yet so little is known about them that fiction tends to override fact and fantasy often takes precedence over common sense.

OF GYPSIES, REAL AND IMAGINED

My first encounter with attitudes towards Gypsies in England was during a two-week holiday in the early 1990s. I was travelling on a rural road in Devon, where I hitched a ride with a young woman and her son of around ten years of age. We talked about the landscape, about the villages, the cattle markets and the tourists. I expressed an interest in whether there were any Gypsies in the region. There were some indeed, the woman said, though they usually came and went. One Gypsy boy had been her son's classmate. 'Do you remember how he used to steal your things?' she said, glancing through the driver's mirror at the boy who was sitting behind her; though she was quick to add: 'But real Gypsies are Romanies; they don't steal!' This left me puzzled. She seemed to draw a distinction between 'real Gypsies' and 'other Gypsies'. In what way were the Romanies more genuine than the 'others'? Apparently, she was keen to defend the Romanies against a negative image. Yet she herself seemed to entertain a negative image of 'other Gypsies'.

The intricate web of labels and attitudes followed me several days later, when, visiting East London, I walked past a pub that carried a sign on its door saying 'No Travellers'. I mentioned this to an acquaintance, an activist who was a member of one of the British Romani associations. Why didn't his organization challenge such signs, so obviously discriminatory? It had tried many times to get the authorities and the courts to ban them, he replied. But in Britain, recognition as an ethnic group was afforded only to 'Romani' people. If a sign said 'No Romanies', then a case of racial discrimination could be made against the owners. But 'Travellers', though considered by most people to be synonymous with 'Gypsies' and hence with 'Romanies', was not recognized as an ethnic label. Excluding 'Travellers' would therefore not be regarded as discrimination in the legal sense. Of course everyone knew and understood that the sign targeted Romani Gypsies. But the law accepted only Romanies as a genuine heritage group, and that is perhaps what the lady in Devon meant by 'real Gypsies'. The term 'Travellers' was ambiguous: it avoided singling out a group that enjoyed legal recognition as an ethnic minority and referred instead supposedly to a lifestyle, which everyone in Britain associated with that particular minority. This gave the pub owners discretion to turn away people who, based on their appearance, were assumed to be Romani Gypsies.

In the autumn of 1997, British media reported extensively about a group of Romani families from the Czech and Slovak Republics who had arrived in the English port city of Dover and applied for refugee status, claiming that they were suffering discrimination in their home countries because of their ethnic background, and that the authorities there were unable or unwilling to offer them protection. The media seemed to treat their arrival as a major invasion. The Minister for Immigration gave interviews in which he promised to put a stop to the influx of these people, whose claims, according to him, were 'unfounded'. It struck me as rather exceptional that the minister was pre-empting the legal procedure; there hadn't been time for the authorities to process the claims and to establish whether or not they were justified, yet at the political level there appeared to be an urge to deny their legitimacy. In the months and years that followed, the British government had agents posted at Prague airport, screening passengers whose destination was the UK and picking out those with a Romani appearance.

Once again I found myself asking how this could be reconciled with anti-discrimination laws. It was true that these Romani people were Czech and Slovak citizens and therefore not subject to UK laws or the protection they offered against racial discrimination. But other Czechs and Slovaks, those with a European appearance, were allowed to travel to Britain unhindered. Here were people leaving the countries in which their families had lived for centuries because they did not feel safe. They were heading for the UK, where they thought that safety was guaranteed. Yet discrimination caught up with them even before they managed to board the plane to reach their destination. In defence of these measures, politicians said they had to prevent the realistic threat of a tidal wave of Romani immigrants who, they claimed, if given the opportunity, would swamp the UK. In fact, just a few years later, in 2004, the Czech and Slovak Republics joined the EU. Their citizens, including the Roms, have since enjoyed freedom of travel and freedom to relocate within the EU, including to the UK. Some came to live in Britain, but there was no mass immigration and no tidal wave. Media and politicians alike had engaged in pure scaremongering.

The reality of Romani fears and insecurity caught up with me once again on one of my first visits to a caravan site occupied by Romani Gypsies in the north of England. 'When my children misbehave,' said the father of a family, 'I say to them: "Stop that, because if they see you behave like that they might deport us!"' We sat in silence for a moment, and then he added, 'But they can't deport us, we are British citizens!' Centuries in this country, yet the fear of being seen and treated as outsiders still prevailed. His family had lived in Britain longer than the family of the then serving foreign secretary and longer than the managers of many of the largest banks in London's City. Yet he was raising his children to fear deportation by their own govern-ment to some unknown destination. I thought about how this fear was likely to stay with his children until their adolescence or even beyond, to be passed on to the next generation when they raise their own children.

In the northwest of England, the A66 passes through Appleby in Cumbria. Once a year, a fair is held in the town and the surrounding hills. It's called the Appleby Horse Fair and it is widely celebrated in the area. In the days leading to the fair, in early June, road signs on the M6 motorway heading in the direction of Appleby warn motorists to look out for horse-drawn wagons. Thousands of Romani Gypsies and Irish Travellers attend the event. For five or six days their caravans fill the green fields that overlook the town and traditional horse-drawn wagons race through its main street, under the railway bridge and down towards the river, where the horses are allowed to bath to the cheers of the crowds and under the supervising eye of uniformed officers from the Royal Society for the Prevention of Cruelty to Animals. The locals sell lemonade along the road and charge visitors a hefty fee to park their cars for a few hours on one of the nearby meadows. Tourists stroll among the market stalls and have their fortunes told behind one of the signs that advertises the services of an accredited 'real Romani Gypsy' clairvoyant.

The road to Appleby and the small towns and villages nearby are generally known as the 'Gypsy Trail'. Local bookshops tend to have a whole shelf devoted to picture books and adventure stories that feature Gypsies. Quite tellingly, the 'Gypsies' bookshelf is usually accommodated either in the section on 'Landscape and the Countryside', or sometimes even under 'Nature', side by side with books about the region's flora and wildlife. In the English countryside, Gypsies are considered to be part of the natural landscape, to be enjoyed and admired for their colourful liveliness and their predictable, cyclical behaviour.

Like that of Appleby, the annual Gypsy Horse Fair in the town of Stow in the Cotswolds has a long tradition, one that goes back to the fifteenth century. Walking among some 10,000 regular visitors, almost all of them British, you cannot escape the impression of being surrounded by a very different culture. The gesticulation, the accents, the fashions and the bartering at the many stalls are all very different from the everyday scene at an English country market. Towards the end of the one-day event, young girls and boys gather in segregated groups to face one another in the town square. To the outsider it seems an almost primordial form of courtship. But the group offers protection and at the same time encourages its members to set aside their inhibitions and make the most of the little time that remains before sunset to fix their eye on a potential partner whom they can look forward to meeting again when the families set their caravans in motion in a few months' time and head for the next scheduled gathering, somewhere in the English countryside. For 500 years Romani Gypsies have been taking their business to Stow, regulated by a Royal Charter. Yet the local shopkeepers are reluctant to join the celebration. With the exception of a single family-run café facing the fairgrounds, whose owner announces proudly that she adores her Romani customers, all the shops appear abandoned on the weekday on which the fair is held, carrying a uniform sign: 'Closed for renovation; open again tomorrow'. After 500 years, they still fear the Gypsies.

My first visit to a Romani caravan site in the north of England was at the invitation of a man who had phoned and asked for advice on learning the Romani language. His relatives used it, but only in isolated phrases, he said. Having become aware of the language spoken by Romani immigrants from eastern Europe and the similarities it had with his own family vocabulary, he was keen to explore it further. I suggested books; and perhaps I could help organize a summer school. 'But our people don't read,' he said. Here was a middle-aged man in twenty-first-century Britain who admitted that he and his community peers were factually illiterate. We decided to meet to discuss putting together a teach-yourself audio CD for Romani. I invited two of my students along, and we drove north.

We had been told the caravan site was hidden away from the road, on the outskirts of a small town, and we later learned that this is typical of all Romani sites. They are invisible to outsiders, much like the internal world of the Romani people who reside in them. We agreed to meet at the entrance of a nearby stadium, where our host would be waiting in his car to lead us to the site. But there was a very long line of cars in front of the stadium when we arrived, many of them with lone drivers waiting, apparently, to pick up friends or family, and we had no description of our host's vehicle. How would we recognize him? As we crawled slowly along I examined the drivers one by one, and my eye finally caught somebody who resembled a person I knew. Was it one of the members of a Polish Romani family I had befriended some years ago, or did he just look like one of the Romani men I had met in Germany? There was no doubt that this person, a total stranger, had a 'Romani appearance'. And indeed, he was our man. But what is a 'Romani appearance'? There was no recognizable dress fashion, no distinctive jewellery or hairstyle, and yet there was something very familiar. I have heard people deny that there is such a thing as a 'Romani look'. These are usually people who feel offended when others make sweeping generalizations about other nations. Surely they have a point. But those of us who have spent much time with the Roms know that we often, even if not always, recognize them even before we hear their Romani speech or learn about their family affiliation. And of course the Roms can pick out one another in a crowd, too.

Family members surrounded us when we arrived at the site and I was in for a surprise. Romani women in the communities I was familiar with always wore long skirts, so I had asked my two female students to do the same as a sign of respect for Romani traditions. Their fellow students usually wore jeans to university, and on an evening out in the city centre you would see them in very short skirts, so the two young women looked quite odd in the long skirts. But they had made the effort so as not to offend our hosts. Yet at the caravan site almost all the women were dressed in shorts or tight trousers. This was a very different kind of Romani community. Their home was a caravan. Some of the families occasionally pitched a specially decorated caravan at fairs, and the women used it as a shop to tell fortunes. The Romani people I knew from central and eastern Europe spoke Romani, but lived in houses. The women wore traditional long skirts and headscarves, but they never engaged in fortune-telling. Here in the northern English countryside, the Romani Gypsies lived and travelled in caravans, but spoke their very own form of accented rural English with just the odd Romani word here and there. The women on the site wore shorts and trousers, but made a living telling fortunes. Which group was the Gypsy stereotype based on? Which group could best match the romantic image of old traditions kept intact?

ALL IN A NAME: THE SOURCES OF A LANGUAGE AND PEOPLE

Words have special powers when we use them as labels. They help us divide the world into categories. This gives us the comforting feeling that we can map, index and understand the complex reality that surrounds us. But when it comes to Gypsies, the labels seem to play tricks and the mapping exercise yields a kaleidoscope rather than a smooth pattern. My friends at the caravan site and their people who frequent the annual horse fairs use the term 'Romani Gypsies' to capture their separate heritage. Their government recognizes them as 'Romanies', yet in popular perception they are 'Travellers' because they live in caravans. They feel attached to a language that they know their ancestors spoke and of which they can recall only several dozen words, and they feel attached to the people who enter their country as immigrants from eastern Europe speaking that same Romani language, in which they refer to themselves as 'Rom'.

In order to understand the Romani people we must first sort out the labels. The terms 'Rom' and 'Gypsy' are a key to a long story of conflicting images and representations. 'Rom' stands for the insider perspective. Until recently, few outsiders were even aware of the existence of this name as the self-designation of a people. Today it is broadcast more publicly and we have come to associate it with something 'genuine', 'recognized' or 'politically correct'. It is even used by the Romani fortune-tellers at Appleby market and elsewhere to brand their market stalls as 'authentic'. The label 'Gypsy', by contrast, stands for the outsider perspective. It represents an image that is not always coherent with reality but which fuels our imagination. In this way it helps brand our own passions as exotic and spicy. It is often so remote from reality that many Roms despise it and refuse to be associated with it. Yet some, such as my friends at the English caravan site and the folk at Appleby fair, have embraced it and see no contradiction at all in calling themselves 'Romani Gypsies'. Both labels have a history and a story to tell. Understanding the labels is a key towards understanding who the Romani people are, and how we as outsiders perceive them.

The girl fortune-tellers I met in San Francisco, their ancestors who immigrated from Serbia, the president of the association in Hamburg and the refugees from Romania who were interested in a cleaning job – they all belong to a people who speak a language that they call Romanes. In that language, they call themselves Rom or Roma. They describe objects and practices that are typical of their own culture and society as *romano* or *romani*, and in some communities they refer to their distinctive set of values and practices as *Romanipe* or *Romania*. For many centuries, outsiders who were not part of the Romani community had little or no knowledge at all about the Roms. Even the name that they use to refer to their people remained unknown except to a small number of individuals, among them academic researchers and Christian missionaries who showed a particular curiosity towards Romani language and culture. In recent decades Romani activists and intellectuals have launched organized efforts to explain more about themselves and their community to the outside world, and many outsiders have begun to take a more intense interest in them. The term Rom or Roma now surfaces in media reports, in government documents and in scholarly references – a token of an emerging public appreciation that this minority, just like other ethnicities and interest groups, deserves to be known by its own self-appellation.

So why do we call these people 'Gypsies', and where do our images of Gypsies and the Gypsy brand come from? One of the key features that defines Romani identity and culture is the Romani language. Dispersed among many countries and living in tight-knit and closed communities, different Romani groups speak different forms of the Romani language. They have different accents, they sometimes use different words, and they very often blend into their own language expressions and phrases from the various languages spoken around them by their non-Romani neighbours. But on the whole, these dialects of Romani are closely related and most Roms can understand one another when talking in their native tongue.

Romani is a language of Indian origin. It remains closely related to the languages of India, as a comparison of basic vocabulary can easily demonstrate: Romani words such as *pani* 'water', *sap* 'snake', *kan* 'ear', *pandž* 'five', *rat* 'night', *mačho* 'fish' and countless others are practically identical to the corresponding words in Hindi, Punjabi, Gujarati and other languages of India. Linguists have also been able to analyse the grammatical structures of Romani and point out the way in which they derive directly from the grammar of older languages of medieval India. Languages rarely travel from one continent to another without a migration of people. It is inconceivable that a European population simply took up the study of an Indian language in late medieval times and adopted it as its everyday domestic speech form. Nor is there a historical record of an Indian invasion that would have forced some Europeans to take on a foreign tongue. The Romani people speak a language that is related to those of India because their ancestors emigrated from India to Europe in the Middle Ages and because they maintained their separate identity as a group, with language figuring as a central component of their distinct culture.

The self-appellation Rom resembles 'Romania', a country that has a sizeable Romani minority. But this similarity is coincidental. There is also no connection with Rum – the Ottoman designation for Byzantium or western Anatolia and its capital Constantinople. Like the language, the name Rom is of Indian derivation. It goes back to the name of a social caste called Dom. Members of this caste are found in various regions of India and they speak different Indian languages. Their common characteristic throughout history was their specialization in certain trades, mainly services such as tool-making, cleaning and seasonal agricultural labour. The status of the Dom and their occupational profile were tightly regulated by the Indian social caste system. They did not own land and they frequently migrated from one area to another in search of employment opportunities. The emigration of various groups of Dom from India is well attested, and groups carrying similar names, speaking Indian languages and specializing in a similar set of trades can be found as far north as central Asia and as far west as the Middle East and the Caucasus. Their group names reflect their origin: Dom, Dum, Dom and Lom. It is the same word from which Rom derives.

Alongside the Indian core of the Romani language there is a strong component from Greek, which testifies to a prolonged period of coexistence with Greeks, over many generations. Linguistic analyses give us some insights, although it is not possible to establish the precise dates or the precise length or intensity of contact with Greeks. Languages often borrow words from other languages for new concepts or objects – such as 'philosophy', 'coffee' or 'banana'. But words that have basic, everyday meanings are borrowed much more rarely and usually only in situations where the entire population is bilingual. Romani has Greek terms for concepts such as 'tomorrow', 'again', 'backwards', as well as 'flower', 'road', 'grandfather' and 'bone', and for the numerals 'seven', 'eight' and 'nine' among many more. These and other Greek words are found in almost all Romani dialects regardless of the country in which they are now spoken. This gives us an indication that the Romani language was more or less uniform during the period in which it was spoken in proximity to Greek, in all likelihood during the Byzantine era, roughly between the tenth and fourteenth centuries. It is likely that the Roms formed a single minority population whose various communities interacted with one another frequently and intensively. Had this not been the case, it is likely that the Greek language would have left different traces in the speech of each and every Romani community. We can therefore conclude two things. First, the Roms spent a prolonged period of many generations in the Byzantine Empire, during which they had a stable relationship with the majority, Greek-speaking population and were integrated to such a degree that they were all or mostly bilingual in Romani and Greek. Second, the Roms formed a tightly consolidated community within Byzantium, despite being geographically dispersed and in all likelihood split into family clans.

In Byzantium, and later throughout the Balkans and southeastern Europe, the Roms were perceived as an immigrant race from overseas. With no indication of any collective awareness of their own Indian origin, nor any historical record of their immigration route, they were associated with the non-European civilization that was at the time most famous and most mystical – that of Egypt. The earliest known records of the Roms, from the thirteenth-century Byzantine capital Constantinople, refer to them as 'Egyptians'. In Greek they are still known as Yifti, derived from the medieval Greek word *Ægypti* 'Egyptians'. Fourteenth-century sources from Bulgaria refer to them as Agoupti or Gupti, and Ottoman Turkish sources from the sixteenth century onwards name them consistently Kibti, also meaning 'Egyptians'. The term made its way into western Europe, accompanying the migration of the Roms to these parts. Safe-conduct letters carried by travelling Romani clans in fifteenth-century Transylvania, Germany, the Netherlands, Italy, Spain and later Denmark identify them as originating in a mysterious region called 'Little Egypt'. In an almost literary improvisation on the same concept, some chroniclers of the time call them Pharaoneans. Spanish, Hungarian and English edicts from the sixteenth century continue to refer to them as 'Egyptians', the term eventually taking on shortened versions such as the English Gypsy and the Spanish *Gitano*.

A separate name, *Tsigan* or *Cigan*, began to appear in the Balkans in the fourteenth century. It accompanied the description of the same people labelled elsewhere as 'Egyptians': family clans travelling in groups of typically around one hundred persons, who are described as dark-skinned, with foreign appearance, colourful clothing, and having artistic skills and crafts. Although individuals belonging to these groups, usually their leaders or spokesmen, were sometimes referred to by their first names, the self-appellation Rom is practically never cited and it appears that chroniclers of the time were entirely unaware of it. Beginning in the fifteenth century we find texts – from Germany, Spain, England and Turkey – that not only describe the people but also include sample phrases in their language. They provide us with unambiguous proof that the people referred to as 'Egyptians' or 'Tsigan/Cigan' were indeed the Roms.

The term Tsigan took on a variety of forms in different languages: Greek, Latin, Turkish, Italian, Russian and German all have labels for Gypsies that are based on this word. We know that the term was often interchangeable with 'Egyptians'. The two appellations appear in connection with descriptions matching the same people, and in some documents both names are actually used together. An order issued by King Vladislav II of Hungary in 1500 refers in Latin to *Egiptii seu Cigani* meaning 'Egyptians or Cigans'. A late medieval edict in Italy, the declaration of the Synod of the Diocese of Syracuse from 1651, refers to 'Aegyptians, who are known in the vulgar language as Zingari'.

A tradition has established itself in texts about the early history of the Roms, which associates them with a religious sect, the Melchisedechians of the province of Phrygia in western Anatolia. These are referred to in Medieval Greek sources as *Athingani* (*Athinganoi* in the Greek spelling), meaning 'Untouchables'. The basis for the association of this group with the Gypsies is the superficial sound resemblance between the Greek appellation and the word Tsingan or Cigan, especially its Latin form *Acingani*. The other link, supposedly, between the two groups is their social image. The term 'Untouchables' suggests that the Melchisedechians were social outcasts and that their status therefore resembled that of the lower-status castes in India. In fact, the Melchisedechians were assigned this name because of their religious practices, which forbade them to touch other human beings who were not part of their group. The likely historical link with the Indian Ḍom suggests that the ancestors of the Roms may have belonged to the untouchable sects before leaving India. But we know next to nothing about the scale of the Roms' actual integration and social participation in Anatolia and the Greek provinces during the Byzantine period. There is therefore no historical evidence at all for any connection between the Roms of the Byzantine Empire and the sect of the Melchisedechians or Athinganoi. In fact, a letter written by the Patriarch of Constantinople, Gregorios II Kyprios, who reigned between 1283 and 1289, mentions taxes that are to be levied on the 'Athinganoi *and* Egyptians', implying that they were two separate populations.

The sound similarity between the two names, Athingani and Acingani or Tsingani, is in all likelihood coincidental. In fact, it is likely that the label Tsingani had its origins not in Greek, but in the Turkish word *Çingene*. There are many Turkish words in the Greek language. Those that begin with the sound *ç* in Turkish often start in Greek with *ts*: Greek words such as *tsai* 'tea' and *tsanta* 'handbag' have the Turkish equivalents *çay* and *çanta*. The Greek word Tsingan for 'Gypsy' could easily derive from the Turkish Çingene following exactly the same pattern.

While the origin of the Turkish appellation Çingene remains unknown, there is indirect evidence that the Roms had contacts with the Turks long before they arrived in Byzantium. In the Balkans, the

Romani word for 'Turkey' is *Koraxaj* (pronounced 'ko-ra-hay'), which appears to derive from the name of the Karakhanid Turkish dynasty that ruled parts of central Asia during the tenth and eleventh centuries. Many historians speculate that it was the establishment of Seljuk Turkish reign in Anatolia in the tenth century that brought the ancestors of the Roms and of other populations of Indian origin to the region, as artisans, craftsmen and providers of various support services to the Turkish armies. The circumstances under which the Roms separated from the Turkish legions and settled in Greek-speaking Byzantine society remain unknown, but the linguistic evidence suggests that immersion with the Greeks was much more prolonged and intensive than the earlier contacts with the Turks: there are hardly any Turkish words in the Romani dialects spoken outside the Balkans, but the Greek influence, as described above, is prevalent. Nevertheless, it appears to have been the Turks who first introduced the appellation Çingene to the region.

The word then made its way across the various tongues of the peoples of Byzantium and neighbouring territories. Among some populations, the meaning of the label was modified and it acquired some very particular negative connotations. In Romanian, the word became synonymous with 'slave' because the first Roms who arrived in the Romanian principalities Wallachia and Moldavia were slaves brought from the Bulgarian territories south of the Danube in the fourteenth century. In eighteenth-century Germany, law-enforcement agencies took an intense interest in monitoring and controlling the movements of various nomadic groups. The German term *Zigeuner* became a generic designation for travellers and vagabonds of various origins, ethnicities and cultures. It continues to evoke associations of lawlessness and wandering in the language today and is therefore avoided by most Roms in public references to their community. In sixteenth-century England and Spain, laws were passed threatening to punish people 'associating with Egyptians', indicating a perception that Roms were attracting followers among the local population. In England today, the popular notion 'Gypsies and Travellers' or 'Traveller Gypsies' groups together different communities in a single category.

A confusion of terms has thus arisen in almost all European languages. On the one hand, 'Gypsy' refers to a very specific population

– the people who call themselves, in their own language, Rom, and who were referred to as 'Egyptians' in earlier documents. On the other, 'Gypsy' (and its various equivalent terms in other languages) is taken as a way of describing certain social characteristics that were associated with the Roms, but also with other populations: slaves, foreigners, and especially travellers and migrant nomads.

POLITICS AND POLITICAL CORRECTNESS

This latter image of Gypsies as a chosen lifestyle, as a social rather than an ethnic attribute, has become so entrenched that some regard the introduction of the label 'Rom' not as a way of referring more accurately to the Romani people, but as a mere politically correct reformulation of the popular concept of Gypsy. As a result, we find an array of contradictory labels and definitions employed in the media and popular speech, as well as in legal documents and political resolutions. In 2004, the European Commission's Directorate-General for Employment and Social Affairs issued a report on 'The Situation of Roma in an Enlarged European Union'. In the preamble, the authors explain the terminology they use to refer to the Romani population:

> At a number of points in this study, the term 'Roma' or 'Romani' is used as shorthand for the broad umbrella of groups and individuals. In no way should this choice of terminology be taken as an endorsement of approaches aimed at homogenising Roma and other groups perceived as 'Gypsies' in Europe or at eliminating the rich diversity among Roma, Gypsies, Travellers and other groups perceived as 'Gypsies'.

The Commission is almost apologetic about choosing to use the term – 'Rom' or 'Roma' – that they themselves employ to refer to their own people in their own language. It takes the trouble to emphasize that in fact, it is not limiting its comments to the Romani people, but extending them to a variety of other populations, which are known to most Europeans under a collective but rather vague term – 'Gypsy'. Since the fall of communism, European institutions have taken an intensified interest in the situation of the Romani minority, especially in the countries of central and eastern Europe. But ambiguity in the reference to Roms is common in European reports and resolutions of this kind. In April 2011, the Council of the European Union issued a communication entitled 'An EU Framework for National Roma Integration Strategies up to 2020'. Its goal is to set out policies for the social inclusion of the Romani minority. This document, too, contains a clarification of terminology:

> The term 'Roma' is used – similarly to other political documents of the European Parliament and the European Council – as an umbrella which includes groups of people who have more or less similar cultural characteristics, such as Sinti, Travellers, Kalé, Gens du voyage, etc. whether sedentary or not; around 80% of Roma are estimated to be sedentary.

Note the contradiction: on the one hand, the Council uses the term 'Roma' as a wholesale designation for different populations who supposedly have a similar 'culture'; it does not specify what these similarities are, but at least two of the sub-groups named, the 'Travellers' and the *Gens du voyage* or 'Travelling people', are characterized by a nomadic lifestyle, and one can infer that it is this kind of lifestyle that the Council suggests is shared by the various groups belonging to the umbrella 'Roma'. Yet in the very same statement we are informed that 80 per cent of Roma are not nomadic at all, but sedentary. So what *are* the cultural characteristics that are shared by these different groups? The Council of Europe's Commissioner for Human Rights sheds some light on the issue of terminology in a statement on 'Human Rights of Roma and Travellers in Europe' from February 2012:

> The minorities labelled 'Roma', 'Gypsies' and 'Travellers' in fact comprise a multitude of ethnicities and distinct linguistic communities, heterogeneous groups that are viewed as a unit primarily by outsiders.

Here, a distinction is suggested between the outsider perspective, which groups different ethnicities together, and the insider perspective of the populations themselves. 'Gypsy' is a concept that has been created and shaped by outsiders. Although the statement suggests that it is synonymous with Roma, in fact the two designations do not always overlap. As we saw before, Roma is the self-appellation of a population whose ancestors immigrated to Europe from India, speakers of a language that they call Romanes (Romani). While some Roms travel, the majority, as the Council of the European Union correctly points out, are sedentary. They are found in dispersed communities all across Europe and in the Americas.

The identity of the Roms as a people is difficult to conceptualize if one's understanding of nationhood is bound to territory, national sovereignty and formal institutions. We tend to think of a nation as having a land, a state, an official language and a recorded history. Regional minorities, too, have an area – a district or a province that they can call their own, and perhaps also some form of self-government. Both nations and regional minorities have at their core a population that has maintained its base in a particular territory for generations and centuries. Most modern nations have recently developed, or are in the process of developing, from a largely agricultural society where work was based in the home, to an industrialized and increasingly urban society in which people rely on training and employment outside the home.

The Roms present us with a paradigmatic dilemma. They have no fixed territory but are dispersed. They have no tradition of agriculture or ownership of land, and even in urban settings their choice of occupation tends to be distinct from that of the majority. Rather than having a territorial base or allegiance towards the symbols and institutions of a particular state, what defines Romani identity is a distinct language, a set of values and beliefs, a form of family organization and a particular outlook on the relations between their own community and the outside world. In this view of the world, outsiders, whom the Roms usually call *Gadje*, are a source of income and are in control of resources and the overall organization of society. The daily challenge facing the Roms, at least in historical perspective, is how to maintain contacts with outsiders in a way that would allow the Roms to make a living, for example by carrying out skilled services that are of use to the Gadje, while at the same time protecting their own community, family structures and spiritual values.

The Roms are not the only population that defines itself primarily through kin structures, strict community values and a niche service economy that resists assimilation into the majority culture. Populations such as the Irish and Scottish Travellers, the Gens du voyage of France, the *Jenische* (*Yenish* or *Yeniche*) of Germany and Switzerland and the Italian *Camminanti* 'Travellers' all have a history of specialization in service trades organized in a family-based economy, and their loyalty to their kin group is the strongest aspect of their social organization as a community. It is this surface resemblance between the Roms and a number of other populations that is behind the wholesale categorization as Gypsies that appears in some of the political reports and resolutions. The Roms are of course conscious of these similarities, and throughout history there have been bonds between Romani families and groups of indigenous Travellers in various countries. Yet the Roms are also very much aware that their culture is distinct from that of travelling populations, and they will seldom subscribe to the view that all Travellers constitute a single nation or that the Roms form part of a nation of Travellers.

The confusion of terms and concepts arises partly due to the fact that many observers who lack close familiarity with the cultures of the groups concerned are aware of the fact that the Roms themselves are geographically dispersed and divided into different populations whose customs, habits and dialects may differ from one another. This internal diversity among the Roms is sometimes regarded on a par with the multiplicity of populations who constitute distinct ethnic minorities but lack a territory or region of their own, and who tend to specialize in service economies. It is this notion that is behind the thinking that 'Roma' as a cover term is equal to 'Gypsies'. If one takes Gypsies to be an umbrella for different ethnicities with different languages and different origins, then not all Gypsies are Romani Gypsies. As is the case with any other nation, cultural practices among the Roms are diverse and pluralistic. But there are characteristics that define them as distinct from other nations, in particular their language, their origins, many of their customs and traditions, and in recent years also their political aspirations.

Throughout history, majority society has projected onto the Roms an image that tends to be based on the negation of the way it understands itself. Because the Roms have no country, they are seen as rootless. Because they are not employed by others, they are regarded as work-shy. Because the laws are hostile to them and they in turn often refuse to bow to them, they are viewed not only as free but also as lawless. When majority society feels imprisoned by its own sexual morals and the restrictions it imposes, especially on young people and on women, it fantasizes about the supposedly seductive and promiscuous behaviour of Gypsy girls. Self-restrained in its expression of emotion, the urban middle class envies the passion that Gypsies project through their music and their colourful and ornamented appearance. Trapped in the responsibilities of routines and regulations, the mainstream stares with romantic indulgence at the Gypsies as children of nature. Yet since this fictional image represents the opposite of majority society's own values, the Gypsies are equally regarded as a threat and treated with suspicion.

MEETING THE 'LUCKY PEOPLE'

In the early 1970s, a group of intellectuals of Romani descent established an international network of activists, which later came to be known as the 'Romani political movement'. They set out to challenge majority society's perception of their people as nomads and social outcasts and to inform about their true origins, the century-old suffering and persecution that they had endured, and their aspirations to gain respect and recognition as a nation that is dispersed across many lands. As emblems of their nationhood they adopted a flag and a national anthem. Their flag had two background colours: green representing the ground below, and blue for the sky above. In its centre it depicted a wheel: this symbolized the image of the Romani people as travellers and, resembling the 24-spoke wheel known as the Ashoka Chatra which features in the centre of the flag of India, it served as a reference to the Roms' historical country of origin.

'I travelled long roads and I met lucky people' is the first line of the song 'Gelem, Gelem', now known as the Romani national anthem. It was written in 1949 by Žarko Jovanović, a Serbian Romani musician who had been imprisoned in three concentration camps during the Second World War and who lost most of his family and friends to the purges of the Nazis and their collaborators. The song was chosen by the activists as an anthem in order to inspire a feeling of solidarity and shared destiny among their people. It tells the story of an encounter with Romani victims and survivors of persecution and describes how, despite their suffering, which was beyond imagination, they maintained a spiritual conviction that clinging to their customs and values bestowed them with good fortune.

I decided to write this book because my own encounters with Romani people have enriched my life in a unique and remarkable way. I have learned from the Roms how sorrow and agony can coexist with generosity and a feeling of security through mutual support. I witnessed an astounding ability among the Roms to react quickly, spontaneously and with flexibility to new situations, and yet at the same time to remain protective of the ideas and values that define who they are. Most of all, perhaps, the time I spent with the Roms and the many years I spent researching their language, culture and history have taught me important lessons about the majority population that surrounds them – our own society: its fears and insecurity, its fantasies and superstitions, and the secret passions and desires that majority society suppresses and projects onto the Gypsies in fairy tales and poems.

You can go on holiday to Tunisia, on an adventure trip to Brazil, on business to Singapore or for a study leave in Berlin. In any of these places you can meet people with different customs and languages who do things in different ways. You can go back home and relate your encounters to your friends and colleagues, and they will usually listen and try to absorb your experiences with a more or less open mind. Yet nobody reacts in a completely neutral way when you tell them that you have been meeting or working with Gypsies.

As a PhD student in the early 1990s I once attended an academic conference in Germany. A distinguished professor there asked me about the topic of my thesis. When I mentioned that it was about the Romani language – I had to explain that this was the language of the people known to him as Gypsies – he immediately asked whether I had been able to uncover why they steal, why they lie and why they all want to immigrate to Germany. Years later, after I had become a professor myself, my ten-year-old son accompanied me to visit acquaintances at a Gypsy settlement in the north of England. When he told his friends at school about the experience, they were shocked.

'You met *real* Gypsies?' they asked, as if he had reported an encounter with aliens or with a famous Walt Disney character.

One of the main challenges in writing about the Roms is that people usually think that they already know who they are and how they behave. To inform about the Roms means by necessity also to inform about who they are not. People's views about Gypsies have been shaped over many generations by literary images, which are so powerful that people often dismiss the reality of real-life encounters with Roms.

And yet over the years I have seen generations of students who took a genuine interest in Romani customs and history and who were prepared to engage with society's prejudiced attitude and to make this the topic of their essays and projects. They followed the narratives of Romani friends whom I had invited to the lecture room with suspense. Many of them took it upon themselves to enlighten colleagues and acquaintances about this vulnerable and marginalized minority once they graduated and took up various professional careers.

Some years ago I was contacted by the head teacher of a local primary school in a deprived area of Manchester. The school had been taking on a large number of pupils of Romani origin for over a year. Their families came from Romania, often after spending several years in Spain, Germany or Italy. The school wanted to know more about their cultural background and how best to communicate with the families to improve the children's attendance and academic attainment. I met with the teachers and was impressed by their curiosity and open-mindedness and their willingness to take on board my suggestions on how to approach the Romani parents and their children. Of course you would expect this from primary school teachers in an ethnically and socially diverse neighbourhood. But, when it comes to the Romani people, I had become accustomed to displays of ignorance and hostility even among professionals. My meetings with the teachers and my years of working with students encouraged me to believe that there are those who are prepared to question the traditional stereotypes that society entertains and to seek instead information about the reality of the Romani people.

The problem is that much of the information about the Roms remains scattered, accessible only to specialists, fragmented or even contradictory and unreliable. Websites and media reports offer a huge range of descriptions and ideas, but the source of their information is not always transparent or verifiable. Academic researchers tend to specialize in the cultures and languages of individual Romani communities in particular locations, and very few have written about the Romani people as a whole. Ethnographers write about culture, linguists write about language, historians concentrate on particular Romani populations within a certain country and period, and political scientists have begun to write about Romani activism. There are many useful and important insights in these scholarly works, but they are seldom combined into an integrated perspective.

My aim in this book is to provide an overview of Romani communities, their customs, their social organization and their history. This is a huge challenge, and an enormous sense of responsibility accompanies me in this task. First, a genuinely comprehensive overview of the culture and lives of the many Romani groups would require an encyclopaedia. All I can deliver in the present format is therefore a selection. There will be gaps, since there are periods in the history of Romani populations in certain countries that have not yet been researched and we know little about them, and there are communities that I have not visited and about which I have not heard or read any reports. In the following chapters I wish to give a general picture about who the Romani people are. But here too there are pitfalls. It is very difficult to generalize about any culture, let alone that of a people who are widely dispersed and who have come under the influences of so many different populations in a number of countries. What do women who live in houses, wear traditional long skirts, speak Romani to their family members and are offended when somebody calls them 'Gypsies' have in common with women who live in caravans, wear shorts, use only the occasional Romani word and refer to themselves as 'Gypsies'? What does a Romani coppersmith in Bulgaria share with a Romani used-car dealer in Los Angeles? How can a Spanish musician of Gitano background feel represented by a Hungarian Romani member of the European parliament?

Challenged by a growing international network of Romani political activists and their calls to unite the Romani nation, it has become fashionable among some civil servants, politicians and academics to emphasize the diversity of Romani groups and even to deny that they have much in common beyond their traditional image in the eyes of the majority population. Some even go as far as to claim that the idea of 'Gypsies' is a construction of our imagination, which leads us to lump together strangers of many different backgrounds. But try entering the home of a Romani family and saying to their face: 'You are not really Roms, you are just a construction of our imagination, a product of our romantic fantasies; there are no real Gypsies' (as my son's classmates seem to have thought).

In this book I also aim to challenge some popular stereotypes about Gypsies. I will try to explain how they originated, how they have been reinforced and disseminated over the centuries, and what effect they have had on relations between the majority society and the Romani minority. I will try to address the complexity of Romani society itself and the complexity of its relations with outsiders, and I will try to do this without being either judgemental about individual Romani customs or apologetic about them. I believe that it is not beneficial either to idealize Romani culture or to treat it as exotic. Romani culture is not simply Indian or Asian, though some aspects of it clearly reflect its historical origins in India, language being one of the most obvious. Nor is it inherently a culture of poverty or a culture of resistance or defiance against mainstream norms.

A discussion of Romani society that aims at being non-judgemental and as far as possible objective can easily find itself caught between two extreme ends of the debate. On the one hand, the Roms have often been accused of isolating themselves and defying mainstream society's norms, and consequently of provoking bias and hostility against themselves. On the other, some contemporary Romani activists, understandably frustrated by the continuous intensity of prejudice and discrimination against their people, seek to blame oppression by outsiders for the day-to-day decisions that the Roms take when organizing their lives, or indeed for the fact that the Roms remain distinct in many of their values and attitudes. The truth is that most Romani people feel 'lucky' or fortunate to be Roms despite the hardships they endure, and that it is for this reason that they do not wish to give up who they are. Despite the differences among them, they share a sense of solidarity and common destiny. They are aware of similarities in language, customs and values, and in attitudes to family, work, shame and honour.

In light of the contradictory definitions and conceptualizations surrounding Gypsies, it feels almost as if a book about Romani Gypsies must do more than tell us who the Romani people are. It must also tell us who they are not, because we all entertain an image of Gypsies that we have acquired through our exposure to the everyday culture, songs and stories that surround us. The chapters that follow are based to a large extent on my own immersion of many years with Romani families and individuals from various countries and regions. In part, it draws on the research of a long list of distinguished scholars who have devoted many years of their careers to exploring and describing many aspects of Romani culture and history. Like other nations, Romani communities are diverse. Describing what is typically Romani is certainly not easier than describing what is typically Italian, Mexican, Swedish, Puerto Rican or Texan. If we are not careful, we end up with stereotypes. In the case of the Romani Gypsies, who are spread among the other nations and absorb many of the customs and habits of the people around them, making generalizations is even more difficult.

My agenda in this book is to try to capture these similarities, to discuss their historical origins, as far as possible, and to examine how the Roms have maintained their distinct identity amid the historical events that have had an impact on them. The following chapters are the very first attempt to deliver an integrated overview of Romani society and customs as practised in different Romani communities. I specify some of the things that are common to most or at least many Romani communities and survey the history of relations between majority societies and the Romani minority. I identify some of the origins of popular present-day images of the Gypsy brand and describe the efforts that many Romani people today are making in order to challenge that image and to provide a more realistic picture of themselves, striving to achieve acceptance as equals in a society that has often approached them with a charged and emotional mixture of fascination and hostility. This book is not a political manifesto and I do not intend to use it in order to advocate any particular policies to support Romani participation and social inclusion, and certainly not to restrict the practice of Romani culture or to change Romani values and attitudes. But I do hold the view that we need to rethink and revise our picture of the Romani people and to move away from the literary images and brands, and on to understanding the real everyday lives and aspirations of a real people.

2

Romani Society

WITHOUT A PROMISED LAND

Traditional Romani culture is strictly oral, with no documents or scriptures that outline either the people's history or the rules and values that govern their lives. The Roms tell legends about their origins that are often characterized by humour and self-irony as they try to explain the relations between themselves and majority society. One such legend places the Roms at the scene of the crucifixion. Overwhelmed with pity, the Roms stole the nails off the cross in order to ease Christ's suffering. As a reward, God granted the Roms the right to steal from other people. Another story tells of the Creation. When God asked all nations what kind of dwelling they would like, most opted for brick, stone or wood. But the Roms were greedy and asked for their houses to be built of cheese. When their request was granted, they wasted no time and ate the cheese. They were then left to travel the roads with no permanent dwelling. The anthropologist Michael Stewart reports a tale that is widely known among the Hungarian Roms: when God gave out wheat to all humans the Roms could not gather any since they were poor and could not afford to buy a sack. And so they asked God to pour their share of wheat into the sack that belonged to the non-Roms, the Gadje. But the Gadje then withdrew without giving the Roms their portion and so the Roms have since had to earn their living by stealing from the Gadje.

These stories do not, of course, represent any firm beliefs about the true origins of the Roms or about their genuine culture or habits. Rather, they show how Romani tradition has to some extent internalized and accepted century-old marginalization and stigmatization by outsiders as a given fact. From the Romani perspective, the world is divided into Roms and non-Roms. Romani people are those who do things in a Romani way, which the Roms refer to as romanes. Not just the Romani language is romanes, but also the way of showing respect to elders, the way of resolving conflicts, the manner of dress, and even the way in which mothers pick up and carry their infants. Every Romani community has a cover term to designate all outsiders or non-Roms. Most often they are called Gadje (pronounced 'ga-je'), but in the Romani dialect of the German Sinte the word is *Xale* (pronounced 'ha-le'), and the Gitanos of Spain call outsiders *Payos*.

The strong sense of culture and identity that is symbolized by the contrast of the words Rom and Gadje does not contradict the need felt by many Roms to remain invisible and unidentifiable to outsiders. In America, Roms often claim to be Greek, Mexican or Indian. When my English Gypsy friends are overheard using Romani words among themselves, they tell eavesdroppers that they are Italian. When I first heard Romani spoken by Yugoslav Roms in Germany and enquired about their language, they replied that they were talking 'Bulgarian-American'. My Romani friends in the northwest of England often describe how they claim to be Irish or Scottish when ringing the doorbells of potential customers to offer services such as surfacing driveways or pruning trees and bushes, for fear of being identified as Gypsies: 'We make a living by denying who we are.' Perhaps the key challenge facing the Roms throughout the centuries, apart from mere survival in the face of persecution and exclusion, is how to maintain their own culture and identity in the absence of a territory and formal institutions.

Romani culture is often associated with travel. In fact, the great majority of Roms do not travel and their families have lived in permanent settlements and dwellings for many centuries. The roots of this idea can be found in two distinct features of Romani society: geographical dispersion and a flexible and often mobile, family-based service economy. The Roms' geographical dispersion is a result of historical migrations, though we must distinguish between 'migration' and 'nomadism'. Migration is in most cases a once-in-a-lifetime event in the history of some families or groups of families, who, due to particular circumstances, decide to leave their region of residence and settle elsewhere. The Californian Roms are migrants in this sense.

Their families arrived from the East Coast and travelled the breadth of the United States like hundreds of thousands of other immigrants. Their ancestors came from eastern Europe, many of them from Serbia and Russia. Although we have no documentation about their origin communities in Europe, their customs and the Romani dialect they speak are shared with the Roms of Transylvania in western Romania and eastern Hungary and it appears that their ancestors left that region in the nineteenth century. Romani settlements in those areas, in turn, emerged after Romani migrations from the southern Balkans during the Byzantine and Ottoman periods.

There have been numerous other migrations in the history of the Roms. A large wave of migrants in the fourteenth and early fifteenth centuries brought the Roms into various parts of Europe from the Balkans. Roms from Germany emigrated to German colonies in Russia, Hungary and Romania during the eighteenth century. Russian Roms joined Russian colonies in Harbin in northeastern China in the nineteenth and early twentieth centuries. The political upheavals in late nineteenth-century Romania led thousands of Roms to emigrate to Russia, Sweden, France and Germany and as far away as Mexico, Colombia, Venezuela and Australia. Thousands of English Roms or Romnichals left Britain for the United States in the first half of the twentieth century. The aftermath of the Greek–Turkish War in the early 1920s saw a massive exodus of Muslim Roms from Greece to Turkey and a migration of Christian Roms from Turkey into Greece as part of a large-scale population exchange between the two countries. Polish Roms who were displaced after the Second World War immigrated to Sweden and other countries, and Yugoslav Roms arrived in Germany, France and the Netherlands in the 1960s in search of employment opportunities. Many thousands of Roms made use of the freedom of movement within the European Union when it was extended to include Poland and Slovakia, among others, in 2004 and Romania and Bulgaria in 2007.

These migrations closely resemble the movements of other populations in search of a better life, especially during times of social and political uncertainty. One major difference is that the Roms leave behind regions that are dominated by others and which they cannot call their own. Their memory of their place of origin might be passed on for one or two generations, but ultimately it is their sense of belonging to a distinct Romani community with its spiritual beliefs and unique practices that defines who they are, not the region their ancestors left behind.

Romani communities have sometimes been referred to as 'diasporas'. They form networks that are geographically dispersed but maintain social and cultural bonds. Contacts are often kept through seasonal travelling and participation in festivities, weddings and funerals. In recent years, mobile phones and the internet have come to play an important role in supporting regular communication among Romani families and clans. Roms often identify with other Romani groups in a way that transcends national boundaries. There is no single territory around which Roms can rally and unite. The awareness of an Indian origin plays a role mainly for Romani political activists in their attempts to consolidate international solidarity with the Roms and among the different Romani communities. But for the majority of Roms, even those who are aware and informed of the early history of their people, India remains an abstract and academic aspect of their identity.

In this respect it is probably correct to identify the Roms as a 'non-territorial' nation. This does not mean, however, that the Roms are 'homeless' or 'rootless' as they are often portrayed. While maintaining their own culture and separate identity throughout the centuries, the Roms have always been immersed to some extent in local traditions and economic networks. Their daily lives, rituals and beliefs are influenced both by their own ancient cultural inheritance and by the traditions and activities of the surrounding populations, often acquired in different places and at different times. They are bilingual, speaking the language of the territory in which they reside alongside their own Romani language. They adopt many celebrations and customs from neighbouring populations, and as their livelihood depends on a steady network of contacts and relations with the other nations they tend to take on the religion of the majority. The anthropologist and ethnomusicologist Carol Silverman has suggested that the Roms may be regarded as having multiple homelands: their current place of residence, the areas they frequent to visit relatives or to take up work opportunities, the places their ancestors resided in, with which they are connected through family and social ties, as well as countries and regions that have played a role in the shaping of the customs and traditions of their communities in the more distant past. The term that best captures this mixture of influences from various places and regions is 'cultural hybridity'.

Probably the most common popular image of Romani society is travel in caravans. Although travelling is limited to a minority within the Romani population, it is characteristic in the sense that it draws on all the key elements of Romani society: geographical dispersion and lack of territorial claims, flexibility in the choice of trade and ability to access local markets and clients, and the organization of work around family life. Travelling in caravans enables Roms to seek new livelihood opportunities without separating from family members. It allows families to maintain a network of contacts with other Romani families through relocation, visits and seasonal gatherings. Historically, travel in caravans has also protected the Roms from hostilities and enabled them to cope with frequent evictions without compromising their possessions and the basis of their livelihood.

On the whole, however, travel tends to be seasonal. Roms travel in order to meet other Roms at annual gatherings and fairs during the spring and summer months and to explore market opportunities. In the travelling season, travel takes precedence over other commitments such as school attendance. This makes travelling an important part of the lifestyle and cultural ideology of many Romani communities. Many Roms who live in permanent dwellings in houses and apartments keep caravans for use during the spring and summer months. Quite a few Roms in the Netherlands, Belgium, Italy, Germany, and especially in England and Wales live in caravans but travel only during certain months. Travelling Roms depend on their familiarity with roads and stopping places and with the customs, languages and cycles of markets and fairs of their region. They also depend on a regional network of trade contacts, and so travel is therefore seldom random. Most travelling Romani communities have remained in the same regions for generations and centuries.

Life in the caravan has a meaning beyond mobility. Caravan sites allow related families to maintain a tight-knit community and to share resources, tools and even cooking facilities in a way that is not possible in most urban settings. An English Romani friend once reflected on how important it was for his family to know that the caravan offers the option of escaping local hardships or hostilities, even though they have been living on the same site for thirty-seven years. His wife described to me how the caravan gives her a sense of safety and security. Wherever she stands inside the caravan she can look out of a window and see where her small children are playing. Living in a house, separated by walls from her children, she would feel uncomfortable and anxious, unable to reassure herself through a single glance that no harm has come to them.

The Roms are not the only population that maintains a service economy and whose social and economic structures partly depend on or are served by travel in caravans. Other communities, often known collectively as 'Travellers' and indeed quite often referred to indiscriminately as 'Gypsies', show similar structures. For many, travelling is the essence of their distinctive culture. The Irish, Scottish and English Travellers use this term to designate themselves, as do the French Gens du voyage, the Camminanti of southern Italy, and the Dutch *Woonwagenbewoners* or 'caravan dwellers'. The Jenische (also Yenish or Yeniche) of southern Germany, Switzerland and Austria live in permanent dwellings, often in secluded villages, but make a living as travelling salesmen, as operators of rides at fairgrounds and as performers at seasonal events.

The Roms are conscious of similarities between certain aspects of their practices and those of Traveller communities, but they emphasize that their own culture is distinct and very different from that of Travellers. The principal emphasis is on language and on cleanliness rules. The Roms maintain prohibitions on eating certain animals and on keeping some animals as pets or even having images of them in their homes. They also have strict rules to do with washing and food preparation (I will discuss these in more detail in Chapter 3). These rules are usually not observed by non-Romani Travellers. Language is another key defining factor. Some Traveller communities have a special in-group vocabulary of words for everyday concepts that they use when communicating among themselves. These vocabularies are distinct from Romani, although some of the words may have Romani origins, testifying to historical contacts among the different populations.

Roms sometimes share caravan sites with Travellers. In Britain, Romani Gypsies and members of Traveller communities often take part in the same gatherings and traditional fairs, and the Romani evangelical missionary movement targets all populations of Gypsies and Travellers in the country. Marriage between Romani Gypsies and Travellers is not uncommon, either, but the rule is for a wife to join her husband's family and so few family links are maintained that transcend community boundaries. Roms will often express a sense of shared destiny between their own people and travelling communities. This notion of a special relationship is triggered partly by similarities in lifestyle and socio-economic organization, but it is based mainly on similar attitudes towards the settled majority population and its institutions and norms, and especially on a shared feeling of marginality and exclusion. It is this sense of shared destiny that is flagged in the title of the European Roma and Traveller Forum (ERTF, an organization established in 2004 to represent both populations at the Council of Europe).

KINSHIP

Being a Rom means being part of a family and a larger kinship-unit or clan, whose culture and language are Romani. We might therefore describe traditional Romani society as based on a kinship ideology, which prevails even though most Roms lack terms for the notions 'clan' and 'tribe'. Instead, they simply call their group by name – the Lalere people and the Pikuleški people, for instance, are examples of clans. Each consists of a number of extended families that can trace their relationship to a shared ancestor. The Sinte, the Lovara and the Kaale are larger groups that unite people who share customs and values and who speak the same dialect of the Romani language. Unlike clans, they are composed of numerous families who live across larger areas, and they no longer maintain any recollection of shared ancestry.

In such a kinship-based society, the structure of sub-groups is not static. Individuals marry across clan and tribal boundaries, creating new bonds and giving birth to descendants of mixed lineage. Families may move from one territory into another, splitting away from their historical clan and sometimes joining another. Ethnographers Elena Marushiakova and Vesselin Popov point out that Romani groups throughout history have often segregated themselves from one another, only to undergo consolidation with another group elsewhere several generations later.

The Romani clan of the Gabor in the Romanian province of Transylvania is a good example. The Gabor have become economically successful and over the past forty or fifty years have earned a special reputation among other Roms for their work ethic and family values. As a result, they have attracted new families keen to join them. These newcomers have made an effort to marry their daughters into the clan and to adopt the clan's customs and values, and many have moved close to the villages that were traditionally inhabited by Gabors. Others travel frequently to these villages, maintaining close ties with their new relations. And so within two to three generations the clan of families who descend from the common ancestor Gabor have become a 'nation' or sub-group of many thousands of people who live scattered among many villages, some of them even in nearby provinces.

The Vlax Roms (pronounced 'vlah-h') emerged as a group in the Romanian principality of Wallachia sometime around the fifteenth or sixteenth century, and they are now one of the most numerous and geographically most dispersed of all Romani populations. They recognize different levels of division among their people. A larger group is known as a *natsya* or 'nation'. Members of a nation share customs such as funeral and marriage rituals and the procedures that regulate the work of the Romani court. They may also share dress codes such as the length and colour patterns of women's skirts or the style of men's hats. Additionally, members of the same nation tend to have a preferred set of trades and a very similar Romani dialect. The most well-known Vlax Romani nations are the Kelderasha, who have communities in all European countries as well as in North and South America, the Lovara, who reside mainly in central and western Europe, the Machwaya, who constitute the largest Romani group in the United States, and the Churara, whose communities are found mainly in the northern Balkans, central Europe and the United States.

Within the natsya there are kinship units, each called a *vitsa*, which is essentially a clan. Each vitsa includes a number of extended families, meaning that the criterion for belonging to the vitsa is descent. Members of the vitsa share a male ancestor and usually derive the name of their vitsa from that ancestor – this name serves among the Vlax Roms as a kind of identity badge or family name, which people use to introduce themselves to other Roms. A new vitsa may emerge when the group of descendants has reached a significant number of families. Alternatively, a vitsa can disintegrate once collective memory of the shared ancestor has faded away, usually after four or five generations. Member families belonging to the same vitsa do not necessarily maintain contact with one another. Rather, the defining aspect of the vitsa is the awareness of shared ancestry.

Another sub-division of the Vlax Romani nation is the *kumpanya* or 'company'. This is an association of unrelated families who live in the same region or town and maintain social and economic ties with one another. Among travelling Roms, members of the kumpanya share stopping sites and favourite travel destinations and routes. They also participate in events and celebrations such as weddings and Saint Day festivities and they share information on business opportunities. The smallest social unit is the *familya* or extended family. The Vlax Roms often refer to the family as *tserha* meaning 'tent' – a reminiscence of earlier dwelling in tents during the period of slavery in the Romanian principalities.

Romani populations have different perceptions of the clan, its role and its composition. In Slovakia, rural Romani settlements or *osadas* tend to be divided into a small number of clans whose members live in separate quarters. Sometimes, however, families of the same clan affiliation take up residence in another village and the clan then becomes dispersed. In some communities, the importance of ancestry as the string that binds together families into a clan is rather loose. The English Gypsies, for example, speak of 'breeds', by which they refer to a rather loose network of families from several parts of the country that share customs, habits and fashions. Ancestry does not play a direct role in defining the network, but individuals are very much aware that certain families and persons belong to the 'right' or 'wrong' breed. Such networks of preferred alliances with other families have a long history. It may include instances of intermarriage and mutual support as well as of feuds and conflict, the details of which have long been lost from collective memory.

THE ROMANI HOUSEHOLD

The basic and most important social framework in Romani communities is the extended family. The father is the head of the household. After his passing it is not unusual for his spouse to take over that role. The extended family consists of the parents, their married sons, and each son's nuclear family (wife and children). Married daughters typically leave the household and move in with their husbands and in-laws, but unmarried siblings stay on and are also part of the extended household. The brothers' married sons will bring their wives into the extended household, too, and their children will constitute the fourth generation. In many Romani communities, marriage takes place at a very young age, and until quite recently it was not unusual for couples aged sixteen or seventeen to marry and have children (though this is now changing in many communities). Consequently, a single extended family might contain four generations: the parents or heads of the household, their adult children, their grandchildren and great-grandchildren. Traditionally, Romani communities tend to have large families and so a typical extended household will have anywhere between forty and seventy members.

In many Romani communities in central and eastern Europe, members of the extended family share living quarters. Usually, each nuclear family has its own one- or two-room space. These areas surround a courtyard, which is used as a communal area. This is where food is prepared, often on an open fire, and where members of the family sit together and entertain guests. Most traditional Roms have strict rules on cleanliness. These rules require public scrutiny of activities involving food preparation and washing and this is an additional reason for performing such tasks outdoors, in view of all members of the household. Toilets must be separated from living quarters and especially from areas in which food is stored and prepared. Traditional Romani settlements in central and eastern Europe and caravan sites have outdoor toilets. In houses and apartments, Roms try to modify the residential layout as far as possible to create a large reception room, usually with sofas and chairs arranged along the walls, often decorated with colourful rugs. Other rooms such as the kitchen and bathroom are located in the back of the house and are private and used only by family members and close friends and relatives. Sometimes just one single separate bedroom is maintained, but even this room is often used only for storage and the family shares sleeping quarters in the reception area, which is transformed into a sleeping area at night by opening sofas and spreading mattresses. This strongly resembles the living arrangements in western Asian cultures.

In travelling communities or among those who travel seasonally, members of the extended family tend to travel together in several caravans and share temporary stopping sites. Groups of five caravans or more were once a frequent sight on Europe's roadsides before restrictions were imposed on travelling and stopping. When stopping, caravans or trailers are usually arranged in a circle, for protection and for privacy, with the communal fire and cooking spot set up in the middle. Washing of laundry and rinsing of cooking and eating utensils are carried out in front of or at the side of the trailer, using separate tubs for different categories of items. Modern caravans are usually equipped with a sink as well as with showers and toilets, but Roms who travel carry out most cooking and washing outdoors, where there is no risk of defilement and where public scrutiny will ensure that no rumours emerge alleging the family's failure to adhere to cleanliness rules. Modern caravan sites are semi-permanent, that is, they are used for regular and continuous dwelling. People move on and off the site in much the same way as settled people might sell their house and move into a different one. Sites are usually equipped with toilet, cooking and washing facilities and these are shared by two or three nuclear families belonging to the same extended household.

Modern sites for travelling communities vary in size and in administrative organization. During the late 1960s, pressure on Travellers increased across Europe to avoid stopping on private land and on roadsides. Landowners frequently turned to the police to evict Travellers, and lawmakers were lobbied to make stopping on undesignated places an offence. In reaction to this development, European governments were encouraged by a series of resolutions issued by the Council of Europe to set up specially designated sites for Gypsies and Travellers. At first, local authorities took on the responsibility of administering the sites. However, gradually they were contracted to private companies. Most Roms who live on caravan sites prefer to have the entire site for their own extended family. Family relations do not regard individual caravans as secluded private spaces. Knocking on a caravan door to request permission to enter is considered dishonourable because it creates artificial demarcations within the extended family. During the daytime caravans are accessible to all family members without prior announcement. In countries such as Britain, France, Germany, Norway and the Netherlands, a typical site will contain pitches for anywhere between ten and fifty caravans. Quite often a nuclear family will occupy two trailers: one for the parents and the youngest children, another for the older children, and when sites are divided among extended families, close relations tend to occupy adjacent pitches.

In the years of economic renewal following the Second World War, many Roms in eastern European countries were resettled from rural communities into major cities and industrial districts. They were forced to move into newly built blocks of mass housing, which accommodated workers in the new industrial estates. Severe restrictions were imposed on travelling during that period and many Roms were forced to settle in such state-built apartment blocks. Urbanization and the abandonment of a travelling lifestyle also led Romani households in other parts of Europe to move into single-family apartments and terrace houses.

A way to avoid the break-up of extended households as a result of such changes in accommodation style is to rent clusters of apartments or single-family homes in close proximity to one another. Romanian Roms who immigrated to Manchester, England, for example, made an effort over several years to rent entire rows of adjoining terrace houses, whereupon some local residents accused them of creating a segregated environment. But even in adjoining terrace houses it has proven difficult for related families to share facilities and communal spaces. Cooking and washing as well as social gatherings continued to be carried out outdoors, often on the pavement in front of the houses.

This attracted condemnation from nearby residents, who regarded the practice as an inconsiderate occupation of public space by the Roms. In an effort to avoid such conflicts, more affluent Romani families have built their own houses in the margins of residential neighbourhoods. These houses are big enough to accommodate several nuclear families. Less affluent Roms have often been content to be assigned state-sponsored accommodation (such as council houses) on the fringes of large residential estates. In this way, the Roms can maintain important aspects of their culture without risking conflict with non-Romani neighbours.

The extended family is not just a residential unit where relations live together, eat together and share everyday experiences. It is also the framework within which Roms care for young children and teach them every aspect of their culture from speaking their own language, Romani, to learning to support the family. Above all, the extended family is the economic unit within which Romani people make a living. Work and income, as well as resources such as tools, household utensils, food supplies and individual meals, are typically organized and shared within the larger family. If a woman is cooking a meal and requires a particular pan, for example, she might fetch that pan from her sister-in-law's rooms, where it had last been placed by one of the daughters who helped out with the cooking. She would not borrow the pan or ask permission to use it, nor will she promise to return it to her sister-in-law's possession once she has finished using it for her ongoing task, since the pan is part of the possessions of the extended household. In this way, resources within the household are shared. Likewise, if a boy has been sent by his mother on a minor shopping errand but was not given enough money for the purchase, he could turn to any of the adults in the household to ask for more. Money earned by one member of the household and given to another to purchase an object that is needed for the household, such as a light bulb, food or a piece of furniture, would not constitute a 'loan' and there is no expectation that it should be paid back to the 'lender'. Earnings from work are brought back and shared with the extended family, and goods purchased from earnings benefit the extended family as a whole. This often continues to be the case even if the members of the extended family no longer live together as a result of resettlement or migration. If one or two families move, then members of the extended household continue to maintain contacts and to function as a network.

Roms cherish the spirit of solidarity and mutual support that characterizes the Romani extended family. They view it as a unique part of Romani culture of which they are proud, and as one of the things that separates them from the customs and habits of the Gadje, or non-Roms. On one occasion, I was travelling in a convoy of a couple of cars with Romani friends. We stopped at a motorway service station to get some food. The party crowded along the cafeteria counter, each member piling up as many plates as he could on his tray, all to be redistributed and shared by everyone once we took our seats at a table of an appropriate size. By chance, I ended up at the front of the queue at the head of a small group that had broken away from the rest. They had filled their trays and were proceeding towards the cashier. I instructed the cashier to add up our entire stack of orders together and hand me the bill. We sat down and were soon joined by the rest of the party, led by the family's elder. He seemed to frown at the realization that his people had apparently each paid for their food separately, relieving him of his duty but also depriving him of the opportunity to demonstrate his commitment to being a responsible and generous family leader who takes care of his group. He was surprised when he learned that I had paid for everyone. Back in the car, my behaviour was commented on. *Naj xandžvalo* ('He's not stingy'), they remarked repeatedly in Romani, acknowledging that it was extraordinary for a non-Rom to show such generosity.

Outsiders often fail to understand and to accept the Romani commitment to collective responsibility towards young children within the family household. I once made friends with a group of Serbian Roms, an extended family who had travelled through Italy, France, the Netherlands and Germany in search of an opportunity to settle. Among them was a childless couple in their early thirties, an age when most Roms are already parents of teenagers. They were very happily married, good-natured, well respected in their community and always ready to support others. Their cousin, a young woman named Jadranka, had had a somewhat more turbulent history of personal relationships. She had abandoned two or possibly three husbands, or perhaps it was she who had been left by some of them. But she was independent and self-confident, caring for two young children in the secure and supporting environment of her family relations. Then, through what appeared to have been a brief liaison with a Polish Rom who then returned to his own clan, she fell pregnant again. A healthy baby was subsequently delivered, and Jadranka, aware of her cousins' distress at not being able to conceive a child, gave the baby to them to adopt as their own. Biological motherhood duties yielded in this case to solidarity within the extended family. All those involved understood that Jadranka was not simply 'giving away' her baby. The child was, after all, staying in the family.

In England I've seen how the authorities confront such practices with great suspicion. In Manchester, it had come to the attention of social workers that some of the young children they encountered when visiting the homes of Romani immigrants from Romania were not, at that given moment, being cared for in the homes of their biological parents. Rumours began to flourish about child trafficking, nurtured not least by an upsurge of media reports about organized international gangs of child traffickers, which often featured interviews with senior police officers and politicians warning of Romani involvement in such criminal activity. But once the allegations were investigated, it appeared that children and biological parents were all accounted for and were all living peacefully in the same community. Childcare was simply organized among members of the extended family and it was considered a duty to offer support to parents who had to leave their homes in the daytime for work or even to travel for several days to visit relatives in other towns. Collective support is celebrated by the Roms, yet outsiders often insist that each and every Romani practice is a conspiracy against the social order rather than simply a traditional way of organizing their communal lives.

GENDER ROLES

Outsiders have conflicting ideas of gender roles in Romani society. These are shaped in part by the way Gypsy women have been portrayed in popular culture – as passionate, permissive and seductive.

By contrast, some people think of the Roms as a 'traditional' society and that evokes associations of very strict gender roles. The physical appearance of Romani women – the fact that they are often dressed in long skirts and wear headscarves – leads outsiders to associate them with peoples of the Middle East, and that in turn triggers various images of a strict patriarchal society where women have no say and no freedom. While it is true that there are strict rules governing the conduct of men and women in Romani society, these rules are in fact quite different from what most outsiders imagine. For a start, both men and women assume responsibility for generating the family's income, and both men and women engage for this purpose in activities outside the home. There is certainly no taboo in Romani families on women or girls interacting with strangers for work purposes, and there is no expectation that the women or girls should stay at home while the men earn money outside.

Nevertheless, women and men tend to have very distinct roles both at work and within the home. Inside the household it is the women who are in charge of preparing food and cleaning, while the men usually handle any manufacturing that takes place at home, making copperware or other tools that are sold to customers. Women might participate in the production of some artefacts, such as pegs and baskets. Both men and women take care of children, especially when one of the parents is working outside the home. Childcare takes place within the household unit, and so children are often looked after by adults who are not their parents. Both men and women entertain and perform within the household, telling stories, singing and dancing, but only men tend to play musical instruments.

Outside the household, women tend to engage in economic activities that bring them in contact indiscriminately with a wide general public rather than with just a selected, particular network of trade associates. In some countries Romani women collect materials such as plastic bags, rags or metal wires and exchange them for money or other goods, or they engage in door-to-door hawking or selling of small artefacts. In some Romani communities, women sometimes engage in begging and fortune-telling, though these occupations are considered taboo among many Roms. In communities where begging is a frequent source of income, there is usually no specific taboo on begging by men, but it is more often practised by women.

This tells us something about the internal rationale of gender role divisions as far as work is concerned. Traditional Romani economy is a service economy and the Roms are experienced in making use of a variety of income-generating opportunities. The fact that women offer a wider range of services to a wider population of clients has little to do with any internal cultural values of the Romani community. Rather, it reflects the reactions towards women in the mainstream population. Potential clients are less suspicious of women. They tend to be more generous to women when it comes to begging and more trustworthy of them when it comes to door-to-door selling. They also open up their own world of thoughts, feelings, wishes and concerns to women more so than to men. This makes women more successful in fortune-telling, a trade that is essentially based on reading the customer's 'hidden face' and making a mental note of their appearance, side remarks and behaviour to assess their life circumstances, worries and aspirations.

Men, on the other hand, engage in more specialized and targeted trades, which take place at markets or with designated trade partners. Collection of scrap material for recycling is an activity that men share with women, though men will tend to specialize in metal objects. Men travel by car to provide door-to-door household services that require tools and machinery, such as paving driveways, installing gutters or windows, and trimming trees and bushes. Specialized, well-established craftsmen produce musical instruments. Those who are relatively well off among the Romani tradesmen typically sell cars, carpets, art or antique furniture. Both men and women work as seasonal labourers in many communities when there is no other alternative.

Genders tend to be separated in ceremonies and celebrations. In many Romani communities, men and women sit separately at gatherings including meals that are served to guests and anyone outside the family. Conversation topics in mixed gatherings strictly avoid any reference, direct or indirect, to women's health and to sexuality. Parents are often concerned about sending children beyond the age of puberty to mainstream schools, where such norms are not observed. Overt mention of sexual matters, even in the context of sex and health education, let alone in informal conversations among boys and girls, will not only cause discomfort to Romani girls but may be interpreted as a sign of disrespect. Girls who tolerate such talk in mixed-gender peer groups might be regarded in the community as surrendering their own self-respect. This in turn brings shame upon them and their families. Unmarried teenage girls thus become vulnerable as soon as they leave the home, be it for school, on an errand or for social events: they must be in a position to fend off any rumours that they may have been treated disrespectfully by others. For this reason, in addition to the more universal need for company as a sense of protection, teenage girls leave the home only in the company of other girls from the community. If any doubt is expressed about a girl's conduct, the others can then vouch for her integrity. For this reason, school attendance beyond puberty is difficult for girls, especially when they are on their own, without a circle of Romani girlfriends.

The protection of premarital virginity among girls is perhaps one of the strictest expressions of gender role divisions within the Romani community. It might also be regarded as the most obvious manifestation of gender inequality. Sexual experience prior to marriage does not affect the community status of young men, whereas for a young woman to engage in a sexual relationship is, in practice, an act of marriage, regardless of whether the marriage has been sanctioned by the parents or marked by a wedding ceremony. Marriage thus comes into effect through a sexual liaison of a couple that are not yet married. A girl who has lost her virginity is therefore considered married; should she abandon her partner following just a very short relationship, she would be regarded as a young divorcée and more likely an adventurer who is unfit for proper marriage. However, the strictness with which such norms are applied varies considerably among Romani communities. A case in point is a debate that arose in the early 1990s among Roms of central Poland. The Polska Roma are guided by a spiritual leader, who is referred to as the *Šero Rom* ('Head Man'). In a dispute between two families, the Head Man had ruled that the family of a man who raped a young unmarried girl was not obliged to compensate the victim's family if the man agreed to take the girl as his wife. The girl's consent was not a factor. This decision angered many in the community, who regarded it as a free licence to rape with impunity and, moreover, as legitimizing rape as a means of forcefully securing the consent of a girl's family to a marriage proposition that they had declined. A significant part of the community withdrew their loyalty and support from that particular Head Man and elected a new leader. In due course, the new leader's power was extended to the entire group.

The privilege of engaging in a sexual relationship without the commitment to starting a family is thus invariably limited to young men in brief liaisons with women outside the community, or else in hidden relationships with divorced or widowed women within it. But although a reputation for premarital sexual experience might add to a boy's prestige status among his peers, this kind of behaviour is usually discouraged in the community. It is seen as destabilizing traditional morals and so as a risk to the community structure. As in many other traditional communities, the solution to the severe restrictions on premarital sex is to encourage marriage at an early age. Both girls and boys in Romani communities usually marry around the age of sixteen or seventeen. Life following marriage tends to show a greater degree of equality among the genders, inasmuch as both husband and wife can decide to break up the marriage if they wish to do so. Married women continue to be at a certain disadvantage since they are expected to move in with their spouse's family after marriage. This entails, of course, coming to terms with a new environment, getting to know the members of the new extended family, adjusting to the norms of a new household, and above all accepting the authority of the mother-in-law, who takes charge of organizing the work and daily routines of the *bori*, the daughter-in-law.

As the wife of one of the brothers, the *bori* of course carries out the normal duties of a wife and plans her activities in discussion and in agreement with her husband. However, since work, household chores and childcare are typically managed in the context of the extended family, the *bori*'s position in the larger household is crucial in shaping her daily routine. Within the hierarchy of the extended household, the daughters-in-law are answerable directly to the female head of the household, the spouse of the family's head. This lends the female head of family a special position of power. It also makes the daughters-in-law potentially vulnerable to abuse and exploitation, while on the other hand ensuring that their participation in the work of the household is part of a larger, organized team. In this way, a daughter-in-law is protected from dependency on any arbitrary wishes and preferences of her husband and is expected instead to integrate into the priorities of the family collective.

A woman who has left her husband's household will often do so empty-handed, unless the families have come to an arrangement that would entitle her to some kind of compensation. However, she will almost always be admitted back into her parental household, without any shame or disgrace. Having been married once, and in all likelihood borne children, she will have considerably more liberty in her movements than young girls in her household. From the community's point of view, she is also free to remarry at any time. The same applies to divorced or separated husbands.

Dress codes are an external expression of gender roles. There are no specific initiation ceremonies in Romani society, and so adopting adult dress fashion is probably the closest one gets to any overt display of puberty. As in other societies, female dress codes are more sensitive to a variety of status distinctions than male dress fashions. In more traditional communities, it is common for married women (including divorced and widowed women) to wear a headscarf. In Vlax Romani communities, married women wear hair braids over the front of the body whereas unmarried girls leave them to hang over the back. Life stages among the Vlax Roms are marked by different colour patterns on skirts: young girls wear very bright colours such as pink and yellow, married women wear red or orange and elderly women wear darker colours such as green and blue.

In the context of the Romani family, both men and women are outspoken and vocal in expressing their views and opinions. Hierarchical differences between the genders are found mainly in the context of the external representation of families and family interests. At gatherings of community elders and funerals it is the men who represent their families. This is also the case in the internal court system or *kris*. The precise rules differ, but usually women cannot take on a role as members of the court ('judges' or 'arbiters'), and more often than not they are not allowed to testify in the courts, either, though only some communities impose restrictions on their presence at hearings.

While women maintain the control over work organization by the daughters and daughters-in-law, men retain the symbolic power of decision over the household as a whole, and the role of representing the household towards the outside world, be it in negotiations with others or in ceremonial functions such as attendance at funerals. In many traditional Romani communities, this ceremonial power of men is counterbalanced by the power that women have to defile men and embarrass them in public by bringing them in contact with skirts or aprons, or implying in other ways contact with the female lower body, through which men may lose their honour. Consequently, women face various restrictions to prevent them from 'polluting' male members of the family. For example, they are not allowed to cook for others immediately after childbirth or during their menstrual period. These restrictions are strict on younger women and are gradually relaxed once they have had several children.

ROMANI FAMILY VALUES

Age is generally associated in Romani communities with life experience and so with respect and authority. The elderly are the most respected persons in the household. The death of the household eldest in traditional settlements means the break-up of the entire household into new units. For most Roms, memory of the oldest members of their own family whom they knew in their lifetime is equated with their historical memory of their lineage. The life experience of the elderly is considered the most important source of family wisdom and, in the absence of literacy and a culture of documentation, their personal recollection is the only form of collective historical memory. Although age is not the only prerequisite for service as arbiter on a Romani court, it is an important attribute.

There are various ways of expressing respect towards elderly people. They are often addressed in Romani respectfully as 'old man' and 'old woman'. Elderly people are the first to be given the floor in any conversation and are not to be interrupted by younger members of the household. The mention of taboo topics such as sexuality or women's health or of any act of defiance against community norms is avoided in the presence of elderly people. In some communities this extends even to the mentioning of certain animals, such as snakes, monkeys and peacocks, which are considered defiled because of their association with evil spirits. In more traditional communities, laundry is hung to dry only out of the sight of elders, and clothes worn by elderly people are washed and dried separately from those of younger, sexually active members of the household, to avoid defilement. While the elderly may be exempted from engaging in economic activities, they are part of family life and will usually contribute by looking after the smaller children.

This highlights an important aspect of Romani family life, namely the inclusion of all age groups in all activities. Children, too, participate in virtually every social activity within the family with the exception of sex. They are present not only at meals and celebrations but also during disputes. They attend funerals and wakes, and accompany their parents to graveyards to visit the tombs of relatives who have passed away. They are not asked to leave when the adults are arguing, negotiating, drinking or mourning. It is exceptional for children to be excluded from conversations or for their daily routine to be regulated any differently from that of the adults. This makes school attendance and the resulting separation of children from their family for several hours every day particularly difficult and often also a very painful experience for Romani families. The thought of a more permanent separation of children through boarding schools or foster homes is even more troublesome, and Roms in countries such as Norway, Sweden, Hungary and Switzerland are still haunted by the memory of periods in the history of their communities during which the practice of separating Romani children from their families was encouraged by authorities as a means of forcibly integrating the young generation of Roms into mainstream society.

Romani parents tend to be very protective of their offspring and will usually not allow them to spend time unaccompanied outside the immediate vicinity of the family's residence. Older siblings, especially girls, are expected to look after their younger siblings. But the entire extended family shares the duty of protecting and caring for children. This allows parents to be separated from their children for several hours or even for several days if necessary without having to make special childcare arrangements. Outsiders often perceive this as a lack of interest, indeed even as negligence, on the part of parents. But from a Romani point of view absolute trust is put in one's close relatives and so there is nothing wrong with placing children in the care of family members.

Children often go with their parents to work, too. The young ones usually tag along with their mothers; at a somewhat older age, boys help fathers in specialized trades and crafts, while girls accompany their mothers or help out in the household. In families and communities where women contribute to the family income by hawking or begging, they usually take their children with them. The involvement of children in street begging has often triggered criticism. In 2009 in Italy, a court ruling that child begging was a Romani cultural practice and should therefore be allowed triggered a public debate. In response, the Italian Parliament adopted a bill that outlawed begging with children. Members of the Romani community would usually dispute the court's interpretation and emphasize that child participation in begging results from a combination of circumstances. Protectiveness prevents parents from leaving their children while they go to work. Romani family values also dictate that life's reality should not be hidden away from children, and so where begging is a necessity and families depend on it for their livelihood, parents do not shy away from admitting this reality to their children. This does not make child begging a Romani cultural practice, and Roms would strongly contest the notion that there is any element of child exploitation in the way they share their daily routines with their children.

The games that Romani youngsters play often involve imitating the lives of Romani adults and their relations with outsiders. The anthropologist Elisabeth Tauber describes how Romani children playing at a caravan site pretend that they are offering to sell things to customers. Teasing is seen as a way of making children stronger. Adults often tease them with remarks that in non-Romani culture would be likely to cause embarrassment. But in Romani society children are viewed as innocent and hence comments about their bodies, excrement and so on are not considered disrespectful but are perceived as affectionate. Romani children are used to continuous overt and emotional expressions of affection from all adults surrounding them. They therefore often find it particularly difficult to adjust to the school environment. In the classroom Romani children are often passive and assume a protected position in the margins. This is reciprocated by the teachers who often opt not to engage with them and even to exclude them from what is happening in the classroom, regarding them as a potential disturbance to the normal conduct of classes. During breaks Romani youngsters tend to stick together and are often not involved in games and the schoolyard activities of other children.

WORK

Roms usually value their independence and flexibility in earning their livelihood. Independence allows not just more choices but it also facilitates sharing resources within the extended family and it enables individuals to be accompanied by family members during work. In order to maintain this independence, Roms often avoid wage work. However, this has not always been possible. During the communist rule in eastern Europe, Roms were often forced to take up jobs in industry and services, either because the authorities imposed restrictions on independent work, or as part of government-sponsored resettlement programmes.

The origins of the Romani way of organizing work remain controversial. Throughout history, Roms have repeatedly been described by outsiders as work-shy due to their reluctance to commit themselves to wage-based employment on somebody else's payroll and to submit to a regulated organization of working hours. Anthropologists studying Romani society, on the other hand, have often tended to highlight the way in which work is organized in Romani communities as the principal distinctive feature of Romani culture. They have viewed the Roms as just one of several societies whose basis is a service economy, lending support to a wholesale categorization of Roms and travelling groups of indigenous origin as Travellers or so-called 'commercial nomads'. A number of writers have suggested that the Roms were originally a caste of warriors, taken prisoner and brought to Europe against their will, and forced to engage in low-prestige service trades.

The fact that some Roms are known to have served as soldiers in various European armies during the seventeenth and eighteenth centuries is sometimes cited as evidence in support of this theory. However, given the consistency with which Roms prefer a certain set of trades, the similarities between the Roms and other service-providing groups of Indian origin outside India, and the similarities in self-appellation and trade portfolio with the Indian service-providing castes of the Dom, there can be little doubt that such specialization is an ancient feature of Romani social organization.

Roms tend to maintain a flexible and diverse range of trades. Popular trades among the Roms include: hawking of manufactured items such as carpets, household wares, plastic flowers, linen, brushes and combs; trading in second-hand goods such as cars, caravans, furniture and antiques, and horses; and selling fruit, vegetables and flowers, as well as jewellery in market stalls. Roms are often engaged in services such as clearing scrap metal and old cars, removing waste from construction sites, paving driveways, pruning trees, installing plastic gutters and carrying out roof repairs; providing entertainment such as musical performance and dancing, and operating rides at fairgrounds; and supplying seasonal labour in agriculture. In the Balkans in particular, Roms often specialize in manufacturing and repairing small tools such as copper pots and pans, skewers, drills and baskets. Specialized services include selling hand-made pegs, charms and metal utensils, and in the past bear-leading, fortune-telling and knife-grinding.

Self-employment allows Roms to combine work with looking after children and the possibility of personal time management. Work is organized within the family, and family members assist in the production and distribution of products. In this way relatives can provide constant support. Family-based work also enables Roms to avoid a strict division between work time and leisure time, and to take time off at will and as a personal choice rather than in the form of scheduled holidays. Family events almost always take priority over employment, while on the other hand the whole family travels together when work opportunities become available in another location. The family environment provides training and education, and there is no formalized graduation or promotion procedure. Skills are instead transferred among family members, and children accompany their parents and in this way they are socialized into the work routine. In the absence of formal professional qualifications, Roms rely on experience and family networks.

But this pattern of work organization has its risks. They include the absence of steady income, lack of job security, and a negative image that is often associated with *ad hoc* negotiation of services, prices and profits. The anthropologist Judith Okely points out that Romani work is characterized by short-term insecurity due to the need to search for clients, but that there is long-term security thanks to self-employment and permanent and regular support of family relations. Roms usually rely on this support from the extended family rather than on pension plans or savings.

The organization of work is also adapted to new situations. In urban environments, especially in the United States and in western Europe, Roms often earn a living as used-car dealers and carpet sellers, and women tell fortunes in shops rather than on the streets, in markets, or by offering their service from door to door. In modern societies welfare benefits are regarded as a potential source of additional steady income. Roms might turn to a non-Romani acquaintance or to members of public services such as social workers or teachers for help in filling in the necessary forms in order to apply for benefits. The time and effort invested in accessing benefits is considered work, comparable to begging, fortune-telling or even entertainment – something that is produced following a certain script for the benefit of outsiders in order to obtain a financial reward. Over the past two decades, the formation of cultural associations has sometimes been seen among some Roms as a further opportunity to generate income. Romani non-governmental organizations are in many cases family-run enterprises and the grants they receive from governments and charitable foundations are used to support family members by employing them in various functions within the association.

In this way, Romani work often has an entrepreneurial character. Romani people are prepared to take risks, they are flexible and make use of new opportunities, and they support one another within the family structure. Some Roms have been successful in accumulating substantial wealth, which they generally tend to invest in lavishly decorated houses and possessions such as cars, furniture, jewellery and artworks. Historically, Roms have tended to be wary of institutions, and even today many do not hold bank accounts. The money they earn from cash transactions is kept at home, or invested in valuables such as gold or antique furniture. The overt display of affluence among the few families of successful and wealthy Romani entrepreneurs often attracts the attention of outsiders, who misinterpret it as unlimited resources and powers that they attribute to the Romani people. In many ways, this attitude is connected to the envy and suspicion that majority society often feels towards the Roms, viewing them as free, flexible and in control of supernatural powers, but also as tricksters and fraudsters. Media reports on wealthy Romani families often contain an element of protest and criticism of the way Roms are generally thought of as poor and defenceless, yet at the same time members of their community openly display their affluence. In 2012, *National Geographic* magazine published a photo series entitled 'Home of the Roma Kings' that portrayed the extravagant mansions of several wealthy Romani families in a Romanian town. Private internet websites display photo series of 'The Life of Rich Gypsies' and are awash with queries such as 'Why are Gypsies so rich?' In actual fact, the great majority of Roms live below the poverty line. Organizations such as the World Bank, Amnesty International and the European Union's Fundamental Rights Agency have all described Romani society over the past decade as poverty inflected. For the most part, Roms are engaged in a fringe economy, relying on occasional services and very often without any source of steady income.

A typical feature of Romani work is geographical mobility, as it is carried out where markets become available. The composition of work teams is variable, but there are often partnerships with others, and occasionally non-Roms are hired to carry out services for the families. In the early 1990s more established urban Romani families engaged young women from Poland, the Czech Republic and Slovakia as childminders and housekeepers and young men from these countries as drivers and handymen. Roms in western Europe often employ Romani immigrants from southeastern Europe (Romania and Bulgaria) to help out in their trades and services.

The manner in which work is organized in Romani communities is nicely illustrated by the examples of two Romani families with whom

I am acquainted. The first originated in Poland and moved to Sweden and then to Germany, spending a few years in the United States. For many years they lived in a caravan, making a living by hawking various household goods in small towns, before moving into a council flat in an apartment block in a major city in Germany. The children left school around the age of twelve. By then they had acquired adequate reading skills but required assistance to write letters or fill in forms. The family set up a carpet restoration business and would receive hand-made rugs and carpets to take home, where all family members participated in renewing colours and damaged threads. In addition, the children spent their weekends at local markets selling small items such as inexpensive watches, necklaces, pictures and other household ornaments. On occasion they would buy larger quantities of objects such as lampshades and torches and travel to smaller towns, selling the goods at makeshift stalls in pedestrian shopping malls. One of the family's sons formed a duo with a talented Romani guitarist and they performed together for several years. At the same time he opened a carpet shop, which he later closed, but continued to buy carpets from local importers and sell them for cash to individual clients, usually doctors and other professionals seeking to invest undeclared cash in valuable household items.

The second example is a Romani Gypsy boy who was raised on a caravan site in northern England. His father sold household goods and his mother told fortunes at fairs and markets. He too left school at the age of twelve to join his father at work. He had some reading skills but very poor writing skills. Together with his brothers he acquired a set of gardening machinery and he often drives around various towns in the region, approaching homeowners and offering to prune trees and hedges. The brothers have access to tarmac construction equipment, which they sometimes rent for several weeks and then drive through neighbourhoods and villages offering potential customers to renew their driveways. They also have contacts with suppliers of plastic gutters and include gutter and window-frame repair in their range of trades. Occasionally they buy used cars, repair them and sell them on for a small profit.

Work provides the principal, and often the exclusive, environment where Roms have contact with non-Roms. Trades and services provided by the Roms therefore define the relationship between themselves and non-Roms. They also shape majority society's image of the Romani minority. The contrast between the way work is organized in Romani society and the norms and rules that govern work among the majority population in both rural and urban industrial societies is representative of both the reciprocal relations and tensions between majority society and the Roms. For most Roms, work is neither a career nor a value in its own right but a means to support their families, though craftsmen and performers certainly take pride in their skills and professional experience. The gravitational centre so to speak of Romani work is neither a patch of land nor an institution such as a factory or office block with its rules, procedures and hierarchies, but family relations and individual creativity and adaptability. Perhaps most importantly, work is almost always a service for clients who are outside the community and who follow a different set of norms and values.

The Roms' livelihood therefore depends on being able to present themselves and their products and services as useful and attractive to outsiders with whom they do not share values, customs and traditions. Members of the majority community in turn are equally ambivalent about their relationship with the Roms. They take an interest in the services that the Roms provide and they often cherish their flexibility – be it as an opportunity to obtain immediate products and services at a low cost or to invest cash with no questions asked – as well as their unique quality in musical performances and divination. Yet at the same time they are often apprehensive and suspicious, since their own majority culture norms lead them to associate mobility and flexibility with lack of reliability and honesty. Throughout history, majority society has therefore sought to take advantage of the services offered by the Roms, while at the same time trying to intervene in order to change the Roms' internal form of social organization and work patterns.

'I DON'T WANT TO BE REPLACED BY A SCHOOL TEACHER': ON EDUCATION

Traditional Romani families educate their children by allowing them to participate in all family activities. Children observe, join in and gradually assume a share of responsibility for the extended household. There is no initiation ceremony and no formal testing of acquired skills or knowledge. School is seen as a Gadje (non-Romani) institution. It represents everything that outsiders stand for and everything that separates Roms from outsiders: rigid rules; obedience towards a person in authority who is not part of the family; oppression of children's own initiative and spontaneous and open expression of emotion; withholding responsibility from children; imposition of arbitrary schedules; and, perhaps the most difficult of all, separation of children from the rest of their family for long hours. School is thus seen as interfering with everyday Romani life and sometimes even as a threat, since it removes children from their families' sphere of influence and weakens their confidence in the ways and traditions of the Romani household.

The school setting conflicts with Romani morality, with its protection of the family unit, and with the natural direction of education in the Romani home, which teaches children to rely on their own assessment of situations rather than to follow strict formulaic behaviour instructions. For travelling Romani households and those who rely on their children's support in seasonal work, obligatory school attendance also constitutes a practical obstacle. Finally, mixing with non-Romani children in adolescence carries the danger of romantic liaisons with outsiders, which threatens to alienate Romani youngsters from their homes and traditions and even to separate them from their families permanently. In many countries in central and eastern Europe, association with non-Romani children was limited for many years as a result of the almost automatic referral of Romani kids to special needs schools. Such schools only contributed, however, to the stigmatization of the Roms while still disrupting traditional family life and weakening parents' ability to act as role models.

School is of course also one of the institutional settings in which Roms face overt and targeted discrimination. Bullying of Romani children on racial grounds is reported in every single country in Europe, and most Roms whom I have known personally, as well as Roms whose testimonies have been cited in numerous expert reports on the school experience of Romani children, tell of a general reluctance on the part of school authorities to undertake any action to prevent such acts of harassment. Indeed, school staff often contribute to the stigmatization and isolation of Romani pupils by excluding them from everyday school activities, forcing them to sit separately in the classroom, and avoiding to engage with them to help build up the self-confidence that is required in order to overcome prejudice and become involved in academic and social activities. In Manchester, I witnessed how primary schools refused to admit children of Romani background, claiming that there were no places in the classrooms, while at the same time those from other backgrounds encountered no such difficulties of admission. I also saw how children of Romani background were kept in separate classes at a local secondary school so that they would not 'slow down' others' learning pace, and I was approached by a deputy head teacher who enquired whether I might be able to support the school's request to the education authority to exclude Romani children from the assessments on the school's attainment statistics in order to boost the school's image.

In most Romani communities it is now recognized that school cannot be avoided at younger ages. Some families send their children to school only reluctantly, hoping at least that they will benefit from the opportunity to acquire some key skills such as basic literacy, which can prove useful to the family as a whole. Many Romani communities have learned to integrate the presence of the school institution into their way of life. The anthropologist Elisabeth Tauber describes how Romani families have come to regard the school setting as the first opportunity that their children have to observe the ways of the Gadje and to practise the maintenance of a demarcation line between Roms and non-Roms. Traditional Romani suspicion towards schools as Gadje institutions is almost invariably reinforced by hostile attitudes towards Romani children on the part of the majority children and their parents and very often by the teachers and the school establishment. This adds to the pain of Romani parents, who feel reluctant yet forced to abandon their offspring to the emotional and often physical abuse of being an unwanted minority in an unwelcoming environment, ignorant of their needs and values and confident in the supremacy of its own norms.

The strategy that most traditional Romani families prefer to pursue is to send their children to primary school, allowing them relative freedom of attendance and even encouraging them to play truant occasionally as a way of signalling that loyalty to the family and participation in important family events take precedence. As parents, they will attempt to maintain a respectful but distanced relationship with the school, always siding with their children in the event of conflict. This is regarded as yet another way to teach them the value of mutual support and loyalty. Together with their children they will endure any hardships encountered by their kids at school, reminding themselves that this is an opportunity for the children to obtain an understanding of Gadje values and priorities, an understanding on which they can later on draw in work transactions with the Gadje.

Many Romani parents withdraw their children from school before they reach puberty. They often give several reasons for this. The most commonly cited is the fear of drugs, violence and other threatening behaviour that is often associated with secondary schools, especially in deprived areas. Another is the fear of alienation from their home environment. Yet a further, more specific reason is the fear that boys and girls might be called to participate together in sex education classes. In the Romani context, this would bring shame upon them and much effort would be required to restore their honour in the eyes of others within the Romani community. It is not just sex education that is the cause of the anxiety. Once children reach puberty they become responsible and so susceptible to the Romani rules that govern shame and honour. At this stage of their lives, they must therefore return to the community, where every aspect of their behaviour can be scrutinized to make sure that their conduct is honourable. Absence for long parts of the day without being in the company of adults, whether family or neighbours, means an escape from this scrutiny and this might make them vulnerable to suspicions of dishonourable behaviour, whether well founded or not.

Some Romani families feel uncomfortable sending adolescent boys and girls together to school, as they are worried more specifically about romantic liaisons that might emerge outside of the family's control. They also fear that any sexual behaviour or even reference to sex made towards their girls or even just in their presence might dishonour them. Although these issues are of common concern to various Romani communities, they are often handled in different ways. Among the Gabor Roma, girls attend only primary school. Boys usually continue into secondary school in order to learn sufficient reading and writing to pass their theoretical driving tests and obtain a driving licence, which is essential for their businesses. Among Romani Gypsies in England, the practice is often the reverse: boys stop attending school in adolescence and go out to work with their fathers. Boys and men often have great difficulties with literacy and rely on their wives for help with forms and letters. Girls do not go out to work, and so they can continue to attend school until they marry, which is often at the age of sixteen or seventeen. Therefore they often attain higher literacy levels than boys.

Like work, school is also a potential source of tension and conflict between traditional Romani society and the majority's institutional norms and values. While modern societies view school education as a universal necessity, education authorities often fail to recognize that the content of the school curriculum and the way in which learning and discipline are organized in schools are not at all free of cultural bias, and that the imposition of a certain set of norms on members of a minority culture can cause alienation, insecurity and loss of self-esteem – even aggression and hostility. In some European countries, there is much debate on reforming the curriculum and introducing Romani content. This too is controversial. Ironically, many Romani parents have accepted the fact that school is an alien institution, ignorant of and even hostile towards Romani culture. They are prepared to send their kids to school on the understanding that the children will come to regard school as alien territory and thus maintain their loyalty to their family traditions. These families sometimes view with concern plans to introduce sessions on Romani language, history and traditions into the school curriculum. They fear that this will weaken the parents' authority, as it will take away their responsibility for transferring Romani culture to their children. 'I teach my children Romani culture at home,' I heard a Romani father arguing at a public meeting about curriculum reform. 'I don't want to be replaced by a school teacher.'

A NEW DESTINY?

There are no reliable statistics on the number of Roms in the world today. Estimates range from 3 or 4 up to 10 million or more. The actual number is likely to be somewhere in between. There is no doubt that Roms form large minorities of around 200,000 and perhaps more in the United States, and that Romani populations of a significant size can be found in countries such as Mexico, Venezuela, Argentina, Colombia and Australia, the descendants of immigrants who began to arrive there over a century ago. In Europe, the largest Romani population is still in the Balkans. Romania is believed to have the highest number of Roms, up to 2 million or some 10 per cent of the total population. Romani minorities of 500,000 or more are found in Bulgaria, Slovakia, Spain and Turkey. Quite a few countries have Romani populations of somewhere between 100,000 and 400,000: Hungary, Macedonia, Serbia, Germany, Russia and possibly also Italy and Greece.

A survey published by the European Union's Fundamental Rights Agency in 2012 revealed that 90 per cent of the Roms surveyed lived in households with an income below national poverty lines. Around 40 per cent lived in households where somebody had to go to bed hungry at least once a month because the family could not afford to buy food. Some 45 per cent lived in households that lacked appropriate washing and cooking facilities or electricity. The survey also found that, on average, only half of Romani children attended preschool or kindergarten, and only 15 per cent completed secondary school. Some two thirds of Roms did not have a regular income, and a third of the respondents aged between thirty-five and fifty-five reported health problems that limited their daily activities. In addition, half of the Roms surveyed said that they had experienced discrimination because of their ethnic background. European governments are aware of the challenges posed by this state of deprivation and marginalization. At the request of the European Commission, in late 2011 they produced a document, 'National Strategies for Roma Inclusion', setting out measures and policies to improve the situation of the Romani minorities. The challenge facing the Roms today is how to find their place among the nations in a way that ensures the continuation of their traditions and strong sense of identity, while at the same time allowing them to participate in shaping their destiny and making full use of the opportunities that modern societies can offer.

Romani society is currently undergoing what is probably the most significant transition in its history. For many centuries, Roms were marginalized and had no choice but to occupy a very specific niche in the socio-economic, political and cultural world around them. But changes to society, such as growing awareness of ethnic diversity and ethnic tolerance, universal access to education, new communication technologies and more, have opened up new opportunities to the Roms in many countries, and scores of individual Roms and their families make use of these opportunities. Since I began working with Roms I have met a huge diversity of individuals in a range of professions: an American Rom who is a high-ranking army officer, a Polish Rom who is a leading civil servant in the human rights division of a large international organization, a Bulgarian Rom who is a lawyer, a Serbian Rom who is a translator and theatre director, a Hungarian Romni (Romani woman) who is a journalist and television broadcaster, a Romanian Romni who is the author of school textbooks, a Slovak Romni who is a social worker, and countless more. Two of my own former Romani students have excelled in professional jobs. The first, a Romani woman from Russia, graduated with distinction and was appointed coordinator for social inclusion of Romani immigrants from eastern Europe in the municipal council of a middle-sized town in England. The second, a Romani woman from Bulgaria, is continuing her career as a secondary school teacher after she completed her postgraduate studies.

The democratization process that began in post-communist central and eastern Europe in 1990 saw the formation of dozens if not hundreds of local and regional Romani cultural and political associations. Civil society foundations and charities of various kinds have provided support and training to a generation of Romani activists, who have had the opportunity to form transnational networks and to meet in seminars, conferences and online discussion forums. This generation is searching for a new way to define the relations between the Roms and their environment. Their destiny is no longer restricted to a family-based service economy, alienated from school and trapped in rigid gender roles.

This does not mean, however, that they wish to abandon traditional cultural values such as family-based networks and mutual support, respect for elderly people, the Romani language, and the flexibility and adaptability that characterize traditional Romani society. The challenge that they face is how to create a synthesis of their cultural heritage with the opportunities that a modern society can offer. For many, one of the most urgent tasks is to confront society's anti-Romani prejudices, which put obstacles in their way, and to assist their people to overcome poverty and deprivation.

3

Customs and Traditions

APPEARANCE AND DRESS

Conscious of Romani origins in India, some authors have tended to search for similarities between the customs of the Roms and those of the various peoples of the Indian subcontinent. Similarities have been suggested in dress, food preparation, music, dance, burial customs and more. But there is general agreement that Romani culture has been, if anything, more greatly influenced by the numerous contacts that the Roms have had over the centuries with neighbouring populations. These have shaped the practices of the various Romani communities in different ways. Some ethnographers have also suggested that Romani customs have been influenced by the cultures of travelling communities of non-Indic origin. It is clear in any case that Romani culture is not uniform and that the customs practised by Romani people have different sources and origins. Nonetheless, some practices are typical of a large number of Romani communities and may be said to be characteristic of the Roms.

In Romani culture the display of prosperity is considered honourable and a token of good fortune. In some traditional communities women wear golden bracelets and necklaces, and headscarves are sometimes decorated with golden coins. Caravans and apartments often have an altar-like corner in which religious icons are displayed along with fresh flowers and golden and silver ornaments. Roms who can afford them invest much of their money in new and expensive cars or caravans. Generosity is similarly considered honourable and showing hospitality by offering food and gifts is a proper way to celebrate friendship, mark the end of disputes or share the success of a business venture. Generosity towards others in the community is an investment in a network of social contacts on which individual Roms and their families can rely in the event of economic or other hardship. For this reason traditional Roms generally prefer to spend money earned in a successful transaction on gifts and other tokens of generosity rather than to save it in a bank account.

Investments are sometimes made in items of symbolic capital, the value of which is primarily internal to the community. Horses are an example and, although they also have an outside market, they are bred and traded within the community and their worth is determined according to the owner's status. Among some of the Transylvanian Roms silver beakers are traded as investments, with their value determined by their history of ownership within the community; for the English Gypsies, carved wooden caravans are considered valuable collector's items.

As tight-knit social units whose members are fond of displaying success and sharing wealth, Romani communities are very receptive to new fashions in all aspects of life. New styles, commodities and opportunities are shared within the community and members of a group tend to be quick in adopting them once they become available. Joining religious movements may constitute an extreme case of fashion involving a long-term commitment and influencing many spheres of an individual's life. At the same time it also provides a framework within which many traditional values can be preserved and protected. Other fashions are recognizable in the choice of first names for newly born babies, the preferred make of cars and caravans, as well as in migration destinations.

Roms are often recognizable to other Roms not just through language but also through their appearance and dress codes. Women usually wear necklaces, which are often embellished with gold coins. Older Romani men often sport thin moustaches and a hat and sometimes a scarf around their neck. Among Roms in urban communities, shiny suits and ties are worn as a display of fashion, elegance and status. Men, too, wear jewellery such as golden rings and necklaces. The style of the hat and waistcoat is often characteristic of particular Romani nations or clan affiliation. Women wear skirts, the length varying according to group, age and marital status. Among most of the Vlax Roma, married women wear a white apron above their skirt and a headscarf called *diklo*. Skirts are always worn below the knee as it is considered shameful to expose parts of the lower body. Traditional Romani men and women will therefore avoid wearing shorts. Since trousers are associated with men's lower bodies, traditional Romani women will not wear trousers, either. Among the young generation of Romani women, especially in the Balkans, in central Europe, in Spain and in Britain, trousers are no longer considered taboo. While in many communities only unmarried girls wear trousers, it is perhaps a sign of changing times that in Britain, young Romani girls often wear short skirts and even shorts that expose their legs, especially at festivities and gatherings such as fairs and weddings.

GOOD FORTUNE AND SHAME

Outsiders have often regarded the oral traditions of the Roms as an antiquated system of taboos. In fact, life in Romani communities is tightly regulated by a code of practice of traditions and values. These practices vary among Romani groups, as can be expected from an oral culture that is practised in geographically dispersed communities. The main pillar of Romani morality is a symbolic distinction between what is sometimes termed 'honour' or 'good fortune' (Romani *pativ* and *baxt*, pronounced 'ba-h-t') and 'shame' (Romani *ladž*, pronounced 'ladj'). Another way of referring to this polarity of practices is 'pure' and 'impure', or 'clean' and 'defiled'. This particular terminology is not directly present in Romani, though many Romani communities have a concept that indicates 'impure' or ritually 'unclean' or 'defiled': *mahrime*, *maxado* (pronounced 'ma-ha-do') or *magardo*.

The contrast between 'honour' and 'shame', and 'clean' and 'defiled', applies to a range of subjects, including food, cleanliness, the body, conversation topics as well as general behaviour and respect towards other members of the Romani community. The body is generally divided into upper and lower. The upper body is considered free of shame and men and women alike are allowed to expose parts of it without losing respect or disrespecting others (the stereotype of the seductive Gypsy woman, often depicted in arts and literature, derives in part from outsiders' misinterpretation of the partial exposure of the upper body by Romani women as a sexual advance). The lower body, by contrast, is considered unclean and Roms will avoid exposing it. They will also avoid any contact, direct or indirect, between the lower body and the upper body and especially between the lower body and the face. Clothes that cover different body parts must be washed separately and separate washbasins and separate towels must be used to wash and to dry the upper and the lower body. Towels in different colours are often allocated for different tasks such as drying dishes, the upper body and the lower body. Bars of soap used to wash the face and the rest of the body are also distinguished through their colours or shapes. Most Roms avoid bathing since water that comes into contact with the lower body may in this way pollute the upper body and face area. Clothes belonging to women and men and those covering the upper and lower body are washed and hung separately to dry. In some communities, the clothes of elderly people are washed and hung separately, too, as a sign of respect and to avoid defilement through contact with the clothes of sexually active members of the family. In order to maintain this separation Roms in some settlements make extensive use of communal laundry facilities in a way that outsiders often regard as selfish or wasteful. Children are considered innocent and hence free of the danger of defilement and their clothes can be washed together with those of adults.

Food must not be mixed with any item that is considered unclean, such as anything associated with the lower body, the floor or animals. Objects used in connection with food cannot touch the lower body or anything associated with it, such as clothing, and they cannot be rinsed together with them in the same basin. Dishes are never dried with towels that may have come into contact with clothes during washing. Some Romani clans maintain a cleanliness code that requires them to throw away cutlery that has touched the lower body. A knife or a cup dropped on the floor must be disposed of and the same pertains to cutlery that may have slipped accidentally into a basin that is used for washing clothes. Some Romani populations, especially those living in Germany, Poland and Finland, maintain these rules very strictly and will not share plates or cutlery or food with anyone, not even other Roms, who does not adhere to the same specific cleanliness code.

In many Romani communities women are not allowed to prepare food for others during pregnancy, immediately after giving birth or during their menstrual period. This is easily managed by sharing the cooking in the larger household. Among evangelical Roms women will not attend church services for up to three months after giving birth and will not touch the Bible. At the end of this isolation period a ceremony similar to a christening is performed, whereby the woman washes her hands and the baby's face in water and both are then considered clean.

Women's lower clothing such as skirts and aprons is considered especially polluted, as is any association with menstrual blood, both verbal and material. Women's skirts are not allowed to come into contact, even accidentally, with any object that might be associated with food (and so with the mouth), such as a table, a tablecloth, or any cooking or eating utensil. Men can be defiled by coming into contact in public with a woman's skirt or underwear and they can be dishonoured by direct or indirect reference in public to birth, pregnancy or menstruation. Women in turn are dishonoured by public mention of sexual acts. Reference to any such topics is therefore avoided in mixed company. Swearing with sexual overtones is, however, not uncommon among Roms. There are various idiomatic expressions in the Romani language that have a sexual connotation (for example the exclamation 'I will eat your penis/vagina!') and swearing is used as a form of teasing in the home. In public it is sometimes directed at non-Roms who do not understand the expressions. Among Roms, both men and women avoid indicating directly that they are going to use the toilet and will instead use euphemisms such as saying that they are about to wash their hands or take care of an errand. Girls are usually taught to maintain their dignity by showing shame and embarrassment as regards their sexual desirability. They are taught not to look into men's eyes or to make gestures that might be interpreted as sexual. This contrasts sharply with the outsiders' image of Gypsy women as seductive and promiscuous.

In some traditional Romani communities the notion of contact between a woman's lower body and men's food or upper bodies is extended considerably in its symbolism and women are expected to avoid stepping over any utensil that might be associated with food (thus sitting on a dining table or coffee table is strictly avoided), stepping over water sources such as a well or water container, or symbolically stepping over men's upper bodies by walking on a higher floor of a building when men are known to be present below. Many traditional Romani families in western and northern Europe prefer to live in caravans or single-storey houses to avoid a situation where this might happen.

Caravans are also considered cleaner since they enable a clearly visible separation outside the caravan of water sources and spaces that are used for washing and cooking and this prevents any suspicion of contamination that might arise in a house through the adjacency of toilets and kitchens. Romani families who live in caravans will not usually use the shower or toilets installed in the caravan and will instead wash either outdoors or in the public facilities provided at organized stopping sites. Kitchens and cookers installed in the caravan are usually used to prepare only tea or coffee and sandwiches, while cooking is done outside, on a gas cooker or traditionally on an open fire. Dishes are rinsed in plastic bowls in public view and the washing of clothes is also carried out outdoors, both in order to protect the intimate living environment of the caravan and to ensure that neighbours are aware that the family observes the strict rules on separation of dishes, clothes and other items. In central and eastern Europe most Roms live in one-storey accommodation and share washing and kitchen spaces and so suspicions of this kind can be more easily avoided. The symbolic separation of the upper and lower body is also observed in the dress code of women, who maintain a visible demarcation line between the clothing that covers the lower body (skirt and apron) and the clothing that covers the upper body. One-piece dresses are regarded as shameful.

Since non-Gypsies (Gadje) do not observe these rules they are often considered shameless or dishonourable and close contact with them, especially the sharing of food, is avoided. Many traditional Romani people will not eat food that is prepared by Gadje or even by Roms of another ethnic sub-group whose notion of shame and honour might differ in the detail from theirs. Some Roms are happy to offer food to Gadje but will not re-use any food utensils, towels or bars of soap that were touched by their non-Romani guests for fear of ritual pollution. Many English Gypsies prefer to buy linen and towels at Gypsy fairs rather than in shops owned by Gadje (or 'Gorgios', as they call them in their speech), not because of the quality or the identity of the manufacturer but because of the opportunity to show in public that these items are being purchased brand new from other Gypsies and that the buyer is thereby taking every precaution to minimize the risk of symbolic contamination.

I had a close friend in a Polish Romani community whom I used to visit from time to time. The group of related families to which he belonged lived in a series of adjoining apartment blocks. Their children would play on the street and the pavements, and weather permitting, windows were kept open in the flats so that parents could peek out and make sure that all was well. This also meant that comings and goings in the community were visible to all. My friend, a trained school teacher and also a singer in the family ensemble, was not a traditionalist, and on some occasions, when I visited after nightfall, I would be served food and drink at his apartment, usually in the presence of his wife, children and elderly parents. At his younger son's christening, I was even invited to join the men's table and share a drink from the glass that was passed around the table, from one guest to another, along with what seemed like a never-ending supply of bottles of strong spirit. Yet when I happened to visit in the daytime, in viewing range of the neighbours, the point had to be made that the family would not share its food or cutlery with me, an outsider. My host then took me out, waving to the neighbours who were standing near their open windows and greeting them politely, and leading me demonstrably down the street and into a small restaurant, where we sat by the large window for lunch. It was essential that people knew that the rules were being adhered to in his household.

While traditional Romani families will take precautions to avoid defilement, good fortune or baxt is celebrated and it is therefore considered honourable to display success and generosity in public. In addition to the public showing of precious possessions and ornaments such as jewellery and brightly coloured clothing, generosity is expressed by sharing food with other Roms. Romani households typically cook much more than is needed to feed members of the family, as households like to have food ready to offer to Romani visitors, and whatever is offered to guests must not appear to be left over from a family meal. Not to have food to offer to a fellow Rom is considered shameful. Naturally, the extent to which boundaries between Roms and non-Roms are maintained in regard to food and generosity differs considerably across communities and individual families. Some of the most lavish meals I've ever been served were at the tables of Romani hosts. Over a period of several weeks I was invited almost every day to share food and drink with a number of Serbian Romani families. My English Romani friends at a caravan site used to request that I carefully time my visits and announce them in advance to give them an opportunity to prepare a meal, and I have vivid memories of a feast that lasted for many hours, and at which I was the guest of honour, at the home of a Latvian Romani family.

Roms often believe that certain diseases are a result of failure to comply with cleanliness rules and that they represent a state of defile-ment. In addition to availing themselves of modern medical resources, Roms suffering from an illness will therefore often seek remedy from a Romani 'doctor' – usually an elderly woman with experience in healing using traditional medicines such as herbs and leaves.

Certain animals are associated with pollution in Romani culture. Most Romani people do not eat horsemeat, which is otherwise con-sumed frequently, especially in central European countries, although horses are considered 'clean' animals and their images are commonly displayed in Romani homes. Dogs and cats are considered 'unclean' and contact with them and with images depicting them is avoided. Frogs and snakes are believed to be unlucky as they are associated with the Devil, and peacocks are associated with evil eye, hence images of all these animals and even symbols resembling them are not found in Romani homes. Rabbits, hares and hedgehogs, on the other hand, can be eaten. Fur has to be completely removed from the rabbits and hares, while spines are traditionally removed from a hedgehog by baking the animal in a clay shield on an open fire.

An abstract representation of the polarity between good fortune and honour, and shame and defilement, is the conflict between the notions of God (*o del* or *o devel*) and the Devil (*o beng*). There is no specific depiction of either entity in Romani tradition. The name of God is often used in greetings and blessings as the provider of health, strength and good fortune. It is interesting that Christian teaching is adopted rather loosely into Romani discourse, with God and Christ both represented as 'our Lord' (*amaro devel*) with no specific distinction between them. The Devil is more of a figurative attribute to bad persons ('the little devil' suggests an evil, disloyal individual) and in some stories an abstract entity that appears in competition with God.

The notions of shame and defilement also extend to the dichotomy of life and death. Once the mourning period that follows a death in the family has ended, the proximity to the dead is considered quite literally as haunting and as a disturbance of the separation between life and death. Among the Romani clans of England and Wales it was customary until recently to burn a dead man's caravan with all his belongings, and among the French Roms the possessions of the deceased were destroyed. Returning to a place of death or sleeping in proximity to a burial site is believed to carry the risk of confrontation with ghosts, which in Romani are referred to as *mule* or 'the dead'. Most Roms will avoid mentioning dead relations by name and will simply use the general term 'our dead people' (*amare mule*) to denote ancestors who are no longer among the living.

To some people, the Romani notion of ghosts might seem old-fashioned, romantic or perhaps even a stereotype that has no anchoring in reality. Certainly, not all Roms believe in ghosts, but reference to the ghosts of the dead in casual conversation is not infrequent among Romani families. I witnessed the reluctance of some Roms from southeastern Europe who had immigrated to Germany to take part in commemoration ceremonies for Romani victims of the genocide in the Second World War when these were held at the sites of former concentration camps because they feared that the spirits of the dead were still present there. Nonetheless, it was only a small minority who expressed such anxieties and most of the community members participated with no hesitation.

I have heard many stories from Romani friends about their fear of ghosts. One woman told me about her family's trips to the countryside during the summer months, where they would sell small household artefacts such as pictures, lamps and various decorations door to door and at markets. They would leave their homes for a long weekend with the merchandise and spend the nights in small hotels along the way. Once, my friend reported, her mother-in-law came storming into her room in panic in the middle of the night. She had heard somebody knocking on her window. They woke up the entire family and everybody circled the small hotel building in search of an intruder, but found nothing. The next morning they asked the hotel manager about the building's history. It appeared that in the immediate vicinity, hidden away behind a small but dense group of trees, there was an old cemetery. The family now knew who was responsible for the mysterious knocks on the window: it had been the spirits of the dead, the *mule*.

For the most part, this ancient fear of ghosts surfaces merely in the form of a casual expression. Another friend told me about an odd event that occurred while her family was travelling in caravans in Scandinavia. One morning they got up to find that the plastic washbasin, which was kept outdoors at night, beneath the caravan, had disappeared. The children were asked about its whereabouts, but nobody had seen it. 'Where can the washbasin have disappeared to?' asked their mother. 'There were no *mule* here to take it away!'

MARRIAGE

Marriage in traditional Romani communities is often arranged by the fathers of the groom and the bride in consultation with other male members of their families, though women usually take an active role in the search for a suitable partner and in initiating the formal approach to the prospective partner's family. Fathers, especially, often travel long distances in order to find suitable brides for their sons, and seek advice from friends and relations. Marriages can be arranged at gatherings such as fairs, pilgrimages or other festivities in which various families get together and have an opportunity to discuss issues of common interest. Marriage usually requires the consent of the bride's parents, for which the groom's family makes a formal request. In some communities the groom's family pays a so-called 'bride price' to the family of the bride. This does not, however, mean that brides are bought and sold. The Roms actually refer to the bride price as a 'gift' or 'present'. The bride's family uses the money to finance the wedding and to purchase such things as beddings, clothing, and jewellery for the bride, which she then brings with her to her husband's household. This is intended to strengthen the bride's position when joining her husband's family, making her less dependent on their financial support immediately after the marriage. Sometimes the bride's family will use some of the money to pay off debts, another way of supporting the family's independence.

Although marriages are often arranged, the marriage requires the bride's consent and no girl is forced into marriage. However, there is often social and family pressure on both boys and girls not to disappoint the parents, who have made an effort to seek what they sincerely believe to be the best arrangement for their children. One of the most moving personal accounts I have heard of such circumstances came from a young Romani woman in southern Romania. At the age of nineteen she was called by her parents, who, without any previous discussion or even a hint, announced that she would be marrying a boy whom she had known all her life, the son of neighbours from her community. The boy, too, received the news in a similar fashion. The girl cried and tried to persuade her parents to cancel the arrangement, but to no avail. Cancellation would bring shame on the family. On the wedding day she was guided by a number of middle-aged women from her family. They washed her and dressed her, and inspected her body for any wounds or scratches. The custom was to display the bloodstained sheet publicly after the wedding night as proof of the bride's virginity, and any interference and misinterpretations had to be avoided.

The girl, we can call her 'Dorina', turned to the only person who might become her ally: her husband to be. 'Neither of us wants this marriage,' she said to him when they were both delivered together into the bedroom that they were now instructed to share. 'Let's just walk away.' The boy felt the same way, but explained that there would be no future for either of them in the community if they did so. They would end up having to bond together, just as a means of surviving. The only way the marriage could be avoided was if the girl proved not to be a virgin, but Dorina had not been with any other man before. After two days of deliberations, caught in a small bedroom together with relatives waiting outside for the announcement that the marriage was now official, they agreed to do as expected of them. They shared their lives for several years and had two children. Then Dorina's husband left her for another woman. She, in turn, left her home town and moved, together with family, to another country. She remarried, this time by choice. She now feels free to tell the story of the husband whom she never wanted to marry, but who became her friend, and whom she says she still loves.

An alternative to arranged marriages is marriage by elopement. This occurs when a young couple decide to legitimize their relationship by going away together. A negotiation process with the families is then initiated via trusted intermediaries, with the final settlement in most cases being the recognition of the relationship by the families and the return of the couple into the community and into the groom's household. It took me quite a while to understand what one of my Romani friends meant when he jokingly commented about my friendly relationship with his wife: 'One day you two will run away together.' Of course, this had not occurred to either of us, and as a group we spent much time together, sharing eventful times and many laughs. But in my world, if relationships broke up and others took their place, there was no need to 'run away'. In the Romani setting, elopement was the way of dealing with any relationship that had not been formally sanctioned in advance by the community, represented by the elders, the parents or the older siblings of those involved.

In most cases, following marriage, a couple joins the groom's household, where the wife assumes the duties of the *bori* or daughter-in-law: a variety of household tasks, which she carries out under the supervision of the mother-in-law, often together with the older daughters of the family. In isolated cases, a husband may join his wife's household. Marriage within one's own Romani group is preferred, but marriage within the extended family is usually prohibited, and this includes kin up to the level of first cousin. Generally, marriages with non-Roms are looked upon with disfavour, but in cases when they do occur the usual pattern is for the non-Romani wife to be accepted into her Romani husband's household. The children are then considered full members of the family and of the Romani group. Daughters who marry outside the group, on the other hand, typically leave. However, exceptions do occur, and when non-Romani men join the household of their Romani wife their children, again, are considered full members of the household.

From the Romani perspective, a lasting romantic liaison constitutes a marriage as soon as it has the recognition of the families and the community. Marriage is the only way to form relationships, though young couples can also move in together and have children soon after. Girls usually quit school after marriage and boys will have left school and begun to work, usually with their fathers, before they are considered able to support a family and allowed to marry. Roms often 'marry' at a very young age – sixteen or seventeen, but sometimes even as young as fourteen or fifteen, which is below the legal age for formal marriage in most countries in which they reside. For this and other reasons, Roms often do not register their marriages officially, even those that take place in a church and are conducted by a priest. Women do not take their husband's surname even though they move to live with their husband's family, because surnames are considered a formality that is relevant only in dealings with administrative institutions and agencies. Children may assume the surname of either the father or the mother.

The marriage celebrations often go on for several days. In some communities they begin with dancing parties held at the houses of the groom and the bride. On the following day the bride is brought from her paternal home to the home of the groom's family, accompanied by her male relatives and a musical band, intended to attract as much attention as possible and the participation of a crowd of friends, neighbours and onlookers. The central event of the marriage celebration is a banquet. In many communities, men and women sit separately at the banquet. In the Balkans it is often customary, as in the case of Dorina's marriage, to display the blood-stained sheet in public after the wedding night as proof of the bride's virginity and the fact that the marriage has now been consummated, as is the custom in many eastern Mediterranean and western Asian cultures.

In western countries there is usually a church wedding ceremony, a lavish procession that often draws the attention of the local community, and a reception with much dancing. Fancy cars and horse-drawn wagons are often used and the brides' dresses are usually exceptionally extravagant. In recent years Roms have begun to upload videos of weddings onto YouTube and other online forums. In Britain, Romani weddings have received wide public attention through the broadcast of the Channel 4 series *Big Fat Gypsy*

Weddings from 2010, which documented weddings among Romani Gypsies and Irish Travellers. The series followed young girls from both communities in the weeks of preparation for their weddings, and on their wedding day itself. It highlighted the young age of marriage among Gypsies and Travellers, the importance of parental consent to the marriage and of the bride's virginity, and the vast expense a family undertook to ensure that their daughter's wedding day was a memorable event. The cameras documented the logistic preparations and showed the exotic vehicles that took the bride and groom to and from the wedding venue. They spared no detail in the coverage of the main attraction of the wedding ceremony – the voluminous silk wedding dresses, often embroidered with gold, pearls and gems. The series has been criticized, not least within the Romani community, for its sensationalism. Yet few could deny that it has brought Romani and Traveller culture to the attention of a wider public, as the coverage of these over-the-top weddings has attracted huge viewer audiences. But the producers also used the opportunity to tell the personal stories of Romani girls caught between a wish to pursue formal education and loyalty to their families' travelling lifestyle, of Romani families who gave up travelling and were adjusting to life in permanent homes, of evictions of Romani caravans by local authorities, and of Romani protests against restrictions imposed on their annual gatherings. The fascination with Romani weddings offered many people who would otherwise have remained oblivious an insightful, if slightly slanted, view through a window into everyday life in the Romani and Traveller communities.

A Romani marriage can be broken up at the initiative of either of the partners. In some cases, where adultery or another dispute between them is involved, the fate of the marriage can be referred to the Romani court for arbitration. A husband who wishes to divorce his wife may under certain circumstances be advised by the court to return the bride price to her family. If a wife is unfaithful, the husband may bring a case against her and ask the court to rule that the wife's lover should pay compensation to the husband. Men's romantic liaisons outside marriage are, on the other hand, usually considered acceptable. Moreover, if the bride's family insists on breaking up the marriage, they may be asked to pay compensation to the husband. Among some Roms any dissolution of a marriage requires the consent of the Romani court, which will initially attempt to iron out the differences between the couple, and the families often call an elderly member of the community to arbitrate between the partners.

THE 'ETERNAL ROOM': DEATH AND FUNERALS

Funeral customs differ across Romani communities, but some patterns are shared. All Roms hold a vigil for the dead. The vigil reaffirms the brotherhood among the Roms and allows them to signal their allegiance to one another by remaining in the company of the deceased from the moment of death until the funeral. In many Romani communities the vigil continues for fourteen nights. This provides time for relatives to arrive from more distant places and for word to spread among other families, who send representatives to pay their respects. The Roms believe that the presence of a large group of people lends support to the grieving family. Unlike in weddings, no invitations are sent out to funerals or vigils, since members of the community, friends and acquaintances all know that it is their duty to attend. Failure to attend is considered disrespectful and will bring shame on the person who is absent and their immediate family. By contrast, failure to attend a wedding simply constitutes a missed opportunity to meet others and to catch up on news. Weddings are gatherings of mainly relatives, friends and neighbours, whereas participation in funerals is expected even from people who were not familiar with the deceased or his immediate family, as a way of paying their respects.

The mourning feast is referred to in the Vlax Romani communities by the Romanian word *pomana*. In southeastern and central Europe many of the Romani practices surrounding funerals are shared with the neighbouring populations. Both Orthodox and Catholic rites that are common among the Romanians, Bulgarians and Hungarians are replicated. They include visiting the cemetery on particular days during Easter and offering food and drink, holding a feast to mark the end of the mourning period, and, among close relatives, dressing in black and not shaving for the duration of the mourning period and avoiding forms of entertainment such as dance and joyful music. Commemoration vigils for the dead often take place six weeks after the funeral, and then again after one year. In Romani communities in the Balkans, water that has been collected is poured out of the house when a person dies, windows are opened and mirrors are removed or covered with a cloth. Candles are lit within the house and the body is washed before it is placed on display for the wake. In some communities, relatives of the same sex as the deceased are responsible for washing the body, while in others this is the task of elderly women.

During the vigil, the deceased lies in an open coffin in an adjoining room. The body is carefully dressed and in many Romani communities coins are placed on the eyes and money in the pockets of the deceased. The vigil is often held in the family home, or, among some Roms, in a chapel or at the morgue. Usually several tables are set out with food and drinks, while another area of the room or an adjoining room contains chairs and benches. Serving food is the family's way of reciprocating the support it receives from the mourners who gather for the vigil. It is customary not to greet the other visitors or family members upon arrival, as the usual Romani greeting *Te aven baxtale!* literally means 'May you be happy!' so it is considered inappropriate at a time of mourning. Singing, however, is allowed in many communities as an expression of grief or as a way to remember the deceased by performing his favourite songs, but merry songs and dancing are avoided. Drinking is an important part of the gathering and serves to keep the assembled mourners together. Getting drunk at a vigil or a funeral is permitted and often even expected of close relatives and friends of the deceased as a way of expressing their solidarity with one another. Some Romani communities maintain a strict separation between men and women during the vigil, each group being allocated a distinct seating area.

The involvement of religious institutions is often secondary. A priest (or, in Muslim Romani communities, an imam) is invited to bless the deceased and to say a prayer, but the arrangements and procedure of the funeral follow Romani tradition. The centre of the funeral procession is a horse-drawn hearse. Accompanied by mourners, sometimes in vehicles, it will travel through the streets of the village or town on its way to the cemetery. In England such Romani funerals tend to draw large crowds of spectators because they are so lavish and unusual. In eastern Europe villagers tend to be more familiar with this Romani custom. Where there is a significant Romani population the procession will circle the entire village, often stopping at places that the deceased used to frequent such as favourite bars and cafés.

Among some Roms the dead are buried in burial chambers that are often extensive. The construction of the burial chamber varies among Romani communities, but it often consists of brick walls and is decorated with carpets and ornaments as it is considered to be the 'eternal room' where the deceased will remain for ever. Rugs are often placed on the floor. The coffin is lowered into the grave along with a selection of the deceased person's favourite and often most valuable possessions and personal trinkets. Some groups bury only small items for personal needs in the coffin, such as jewellery, a bar of soap, a comb, perfume, bottles of drink, cigarettes, a wallet or coins to accompany the dead person on his way. In other groups larger possessions may be lowered into the grave, such as a musical instrument, artistic artefacts of various kinds, a television set, a tape recorder and even chairs and other furniture.

The chamber is then covered with beams and plastic sheets and earth is spread over the top. In many Romani communities the custom is to avoid contact between the earth and the coffin and the body of the deceased so that the weight of the earth will not be a burden on his soul. The burial chamber is sealed on all sides to avoid contact between the body and underground creatures such as snakes, frogs or worms.

Romani tombstones are seen as an opportunity to display a family's generosity and good fortune. They stand out because of their size and ornaments, usually carrying photos of the deceased and golden inscriptions. Families often reserve a cluster of gravesites within a cemetery, thus creating a Romani area. The cost of vigils, funeral processions and burials are considerable and family members contribute whatever they can in order to be able to maintain the display of generosity and avoid bringing shame upon their clan. Solidarity within the larger Romani community means that the community as a whole is affected by shame that is brought upon a single family. If a family cannot afford the costs of the funeral, others within the community will offer their support, donating cash gifts in order to enable a respectful funeral.

FEAST DAYS AND CELEBRATIONS

Romani festivities are essentially opportunities to gather. This maintains and reinforces group identity. In the absence of a shared territory, formal community institutions or scripted ceremonies that are codified in written form, gatherings are the principal expression of Romani communal identity. They are also a way to stay in touch with relatives and friends who are geographically dispersed. Opportunities to gather include funerals and weddings, but also fairs, pilgrimages and festivities such as saints' days, events that are shared with neighbouring populations but offer an occasion for particular Romani celebrations.

Family occasions give the participants an opportunity to express and to strengthen the bonds among their families. Drinking together is often regarded as a way of establishing and flagging the brotherhood among men. The Polish Roms, for example, sit in a circle and pass the bottle and the same glass from one to another. Each of the men demonstrably empties the remaining droplets onto the ground when he receives the bottle, then pours the drink into his glass, greets the others and is greeted by them in return, saying 'May you have health and good fortune'. He then empties the glass with one single gulp and passes the bottle and the glass to the person sitting to his right, continuing the communal ritual. Among the Vlax Roms a party that is organized for a distinguished guest is referred to as a *pativ*, literally meaning 'honour', which expresses the way gatherings are associated with respect, honour and good fortune.

For Roms who travel regularly or seasonally, attending fairs is a major way of keeping in touch and of identifying potential brides and grooms. Among the English Gypsies entire families travel in caravans to annual fairs, which are the most important event in the Romani calendar. There are several of them across the country. Among the largest, most famous and best established are the annual horse fairs at Stow in the Cotswolds, which has been taking place since 1476, and in Appleby in Cumbria, which began in 1685. Both were launched through the provision of a Royal Charter that continues to give them official status to this day. Both fairs used to be important for the trade in horses. Horses are still on prominent display, but they are now joined by hundreds of stalls offering everything from traditional Romani artefacts such as wooden pegs, baskets, healing kits and specially carved and ornamented wagons, to clothes, beddings, silverware, art and jewellery, as well as modern caravans. Trade, however, is really a secondary aspect of the fairs, and many participants spend four or five days at sites such as Appleby simply in order to socialize with other Romani families and to catch up on family and community news.

The American Roms maintain a tradition of travelling to stay with relatives and friends on particular saints' days, which are referred to as *slava*. This follows a Romani custom that is still common in the Balkans. The general tendency is to adopt several days in honour of particular saints as the main festivals of the local community. Which day is chosen varies among Roms in different countries and regions and sometimes even among the Roms in individual communities within the same region. Saint's day celebrations include the preparation of special food, visits to friends and relatives, gatherings and often ritual cleansing in rivers and lakes. Sometimes animals such as geese or lambs are sacrificed. Many of these customs are shared with other populations of the same region but large gatherings are typical of the Romani way of celebrating.

In the southern Balkans (Bulgaria and Macedonia) the most important festivity is St George's Day (*Gergyovden*), which is referred to by the Muslim Roms as *Herdelez*, *Hederlez* or *Erdelez* (the day of Hazret Eliyah or St Elias's Day). It is generally celebrated on 6 May (in accordance with the Orthodox Calendar), but Muslim Roms sometimes celebrate it on the Friday following the Christian St George's Day. The festivities usually last for three days. The first day starts with a walk to the nearest river at daybreak, where people wash themselves in a ritual manner. Bread is often placed on the water and allowed to float carrying a candle, a sacrifice is made, and special dishes and pastries are prepared. Many Bulgarian Roms celebrate the Day of St Basil, also called *Vassilica* or *Bango Vassil*, on 14 January. Celebrations for this often continue for two or three days and special dishes, bread and cakes are prepared and served on plates that are reserved especially for the holiday.

Pilgrimages occupy an interesting position in the spiritual tradition of the Roms and in their calendar of events and gatherings. A number of general pilgrimage destinations that serve a wide population of believers have been adopted by Roms in some parts of Europe and are considered by them to be characteristic Romani places of gathering. Historically, the religious concept of pilgrimage was easily reconcilable with reserving a specific location in a cycle of travel for spiritual and family gatherings. In this way particular Romani forms of social organization meet aspects of mainstream, institutionalized religion. One of the most famous Romani pilgrimage destinations is the church of Saintes-Maries-de-la-Mer in the Camargue region of southern France. The church is the veneration centre of *Kali Sara* (also *Sara e Kali*) or 'Black Sara', sometimes referred to as the patron saint of the Romani people. She is traditionally believed to have been the servant of one of the legendary Three Marys – Mary Magdalene, Mary Salome and Mary Jacobe – all of whom played important roles in early Christianity. The pilgrimage takes place in late May for the annual ceremony on 24 May, during which the statues of the Marys are lowered from the top of the church. The event attracts thousands of Romani families from across Europe, many of whom arrive in caravans and remain at the site for up to two or three weeks. Among Romani cultural activists it has recently become fashionable to associate the celebration of Kali Sara with cults surrounding Indian goddesses, but the precise origin of the custom remains unclear, especially since Kali Sara is not the only object of reverence among the European Roms. In central Europe, many Roms carry out an annual springtime pilgrimage to Częstochowa, the site of the icon of the 'Black Madonna' (a depiction of the Virgin Mary) which is an important pilgrimage destination for Catholics throughout the region. Roms in Kosovo participate both in the annual Catholic pilgrimage to the Church of the Black Madonna at Letnica, and in the Orthodox pilgrimage to the Gračanica monastery near Priština.

A further meeting place is offered by religious conventions practised by modern evangelist movements, which began to spread among the Roms of western Europe and North America in the 1950s, recruiting a large membership from the 1970s onwards. Local residents and municipal institutions usually respect religious conventions and their organizers are rarely denied permission to lead a large-scale gathering of Romani families assembling in caravans for several days. The convention is a religious event but one encounters the usual atmosphere of a Romani gathering (with the exception of commercial stalls), attracting families who wish to reunite with friends and relatives for a period of several days.

MUSIC: FROM LISZT TO EUROVISION

The debate about the character and origins of Romani music has been ongoing for well over a century. The Hungarian composer and musicologist Ferenc Liszt published an influential book entitled *The Gypsies and their Music in Hungary* in 1859. Liszt expressed his admiration for the independence of Gypsies and argued that Gypsy music was not only a product of their culture of migration and collective influences, but also of the absence of formal education and the prevalence of intuition and spontaneity. He suggested that Hungarians had adopted Gypsy music and fitted the melodies with their own lyrics, and that much of the traditional Hungarian folk music in fact had Romani origins. The claim was controversial and was criticized by another prominent Hungarian composer and musicologist, Béla Bartók, in the first decade of the twentieth century. Bartók attributed the origins of Hungarian folk music not to Gypsies but to Hungarian peasants, basing his argument on an analysis of the different styles of peasant music and Romani music. He suggested that Gypsies played repertoires that were not part of their own Gypsy culture. Rather, they adopted music that had been composed by individuals belonging to the Hungarian nobility, who were unable to perform in public because musical performances were not considered appropriate for their status. They therefore hired Romani musicians to perform their music.

Music is one of the oldest Romani occupations and yet there is no evidence that Romani musical styles share a common origin. Suggestions that Romani music shows traces of Indian musical traditions remain unproven. The 1993 documentary film *Latcho Drom* ('The Good Road') depicted musical styles performed by nomadic or semi-nomadic groups of musicians from India, central Asia and Europe, suggesting a historical continuity of Romani music with Indian and west Asian origins. In fact, Romani musicians often adopt traditional music that is played at a given period in a particular region and maintain it even after it ceases to be part of everyday mainstream popular culture, thus becoming, in effect, the guardians of old traditions.

Some present-day ethnomusicologists such as David Malvinni have pointed out that one of the principal features of Romani music is its reliance on improvisation while still showing artistic virtuosity. This combination, projected onto the general cultural stereotype of Gypsies as free, spontaneous and passionate, lends Romani music its emotional attributes. Improvisation is associated with freedom, mobility and defiance of strict norms of behaviour. The fascination that many modern composers had with Gypsies was inspired by the fact that Romani music is generally driven by the demands of audiences, yet at the same time it is artistic and professional. It therefore stands apart both from the amateur musical performances that answer primarily to audience demand, and from the distanced, tightly choreographed professional performances of the bourgeois concert hall.

For many centuries Romani musicians have been involved in different forms of music in different countries. They have specialized in a variety of instruments, from bagpipes, flutes and drums in the Balkans, to violins and guitars in central and western Europe and harps in Britain. Different metres and rhythms are associated with Romani music in different countries. In some, such as Hungary, Spain and Russia, certain forms of Romani music have become associated with national musical styles. The ethnomusicologist Carol Silverman therefore regards Romani music, like many other aspects of Romani culture, as dynamic and transnational, drawing on multiple sources and inspirations and incorporating various styles and genres. Many of the

Romani songs sung within the family are typically slow and sad with a sorrowful mood that tells of misery and misfortune. They are often cries of grief and calls for help and solidarity, and very different from the fast and merry songs that Roms perform to non-Romani audiences.

There is a long, established Romani tradition of performing music professionally for outside audiences. Records show that Roms served in military bands in the Ottoman Empire. During the period following Bulgarian independence in 1878, sources tell of Romani musicians travelling around the country, performing at feasts and celebrations, such as weddings and christenings, and folk and professional gatherings. Their repertoire consisted mainly of Bulgarian and Turkish songs with some Greek, Albanian, Armenian, Serbian, Russian or Croat influences. Under communism Bulgarian Roms often performed at weddings, maintaining the traditional urban music *chalga* that was censored for a period under communism and adding to it elements from western popular music. In modern-day Bulgaria, as in other countries, Roms are often hired as musicians for celebrations, particularly weddings, and also perform in cafés and restaurants. Budapest is famous for the permanent presence of Romani music bands at such establishments, and Romani musicians move around cities from one location to another, performing several pieces at each one.

Roms have been instrumental both in importing new styles to local and regional audiences and in preserving more traditional styles that are typical of earlier periods or foreign cultural influences. This characterizes the Arab-influenced Flamenco in Spain as well as the Hungarian-influenced Gypsy Swing or Jazz Manouche that became popular in Germany and France in the first half of the twentieth century. In the early 1990s the popular Brazilian dance *Lambada* became emblematic among Romani musicians from the Balkans playing on the streets of western European cities, and in the late 1990s young Romani artists in Austria and other countries followed a trend and produced rap tracks in the Romani language. Gypsy music therefore evokes associations of cosmopolitanism and at the same time an adherence to traditional roots.

Roms also perform in public at music venues and theatres, but on the whole their audiences are local and regional and few Romani musicians have obtained international fame. Among those who have acquired a reputation that crosses borders are the jazz guitarist Django Reinhardt from Belgium, and the singers Vera Bila from the Czech Republic and Esma Redžepova from Macedonia. The Romani singer Maria Šerefović from Serbia won the 2007 Eurovision Song Contest, and the Romani singer Sofi Marinova represented Bulgaria at the 2012 edition. World-famous Romani bands include Kalyi Jag from Hungary, Taraf de Haïdouks from Romania, and the Gypsy Kings from France (whose families emigrated from Catalonia).

Music is a binding factor among Romani communities that have dispersed. In recent years, online radio channels led by famous Romani DJs provide Romani diaspora communities with entertainment that reinforces and shapes the musical tastes of specific Romani groups. They are sometimes accompanied by chat forums that allow users to keep in touch by exchanging messages in an improvised form of written Romani as well as in other languages. Another way music connects communities, other than virtually, is through gatherings of musicians. The Stara Zagora annual Romani Music Festival has been held in Bulgaria since 1993, and has its roots in the Gypsy Ensemble that was set up in the town in the 1940s. The ethnographer Nadezhda Georgieva describes how the idea to organize an international Romani music festival emerged among Romani musicians in the town in the late 1980s, but materialized only in 1993, when the local Roma Confederation received support for the initiative from the Ministry of Culture and Bulgaria's former prime minister Andrei Lukanov. The festival demonstrates how music has become an expression of a new Romani nationalism. It is symbolic of an autonomous cultural space that the Romani minority in Bulgaria is claiming for itself, and also of the Bulgarian Roms' attempt to reach out to Romani communities in other countries. Bands are invited from various parts of Europe as well as from India; the festival organizers and their followers embrace Indian music as an expression of the symbolism of India as the place of origin of the Romani nation and the roots of Romani culture. Another large annual festival of Romani music is the Khamoro, which has been taking place in Prague in the Czech Republic since

1999. Its first patron was the former Czech president Václav Havel, and it brings together musical performances and other cultural events such as art exhibitions and public lectures.

OF ROMANI LEADERS
AND CONFLICT RESOLUTION

As a small minority community, Roms in every locality rely on mutual respect and solidarity among families as well as on cooperation and mutual support among members of the extended family. The Romani people are among the few nations that have never been involved in an armed conflict with another nation. There is no known history of violent dispute between Romani populations, either. Naturally, differences among families and clans arise just as disagreements between individuals may emerge, but there is a strong tradition among the Roms of avoiding overt conflict. Romani families follow strict norms to avoid interfering in other people's lives and other families' internal roles and social and economic organization. If tensions do arise, measures are taken to prevent disputes. Among travelling Roms, families will avoid sharing a stopping place with families with whom they have a quarrel, and they will move away from a site in order to avoid aggravating an existing problem. Rivalries, between families of the Sinte of Germany for example, may last for several generations, long after the cause of the dispute has been forgotten. Families retain an awareness that they should avoid contact with members of a particular clan, and moving to another residence to prevent further conflict, even for settled Roms, is considered honourable within the community.

Since the family is the most important unit in Romani society, the head of the household is the immediate and most relevant leadership figure for most Roms. This role falls to the eldest man in the extended household, though sometimes an enterprising and particularly successful son may take on the practical decisions of the family's priorities, leaving the more ceremonial aspects of representing the family to an elderly father or uncle. Beyond the extended household, leadership is a function related only to specific tasks and contexts.

Many Romani communities maintain the institution of a Romani court (often called *kris*), which is entrusted with conflict resolution in the community. The primary function of the Romani court is to secure the agreement of disputing parties to a compromise solution and thus to resolve the problem without involving outside authorities. Courts have tightly regulated procedures that are transmitted orally between generations, and appear in slightly modified forms in each Romani group. Courts may either propose a compromise or, in the case of an injustice that has been done to one of the disputants, the court may impose penalties on the guilty party. However, court proceedings are ultimately seen as a process of mediation between the families of the two parties involved. Conflicts within families are resolved by the head of the family and are seldom brought before the court.

The Romani court deals with a range of issues, such as theft, but also with economic disputes, such as sellers undercutting one another, and with domestic issues, such as infidelities, that involve individuals belonging to different families. In one case, a Romani court held in Germany ruled against the family of a man who was accompanying a youth on a train journey when the latter committed suicide by jumping off the moving train. The family was held responsible because the court deemed that it had been the duty of their relative to guard the young man and to protect him from his own actions. The court can also deal with issues of honour, such as verbal abuse against girls and women in public, as well as with loyalty questions, such as incidents of Roms cooperating with the authorities against the interests of other Roms. In the event that a crime has been committed by a Rom against another Rom for which the culprit has been punished by the state authorities, the Romani court will often meet after the state's sentence has been completed to try the responsible person again according to the law of the community, and will require the guilty person's family to pay compensation to the family of the victim.

The Romani court is based on the principle of consensus among the arbiters and the quest for a just solution that is accepted rather than imposed by force upon the parties to the dispute. The court verdict is usually expressed in monetary terms, as a payment of compensation by the guilty party to the aggrieved party. The relative wealth of those involved is taken into account when setting the fine. If the court orders a family to pay a fine it also issues a deadline for payment. The court can also declare people who have been found to be at fault in a severe case as *mahrime* or 'defiled', meaning that it is forbidden to associate or share food with them. The court's decision is considered final but can be appealed by the parties if new evidence is found or new witnesses come forward.

Strict procedures are followed in hearing testimonies at court discussions. An important part of the proceedings is the taking of an oath, which all those involved must do. Most groups have a specific wording that has to be repeated. The oath is strengthened by the belief among Romani communities that perjury in front of the Romani court brings misfortune and dishonour. This belief, more so than any penalties imposed for perjury, is the basis for cooperation with the court's proceedings. The judges also swear an oath, promising to be fair.

Courts do not usually have permanent membership. Instead, individuals whose experience and impartiality are recognized and agreed on by the conflicting parties are invited by them to serve as arbiters in the specific proceedings of their case. Among some Romani populations, recognition of these mediators is informal and individuals may simply enjoy a reputation as experienced arbiters who are frequently summoned to participate in courts. Initially, it is often a brother or uncle of one of the parties involved who presides over the court. If a resolution is not reached, then outsiders will be called upon as judges. These can be nominated by each family. The court always consists of several members who have equal status, although one of them will chair the proceedings. The judges are people with years of experience who have gained the respect of members of the community. In most Romani communities, only men can serve as judges, and in some communities only men are allowed to testify or speak before the court, though women can observe the proceedings. Some Romani groups have female arbitrators who mediate in cases of disputes between women that are of a personal or domestic nature, while processes involving issues such as divorce, debt, economic partnerships or theft are referred to male judges. The number of judges in a court case is not fixed but is usually between ten and fifteen. In many communities judges do not receive a fee but the parties involved in the dispute pay their expenses. In some communities they may also receive compensation for loss of earnings for the duration of the proceedings, which may take into account the value of the case under dispute and the wealth of the families involved.

Usually the authority of the court extends only to the ethnic sub-group or Romani nation. But in exceptional cases the composition of the court panel might be drawn from two different groups in order to resolve a conflict between families belonging to different Romani nations. Ethnographers Elena Marushiakova and Vesselin Popov report on the growing importance of the mixed court in the countries of the Commonwealth of Independent States (CIS, or former USSR) due to the urbanization of Roms and frequent contacts among Roms from different groups. Non-Roms cannot raise a claim at a Romani court or even participate in its proceedings.

Among some Romani groups, successful arbiters hold a life-long title, for example the *Rechtsprechari* among the Sinte of Germany. Among the Roms of central Poland the institution of the court is missing. In its place we find, exceptionally, a single person in a position of authority – the *Šero Rom* or 'Head Man'. The title is usually passed on to a son, nephew or other close relation of the predecessor, in agreement with the heads of the larger families. It is thus a kind of combination of hereditary and elected office. There are few other examples of individuals in such a position of authority over an entire community. Many Romani settlements have a recognized authority figure, usually the head of one of the more influential families, who is often referred to as 'Head Man' (*Baro*, or *Rom Baro*). This person's authority is usually derived from his family's status, wealth and influence among the local Roms, and is often strengthened by external recognition from local or regional officials seeking to establish a dialogue with the Romani community.

External recognition gives rise to power and leadership of a very different kind. It allows individuals within the Romani community to act as middlemen, usually negotiating with officials on behalf of a fellow Rom for a fee or other kind of reward, or acting as messengers on behalf of the authorities. Their role is a kind of hybrid between an external and internal appointment. Members of the

Romani community accept them as successful mediators. External authorities and institutions view them as reliable and useful contacts within the Romani population. Throughout history authorities and officials have also appointed individuals as leaders without regard to their status within the Romani community. Although these leaders typically lacked popular recognition, they were able to exercise power if they were in a position to regulate privileges, as was the case under communist regimes, or control access to benefits such as donations from charitable foundations, which are nowadays often essential to a community's survival in some of the poorer regions of southeastern Europe.

Many Romani communities have a history of showcase appointment of kings, dukes and princes. In many cases the main purpose of events such as 'coronations' is to attract attention to a person who is already a mediator or a respected community personality by romanticizing his role in accordance with outsiders' stereotype images of the Roms. Coronations also provide an opportunity to generate income and are thus seen as performances to an outside audience. Most individuals who have been presented as kings and dukes lacked authority beyond their immediate community. Even within its confines, that authority might not have exceeded that of the head of a single household. Romani kings, dukes and princes, therefore, are entertainment figures, mainly for the benefit of outsiders.

WHAT RELIGION ARE THE ROMS?

Due to the necessity of relying on official institutions for burial, Roms have had to join one of the officially recognized mainstream religions present in the various regions in which they live. The overwhelming tendency in a historical perspective has been to adhere to the most influential and powerful religious institution of the respective region. Roms are Catholic in Spain, Lutheran in northern Germany, Orthodox in Romania and Muslim in many areas of the southern Balkans. Typically, the principal – and sometimes the only – religious ceremonies that Roms partake in, and for which they require the services of clergy from the respective religious bodies, are burial and the ceremonies through which they gain membership in the religious order in the first place, namely christening and circumcision. For these events Roms invite an authorized minister of religion and will often make generous donations to the appropriate office or institution. Otherwise Roms tend on the whole not to participate in religious services, whether weekly prayers or religious festivals. Pilgrimages are the exception to this norm, though Romani people tend to congregate on their own specific pilgrimage dates and to utilize the events as an opportunity for a separate Romani gathering. Weddings are usually a private family affair and most Roms do not involve ministers of religion in them.

The Roms' reliance on the church or alternative religious institutions for, effectively, burial only (apart from to gain membership itself) and their continuing adherence to their own Romani values and moral and spiritual code have prompted throughout the centuries expressions of mistrust of what has been viewed as the Roms' 'superficial' adherence to Christianity. Roms have indeed been rather quick to embrace new religious alternatives. In the Balkans switching between Islam and (mainly Orthodox) Christianity accompanied either migration from one region to another or the changing power relations in the region, with the Roms keen to align themselves with the dominant group.

Evangelical or Pentecostal religious movements have been active among the Roms for many generations, but have become especially widespread among Romani communities in America and western Europe from the 1970s onwards and reached the Romani populations of central and eastern Europe following the fall of communist rule in the 1990s. Evangelical Roms usually refer to themselves simply as 'Christians' and to one another as 'Brothers and Sisters'. Inspired by the evangelical movement, they embrace a new view of their own culture. They accept a series of restrictions, including a ban on drinking alcohol and smoking and on traditional trades that are considered 'dishonest' such as fortune-telling and the selling of healing herbs. At the same time, the movement encourages them to take pride in their Romani culture and heritage. It accepts and even institutionalizes the involvement of entire families including young children in its services and accommodates them with the appropriate flexibility. An open atmosphere is maintained, allowing children to move about freely in

and out of the room and parents to give their young offspring attention whenever needed during the service. Much of the service consists
of singing while standing and gesticulating. It relates to the scriptures
but does not rely on literacy. Members of the congregation are invited
to lead songs and prayer and to report on their missionary success
among other Roms and on miracles that they have experienced, and
which they believe have led them to discover God and Jesus.

The movement discourages marriage of young girls under the age
of eighteen, which is otherwise common in Romani communities, but
it accepts Romani traditional forms of arranged marriage and elopement and the lavish displays that are customary in Romani weddings.
The evangelical church is hierarchical in the sense that it recognizes
the functions of preachers and pastors, yet it cultivates informal relationships among its members rather than a distanced respect towards
a separate class of clergy. The churches support Romani culture by
producing CDs of religious music sung in Romani and religious videos in the Romani language. The American Wycliffe Foundation, an
evangelical organization that trains pastors and publishes religious
literature, has produced Romani versions of several series of video
films portraying the life of Jesus and various stories from the Old and
New Testaments. They were released in numerous dialects of Romani
targeting Romani populations in countries including Germany,
Lithuania, Russia, Romania, Hungary, Bulgaria and others.

Baptism is perhaps the most important ceremony in the evangelical
tradition, as it is performed to accept new adult members of the congregation, often as part of annual conventions. Videos of baptism
ceremonies, conventions and regular church meetings are shared
regularly on YouTube and distributed on DVDs among members
and as part of missionary campaigns. The principal event of the
Romani evangelical calendar is a series of national and international
conventions that usually take place during the summer months.
Typically they revolve around a huge marquee in which 'meetings' are
held. These are public worship events that include preaching and singing as well as personal testimonies from followers who have recently
adopted the movement's spiritual beliefs – or in the terminology used
by the movement, have been 'saved'. Romani families arrive in caravans at the site, usually a field that has been rented for the event from

the landowner. They stay for up to a week. The convention centres on religious activities but it tightly replicates the tradition of gathering that Romani people have been practising for many generations. The missionary character of the convention gives it legitimacy with the local settled community and its official institutions and agencies, providing an official licence and protection for the gathering of Roms, much like more traditional events such as pilgrimages to the burial sites of saints and similar places of reverence. Evangelical conventions may attract several thousand families, not all of whom are necessarily practising members of the religious movement. They provide opportunities to meet, to exchange news and fashions, to form personal and business connections and to embark on courtships. The decentralized character of most of the evangelical churches allows the Roms to define an institutional space within which Romani values and family networks can be overtly maintained and celebrated. Romani missionary movements have to some extent rebranded Romani identity by bringing together traditional practices with references to Christianity.

There are various kinds of evangelist movements, including Methodists, Congregationalists, Adventists, Pentecostals, Baptists and others. Missionary activities among Romani communities began in the nineteenth century. Modern Gypsy Pentecostalism emerged in 1957 in northwestern France, when the French pastor Clement Le Cossec established the *Mission Evangélique Tzigane de France* ('Gypsy Evangelical Mission of France'). From there the movement spread to Romani communities in the United States, Argentina, Finland, Spain and Britain, where it became known under a variety of names, including *Iglesia de Filadelfia* ('Philadelphia Evangelical Church') in Spain and Latin America, and *Mission Vie et Lumière* ('Life and Light Mission') in Britain and France. The churches train pastors who carry out parish work in their own communities and leave on 'witnessing missions' to Romani populations around the world.

The commitment to spreading the church's teachings among the Rom has encouraged followers of the movement in countries such as Britain and Norway to try to learn the Romani dialects of central and eastern Europe and to engage with documentary material on Romani history, prompting a cultural revival of a new kind. Romani immigrants from eastern Europe find a warm welcome among evangelical Romani communities in western countries such as Britain, France and Spain. Churches often own or rent buildings in which they hold their meetings. These buildings are often used for educational purposes such as Sunday schools that promote Romani language literacy.

They also serve as a base for a new, modernized way of running Romani community affairs, one that purports to be guided by scripture and the formal training of the pastors. The pastors, recruited among the more charismatic followers of the church, are often young people who have been mentored by those in authority within the church and have usually been sent for training in one of the institutions affiliated with the evangelical movement. In a subtle way they change, or at least challenge, the traditional setup, in which the elderly members of the community have the greatest authority. The pastors have the power and the opportunity to influence the norms of behaviour within the community and the relations among its members. The position of pastor offers work and promotion opportunities to individuals who have the necessary leadership skills and commitment. Formally, pastors are not paid but they receive compensation for 'loss of earning', which in practice amounts to a way of supporting their families. Work on behalf of the church thus has its rewards in an economic as well as spiritual sense. Pastors maintain other occupations and sources of income alongside their religious duties and their service for the church is merely a supplement. Overall, evangelical churches offer Roms a way to maintain Romani identity while escaping the stigma that is associated with it.

I once obtained an interesting insight into how traditional Romani beliefs and values are still reconciled with the teachings of the evangelical Christian movement, and how outsiders sometimes struggle to understand the reasoning that is applied to this synthesis. The church bans fortune-telling, and Romani members of the church had always told me that this was because fortune-telling was dishonest. When I explained this to an English acquaintance, a journalist by profession, she asked whether the Romani church also opposed begging. To her, fortune-telling and begging were both non-mainstream professions that were associated with 'Gypsies'; they belonged in the same category. If a Romani group gave up one for ideological or spiritual reasons, then it seemed logical to expect that it would give up the other as well. But from a Romani perspective, the two practices have little in common except for the fact that both entail some form of performance in front of outsiders who are, for all practical ends, regarded as clients. Begging was not considered dishonest, because it did not capitalize on outsiders' beliefs in the supernatural powers of Romani people, but merely on their sympathy. In the view of the church, mortal human beings do not, and cannot, possess supernatural powers. They are equal before God, and pretending to be able to read the future therefore stands in contradiction to the church's teachings. But the twist came when I discussed the matter with one of the more experienced Romani evangelical preachers, a person of very high standing within the church. Fortune-telling was banned, he said, not because it was a case of misleading the clients into believing that what Romani fortune-tellers said was true. On the contrary, Romani women did indeed have the ability to read the future, and their offer to enlighten clients was genuine. But the powers of divination came to these Romani women as a result of their involuntary possession by the Devil. Romani fortune-telling was harmful because it was genuine and risked a situation where the community would be embracing the Devil for its livelihood.

4

Romanes: The Romani Language

LANGUAGE OR SECRET CODE?

One of the key features of Romani culture is the Romani language. The Rom refer to their language as *romanes*, also pronounced *romaneh*, *roman* or *romnes* depending on the dialect and its location. Literally this means 'in the manner of the Roms'. Another name for the language is *romani čhib* 'the Romani language', from which we derive the designation 'Romani'. Romani people identify one another primarily through their use of a common language; a fellow Rom is somebody who speaks a form of Romani even if it is somewhat different in pronunciation and vocabulary to one's own native variety. In traditional Romani society the language is a symbol of shared values. In the context of modern-day websites, media and international meetings of Romani activists it symbolizes a shared destiny and nationhood.

The Romani language is also the most valuable clue to the origins and the early history of the Romani people. Until the late 1700s there was a widespread belief that the Gypsies spoke a makeshift jargon whose primary function was to deceive outsiders by concealing their conversation from them. Many still believe that there are different Gypsy languages and that each group of Gypsies in each country or region invents its own jargon for such purposes. People are often surprised to hear that Romani is in fact a fully fledged language just like any other, that it has its origins in India, that it is related to Sanskrit, an ancient language associated with Indian scholarship and religion, and that it has been preserved by the Romani populations through oral traditions and in a variety of dialects for many centuries.

Before returning to discuss Romani, its history, its structure, and its place in the culture and everyday life of the Romani people, it is important to dwell a little on the origins of misconceptions about the Romani language. At least one cause for confusion lies in the linguistic reality of indigenous populations of Travellers who specialize in itinerant service occupations. In many parts of the world Travellers make use of a special, in-group vocabulary, a kind of lexical reservoir, when communicating among themselves. This vocabulary remains by and large unknown to outsiders and is often protected as a secretive element of Traveller culture. It usually includes words for everyday items such as food, drink, body parts, basic activities, work and animals. Quite often an elaborate set of designations exists for human beings and especially for persons of authority such as magistrate, policeman, soldier, doctor, teacher, priest and gamekeeper.

The need for a special vocabulary that is not shared with outsiders is in part obvious: it allows members of the group to communicate with one another in the presence of others without being understood. In the traditional lifestyle of itinerant groups, coordinating activities spontaneously with friends, partners and family enabled quick reactions to changing situations and was often a key to survival, in the more extreme cases, or simply to the success of financial transactions. The lexicon was often used to convey warnings to group members who might have been in danger of persecution, to coordinate business dealings in the presence of customers, and sometimes to conspire together to carry out activities that were not in line with mainstream society's norms or values.

Apart from concealing in-group communication, secret vocabularies had additional functions. In a tight-knit community with strictly oral traditions, coining new words and creating new usages is a form of entertainment. Using words that are shared only with close friends and relatives strengthens the emotional bond between members of the group. In everyday conversations in the family circle, the in-group vocabulary might be used to emphasize a point, to persuade somebody to do something or to accept an opinion, as a gentle reminder of family duties, or as a euphemistic expression replacing a word that is likely to cause embarrassment or discomfort.

How are in-group vocabularies created? Broadly speaking, there are three different pathways that lead to the emergence of in-group vocabularies of the kind described here. The first common strategy is to adopt foreign vocabulary that is unknown, or at least not widely known, outside the community of Travellers. In cases where Travellers have a foreign origin or access to a second language – perhaps a major language of regional trade – they will often retain vocabulary from the language of their ancestors, or from that second language, and use it as their own secret code. The Äynu peripatetics of the Xinjiang province in western China (also known as East Turkistan), whose everyday language is Uyghur (a Turkic language, related to Uzbek), use Persian-derived vocabulary in order to camouflage selected words and utterances. The Jewish cattle-traders of pre-war Germany used to incorporate words of Hebrew origin, acquired through teaching and learning of religious scriptures in Hebrew.

Another way of creating in-group vocabulary is to rely on figurative expressions that trigger associations with the intended object. For example, seventeenth-century English 'Thieves Cant' had expressions like *stocks* for 'legs', *stock-drawers* for 'socks', *greenemans* for 'fields', *darkemans* for 'night' and *lightmans* for 'day'. The third strategy is very similar to children's and adolescents' language games and involves deliberate distortion of syllables or parts of the word, for example substituting sounds with other sounds, or reversing syllables. The in-group vocabulary of Irish Travellers in Britain, for example, has *groilet* for 'toilet' and *greep* for 'sleep', but it also inherits Irish words with reversed syllables, such as *rodas* for 'door' (Irish *doras*) and *kam* for 'boy' (Irish *mac*). A further way of camouflaging words is to add an ending or to scramble the sounds in the word. Thus the speech of the Egyptian Halab (primarily metalworkers and entertainers) has forms like *muftāḥiš* for 'key' from Arabic *miftāḥ*, and *mubwābiš* for 'door' from Arabic *bāb* (plural *abwāb*).

Secret or in-group vocabularies of this type, used by indigenous travelling populations, are found in numerous forms and in various parts of the world, including East Africa, North Africa, the Middle East, South Asia, Central Asia, Central America and all over Europe. Considering that settled populations tend to lump together all Travellers as Gypsies, whether they are Roms or of other origins, the source of confusion in regard to the language of the Roms is perhaps understandable. But attitudes also play a role. Suspicion leads many people to imagine that unfamiliar aspects of the Roms' behaviour are in fact directed against majority society and are aimed at taking advantage of society and its resources. When it comes to language, the perception of the Roms' use of unfamiliar words and sounds has often been that of a secretive, made-up gibberish that is intended to deceive and confuse outsiders.

DISCOVERING THE ORIGINS OF THE ROMANI LANGUAGE

In fact, Romani is neither an invented nor a secret language. Nor is it just a vocabulary that is inserted into everyday speech in the respective language of the majority population – although some Romani communities, such as those of Britain, Spain, Portugal and Scandinavia, do use Romani vocabulary in this way. Most speakers of Romani, however, use it as a complete language that has its own grammatical inflections, its own sounds and pronunciation patterns, and its own sentence structure. Romani is a language just like any other. By the most conservative estimate, it is the everyday family tongue of more than three and a half million people.

Romani has its ancient roots in the languages of India and as such it is related both to modern languages of the Indo-Aryan family such as Hindi-Urdu, Punjabi, Gujarati and Bangla, and to older spoken and written forms of the same language group such as Sanskrit and the medieval Pali and Prakrit. However, unlike many of its sister-languages in India, Romani has no history or tradition of writing. It has been transmitted as an oral language from one generation to another over many centuries. Even today the number of people who use a form of Romani in writing is comparatively small.

It is in fact quite extraordinary that a small and socially marginalized minority population has been able to maintain its language over such a long time. There are very few similar cases of nations holding on to their native language in dispersed diaspora communities without the support of religious, scholarly or political institutions and without a tradition of writing. The survival of Romani in dispersed communities around Europe and the New World for over 1,000 years after the departure of the Roms from India provides an indication of the strong position of the language as a marker and a badge of ethnic and cultural identity. There is no doubt that the Roms' protectiveness of their own values and family structures has played a decisive role in motivating them to maintain their language and that the language has in turn served them as a clear demarcation line between their own culture and the world around them. But at the same time we must not see the retention of Romani as an indication of self-exclusion or dogmatic separateness. All adult Roms are bilingual and this will have been the situation for many centuries. They learn the language of the surrounding majority society fluently from a young age and they are rarely ashamed to import phrases, words and sounds from that language into their own. Bilingualism in Romani and the respective state or regional language can be seen as the Roms' way of flagging loyalty to their own culture, coupled with the pragmatism of having to communicate effectively with those around them.

Where did Romani originate, and what does the shape of the language tell us about the early history of the Roms? Word comparisons provided the first clues about the origin of Romani. Scholars began documenting word usages in Romani as early as the late fifteenth century, apparently out of curiosity and academic interest in the diversity of peoples and cultures. As the pool of documented Romani lexical material published in different parts of Europe grew, so did the realization that there were obvious similarities among the vocabularies used by the Romani populations in the various countries. By the early 1700s the belief emerged that the connections between the various forms of speech used by Gypsies could in fact reveal something about the origin of the language they speak and so about the origin of the people. An international network of scholars emerged who exchanged vocabulary samples along with comments, ideas and theories about the composition and origins of the Romani vocabulary. Among them were Hartwig Bacmeister and Peter Pallas in St Petersburg, Christian Büttner in Jena, Johann Biester in Göttingen, William Marsden in London, and Johann Christian Christoph Rüdiger in Halle. Bacmeister and Büttner in particular shared their observations on the similarities between many Romani words and the lexicon of Indo-Iranian languages in their correspondence with other colleagues. Yet it was the German scholar Johann Rüdiger who, in a public lecture in 1777, first pointed out the remarkable similarities between Romani and the language that was then called Hindustani and is today known as Hindi or Urdu.

Rüdiger was Professor of Accountancy, Civil Service, Languages and Philology at the University of Halle. One of his key publications was a compilation of all connections among the languages that were known at the time. Although his main preoccupation was with printed and reported samples of foreign languages, his passionate interest in the Gypsy language turned him into a pioneer empiricist. He embarked on a search of descriptions of remote languages that might be compared with what was then known as 'the Gypsy tongue'. In particular, he followed the lead provided by his mentor Büttner and by Bacmeister, which pointed towards India and Iran. Rüdiger obtained a copy of a grammatical description of Hindustani, authored by a missionary in India. Working with an illiterate Gypsy woman later identified as Barbara Makelin, he extracted Hindustani sentences from this book, translated them into German for his speaker consultant and then noted down her own literal translations of the same phrases into her dialect of Romani. Not only did the words match, but Rüdiger was also able to identify similarities in the inflections of words and in grammatical vocabulary – function words such as prepositions and pronouns – which tend to remain stable in the history of languages. Remarkably he was also able to account for the differences between the languages, demonstrating that various features of the Gypsy language, such as the order of words and the presence of a definite article 'the' (which does not exist in Hindustani), are likely to have been acquired through imitation of the corresponding structures of European languages with which Romani had come into contact.

Rüdiger was thus in a position to demonstrate convincingly that Romani was a language of Indian origin and that it had preserved not just its vocabulary but also much of its Indian grammatical structure. He concluded that Romani was brought to Europe in all likelihood as the mother tongue of a population of migrants from India. These findings were published in Rüdiger's single known article on the subject in 1782. Keeping open the question of what motivated the ancestors of the Roms to leave their ancient homeland, Rüdiger added to his finding a passionate call for the fair treatment and protection of the Romani people and warned against society's prejudice and the racial hatred towards them. 'The mistreatment of the Gypsies has no other cause but deeply rooted xenophobia,' he wrote, adding, 'Nowhere have they obtained full civil status and equality with the rest of us humans – to which they are naturally entitled.'

In the decades that followed, Rüdiger's conclusions became widely disseminated both among the scholarly community and among civil servants across Europe. Much of this was due to the work of his contemporary Heinrich Grellmann. Giving Rüdiger little credit, Grellmann had embedded his colleague's findings into his own book, published in 1783, along with a series of articles that he plagiarized from a variety of sources, most notably from the work of Samuel Augustini ab Hortis on 'The Gypsies in Hungary', which was published in 1775 in the *Vienna Gazette*. Unlike Rüdiger, Grellmann had very little sympathy with the Gypsies. He did not regard them as a marginalized minority that suffered from exclusion and prejudice. Instead, he took the line that the Gypsies had a predisposition towards anti-social behaviour and recommended that they be forced to settle and that they be resocialized and assimilated into mainstream society.

Specialists acknowledged the value of Rüdiger's groundbreaking work. But to this day his essay remains unknown to many, and most popular sources on Romani fail to mention it. It was not until 1986 that Martin Ruch, then a doctoral student at the University of Freiburg in Germany, carried out an extensive study of archive manuscripts and demonstrated in his thesis the value of Rüdiger's original work and the sources from which Grellmann had plagiarized. In 1990, a facsimile of Rüdiger's article was published in Hamburg, making it for the first time widely available to an audience of readers. Ironically, a few of Grellmann's present-day critics have expressed scepticism with regard to 'his' conclusion that the Roms originated in India, primarily because they seem to associate that conclusion with the hostile tone of Grellmann's overall narrative. Rüdiger's work proves that the Enlightenment scholarship had several different faces, and that among them was at least one that combined a passion for the facts and the reality of the Roms' speech with a concern for their social and political status and respect for their right to equality and dignity.

Within the scholarly community Rüdiger's thesis and the linguistic facts that point to the Indic origin of the Romani language remain undisputed. In the decades that followed Rüdiger's publication scholars collected many more samples of Romani speech in different parts of Europe. By 1844 the German August Pott, a Professor of Philology at the University of Halle, where Rüdiger had also taught, was able to publish a comparative investigation and a comparative dictionary of the various dialects of Romani, drawing on information from dozens of published sources. A generation later, in 1872, the Austrian-Slovene Franz Miklosich, a specialist in the philology of the Balkan languages, published a twelve-volume investigation of the dialects of Romani, much of it based on his own field notes, into which he incorporated a discussion of historical sources documenting the arrival of Gypsies in the Balkans and central Europe as well as a thesis about the migration routes of the Romani-speaking populations across the European continent. By the end of the nineteenth century Romani philology had become an acknowledged field of investigation and was attracting leading specialists in the history of Indo-Aryan languages such as Richard Pischel, George Grierson, Ralph Turner, Jules Bloch and Alfred Woolner. Their work was facilitated to a considerable extent by a growing interest in the Romani language among laypeople who made notes on the speech of Romani neighbours and acquaintances and passed them on to scholars for analysis. The English novelist George Borrow (1803–81) included long quotes in Romani in his stories about Gypsies and thus inspired many of his readers to take an interest in the Romani language and culture. The Journal of the Gypsy Lore Society, founded in Edinburgh in 1888, provided an international platform for a scholarly discussion and exchange about the origin and structures of the Romani language and its various dialects.

LANGUAGE AS A MIRROR OF EARLY HISTORY

One of the reasons that both scholars and amateurs became attracted to the study of Romani is that the analysis of the structures of a language is able to unfold a series of hidden facts about the history of its speaker population. The ancestors of the Roms did not write down their language and so we have no direct impressions of the shape it had in its early phases or of the changes it underwent throughout history. We are fortunate, however, to have extensive documentation on related languages of India. From the changes that the literary languages of ancient and medieval India underwent at different historical stages, and which are reflected in the texts preserved from these periods, we can try to make inferences about the earlier history of the Romani language. This can be done by comparing the end result that we find in Romani today with the patterns of structural change that are reflected in the texts at various periods in history.

Written documents in the languages of India go back more than 3,000 years to the liturgical Sanskrit texts of Hinduism and Buddhism. The most ancient literary layer dates as far back as *c.* 1500 BCE and shows a relatively uniform language that continued to be in use for religious and literary purposes for many centuries. This language stage is known as Old Indo-Aryan and is best represented by the Sanskrit religious and scientific texts. Around a millennium later, from *c.* 500 BCE, regional differences begin to appear in a different type of texts, most notably in the dramas called the Prakrits, which represent the vernacular or spoken regional languages of the time.

This historical stage in the development of the languages is also known as Middle Indo-Aryan. The emerging regional differentiation of the Indian languages at that time provides us with the first key to locate the origins of Romani. Some of the Old Indo-Aryan or Sanskrit forms are succeeded by innovations that take on different shapes in the various regions. The comparison with Romani allows us to trace the origins of the language to central India, in the same area where languages such as Hindi, Gujarati and Rajasthani emerged. The structural profile of the language and the forms that it shares with other languages of the region also offer some clues in regard to the time frame. While it is not possible to calculate a language's age with any precision, dated medieval Indian texts give us a rough indication of when and in which region the shape of certain words changed. The comparison with Romani allows us to assume that the language began its history sometime after 500 BCE as a language of central India, and that it left that area sometime before 500 CE.

Romani also shares some features, such as the pronunciation of certain words and the shape of some of its grammatical inflections, with languages that are spoken in the extreme northwestern regions of the Indian subcontinent, such as Kashmiri. This suggests that when the Roms left central India, they did not emigrate immediately towards Europe but stayed for several centuries in the northwestern regions of India. Some grammatical developments indicate that Romani was still spoken in the Indian subcontinent until late in the first millennium CE: Old Indo-Aryan had a very elaborate system of noun inflection, similar to that of Latin and Ancient Greek. This system became simplified in all the modern languages of India, and the seeds of this change can be seen in medieval Indian texts from the ninth and tenth centuries. It is therefore assumed that the Roms stayed in India at least until the ninth century CE.

In this way, structural layers of words and sounds in Romani are able to tell us a story of a population that departed from central India in the first half of the first millennium and settled in the northwestern regions of the country, staying there at least until the eighth or ninth century and perhaps even longer. Language gives us no direct clues as to the reasons behind the migration away from this area westwards. But there is at least one word in the Romani vocabulary that might shed some light on the mystery, and that is *koraxaj* and its extension *koraxano*. Among the Balkan Roms the word is used to denote 'Turks' or 'Muslims'. Some Romani communities in western Europe use the same word for the more general meaning of 'stranger' or 'foreigner'. Its origin appears to be in the Turkic word Karakhan, the name of the dynasty that ruled the first Turkic state in central Asia between the ninth and fourteenth centuries. The Karakhanids, as they were called, converted to Islam at the end of the tenth century and were based in Bukhara in today's Tajikistan. They participated in numerous raids and served as tax collectors in the areas inhabited by Indo-Iranian populations. It is quite likely that the Karakhanids were the first Muslim people that the Roms encountered. It is even possible that it was the Karakhanids who motivated the Roms to emigrate from India. The Roms may have wanted to escape a troubled area or they may have put their skills as artisans, craftsmen and entertainers in the service of the Karakhanid troops. Towards the end of the eleventh century the Karakhanids had joined the Seljuks and it may well have been the Seljuk expeditions westwards, into Anatolia and beyond, that brought the Roms to the gateway of Europe.

Whatever the historical trigger for the migration was, the Romani language illuminates additional stages in the story. Romani absorbed a great number of words and grammatical formations from Byzantine Greek. Almost a quarter of the core vocabulary that is shared by the dialects of Romani derives from Greek. This includes some basic concepts such as *drom* 'road', *pápus* 'grandfather', *zumí* 'soup', *párpale* 'backwards', *panda* 'more', *kurkó* 'Sunday, week', *xolí* 'anger', *čerus* 'time', *apopli* 'again', *ravnos* 'sky', *tajsa* 'tomorrow', and many more, including the numerals *eftá* 'seven', *oxtó* 'eight' and *enjá* 'nine' and in many dialects of Romani also higher numerals above 'twenty'. The grammatical influence of Greek on Romani is massive and is difficult to enumerate. The order of words in the sentence matches that of Greek almost precisely. Imitating the Greek model, Romani developed grammatical function words such as the definite article 'the', which is lacking in the languages of India. Many Greek inflectional endings have been absorbed into Romani, too. All this suggests that there was a very long period of intense immersion in Greek society and culture during which the Roms spoke both Romani and Greek and felt comfortable enough in both languages to mix them freely in conversations among themselves, leading to the permanent replication or 'borrowing' of many structures from Greek within Romani. This in turn suggests that the Roms had acquired some kind of permanent or stable socio-economic role within Greek-speaking society in the medieval Byzantine Empire.

Recall that the Byzantine Empire of the eleventh and twelfth centuries included not only Greece and territories in the Balkans but also Anatolia (Turkey) and parts of Antioch (on the border of present-day Syria). It was a multicultural and multilingual state and the Roms will have interacted with the different ethnic groups within this stratified society. Romani contains up to seventy or eighty loanwords from Iranian languages and up to thirty or forty loans from Armenian. Some of the Iranian loans might be attributed to any one of several Iranian languages, including Persian and Kurdish. They include *avgin* 'honey', *diz* 'town', *baxt* 'luck' and *bezex* 'sin'. Others are specifically

Persian (such as *pošom* 'wool' and *šaj* 'possible') and a small number of words are attributable to other languages such as Ossetian (e.g. *vurdon* 'cart'). Armenian words in Romani include *bov* 'oven', *kotor* 'piece', *xanamik* 'in-laws' and *grast* 'horse'. Some words that appear in Romani are shared by two or more of the languages Persian, Kurdish and Armenian: *mom* 'wax, candle', *tover* 'axe', *zor* 'strength', *xomer* 'dough', *či* 'something' and more. Many scholars have assumed that contact with Iranian and Armenian occurred before contact with Greek – mainly due to the geographical locations of the languages in our present era. But it is also possible, and indeed quite likely, that the Greek, Iranian and Armenian influences were all acquired during the same period in central and eastern Anatolia.

MAKING SENSE OF DIALECT DIFFERENCES

As small Romani populations began to emigrate from the crumbling Byzantine Empire into central and northern Europe in the early 1400s, they took with them a unique language that had been shaped through several centuries of cohabitation with other ethnic minority groups within the Greek-dominated realm of the eastern Mediterranean. Romani at the time must have resembled Greek and other languages spoken in the Balkans in its sentence melody, in many of its sounds, in its manner of organizing utterances and also in much shared vocabulary. Yet it continued to preserve its Indo-Aryan core of basic lexicon and word structure. Even some sounds, such as the typical Indo-Aryan *r*-sound that is pronounced by curling the tongue backwards and is a notable feature of an Indian 'accent', remained a living linguistic testimony to the Indian heritage. The long period of stability under Byzantine rule had now come to an end, and this appears to have led to an almost erratic dispersion of Romani groups from and within the Balkan regions. New relations with settled populations in various parts of the European continent had to be negotiated and for this purpose new cultural and linguistic repertoires had to be acquired. Romani people were again migrating and their immersion with new populations led to the acquisition of new combinations of languages and new forms of multilingualism.

The Slovene scholar Franz Miklosich (1813–91) carried out one of the earliest and most extensive studies of the dialects of Romani. He theorized that loanwords in the individual dialects of Romani that were acquired through contacts with different settled populations provided clues to the Roms' migration history. Since all Romani dialects shared a Greek component, Miklosich concluded that the Gypsies' 'European homeland' had been in a Greek-speaking area. He also noticed that the Romani speech of most groups showed a number of words whose origin is in Slavonic languages such as Bulgarian, Macedonian and Serbian. They include words such as *vodros* 'bed', *dosta* 'enough', *čelo* 'whole', *kralis* 'king', *stanya* 'barn' and *zelano* 'green'. There is no doubt that some Roms at least had acquired Balkan Slavonic languages before leaving Byzantium through contacts with the Slavonic populations. The presence of Slavonic loanwords in most European dialects of Romani outside the Balkans indicates that the migrants who left Byzantium did not come directly from Anatolia but had been settled among the population of western Byzantium, where Slavonic-speaking peoples lived.

It also appears that the migrations that brought Romani populations into their present locations were gradual. The Romani dialects of Britain, Scandinavia, Poland, the Baltic lands and Russia all include German loanwords, though different words are found in the east and in the west indicating two distinct migration routes. Typical German-origin words in Polish, Baltic and North Russian Romani include *štala* 'cellar', *korba* 'basket', *špera* 'trace', *zanta* 'sand', *bilta* 'picture', *frajda* 'joy' and *fraj* 'free'. German-origin words in British and Scandinavian Romani include *varta* 'to watch', *štifo* 'in-law (sibling)', *selta* 'tent', *čifa* 'boat', *vajla* 'while', *šafraben* 'work' and *stakelengro* 'hedgehog'.

Germany, it appears, was an important transit place. It attracted Romani migrants but was also a point of departure for Romani groups heading east, north and west. Those who continued northwards were exposed to the Low German dialects of the North Sea coastal regions for quite some time before migrating further into Scandinavia. Low German was an international trade language and the official tongue of the Hanseatic League of the North Sea and Baltic cities until the seventeenth century. It is not surprising that the

Roms, specializing in mobile trades, acquired this language. The dialects of Romani spoken in Denmark, Sweden and Norway all show heavy influences from Low German, as can be seen by examining the Romani vocabulary that survives today in the speech of Romani populations in these countries. Finnish Romani also shares these and other features with the Romani dialects of the Nordic countries and it is fairly obvious that the Finnish Roms arrived in Finland as part of a Swedish colonization and migration wave. In central Europe, Roms living in the eastern territories of the Habsburg Monarchy acquired Hungarian as their second language. The speech forms of the Roms who remained in the Balkans absorbed heavy influences from Turkish, the language of the Ottoman Empire that ruled the region from the late fourteenth century.

It is likely that the speech forms of different Romani families and clans differed only slightly before they migrated into Europe. Linguistic comparisons among the present-day dialects of Romani allow us to derive various related forms of the same word in a fairly straightforward manner from a single root form that will have been used by the Roms during the Byzantine period. These root forms can be referred to as 'Early Romani'. Since we have no written records of Romani from that period, this remains an academic designation but it is grounded in a comparative linguistic methodology.

Once in their new locations, Romani migrants in the fourteenth and fifteenth centuries acquired local languages, took on local religions and integrated into local and regional economies. Although they were often known as Travellers due to their specialization in itinerant trades, most Roms did not habitually travel long distances but remained in familiar regions, interacting with a familiar population of settled clients. This is confirmed by genealogies as well as by the pattern of dialect development in Romani, which shows regional dialects that are confined to certain locations rather than random patterns of variation. Hybrid identities developed as each Romani population accommodated to its new environment while maintaining its own language, beliefs and customs.

The period that followed migration into the individual regions was one of rapid changes that saw the emergence of distinct regional Romani identities. This period left its mark on the speech forms of the

Roms in various locations. Each community developed its own speech preferences and adopted influences from the new contact languages. The earliest samples of Romani, published between the late fifteenth and the late seventeenth centuries and collected in locations as far apart as Germany, Britain, Italy, France and Thrace in the Balkans, show a relatively uniform language. Documentation of Romani proliferated by the early eighteenth century as scholars' interest in the language intensified. By this time, Romani dialects were already as diverse as we know them today. The changes that shaped them and gave them the structural characteristics that they have now thus appeared to have taken place somewhere between the fifteenth and eighteenth centuries.

One notable factor that led to the emergence of distinct, regional varieties of Romani was of course the impact of the contact languages. When an entire community is bilingual its members tend to mix languages in conversation with a relatively high degree of freedom and to incorporate words and expressions from the surrounding language into the preferred language of the home. Along with these words and expressions come sound patterns and modes of organizing sentences and entire conversations. Within a few generations, each and every Romani dialect had taken on significant influences from its respective contact language: Basque, Finnish, Italian, Serbian, Hungarian, Romanian, Polish, Welsh, Turkish, Albanian and more.

But other changes also appeared in the language, making the divisions among dialects even more pronounced. These are natural changes in pronunciation and the choice of words, which constantly occur as speech habits and usage change. When communities become dispersed and the contact among them weakens they become susceptible to fashions and trends and the differences between them grow. This is essentially no different in Romani from any other language. The Roms, however, tend not to make a distinction between the terms for 'language' and 'dialect', referring to all speech forms as *chib*, literally 'tongue'. This does not mean that they perceive other varieties of Romani as entirely different languages. Aware of some variations they may either opt for a foreign language as a way of communicating with other Roms or make the effort to try to understand speakers of other Romani dialects.

Differences in pronunciation among Romani dialects can be illustrated by taking the example of the Romani word for 'day'. The most widespread form of the word in Romani is *dives*, used in northern and western Europe as well as in the southern Balkans. In some areas of the Balkans the final sound is lost and we hear *dive* or *diveh*. In the Romani dialects of Slovenia, eastern Austria and southern Hungary, the word is shortened even further and we encounter simply *di*. There are large areas in Romania, Macedonia and Bulgaria where it is shortened in another way, by eliminating the sound *-ve-* in the middle. Here we find *dies* or *djes*, sometimes also *gjes*, *džes* or *zis*. Clearly, the oldest form of the word is *dives*. It is most frequent and more widespread geographically and all the other forms can be derived from it. It is also closest to the Old Indo-Aryan form of the word that we find in Sanskrit – *divasa*.

Working our way through the vocabulary and grammar of Romani in this way, word by word, we can try to map the historical developments that have occurred since the dispersion of Romani populations across Europe from the fifteenth century onwards. The picture that emerges is essentially the following: while the speech forms of each location and region have their own particularities, just like in any other language, Romani dialects can broadly be divided into two large groups, southern and northern. The dividing line between them can be labelled the 'Great Divide'. It is not a single line but more like a belt that separates the Romani dialects of Romania, Serbia, Croatia and southern Italy as well as those spoken further to the southeast, from the Romani dialects spoken in Ukraine, Hungary, Slovenia and northern Italy, and the regions further to the north and west. The division mirrors the historical border region between the Austrian Habsburg Monarchy to the north and the Ottoman Empire to the south during the sixteenth and seventeenth centuries. It reflects the patterns of contacts that Romani communities had with one another. New words and structures that emerged in the speech of the Roms north of the border could not spread to the south and vice versa due to the lack of contacts across the political divide during the crucial period at which dialects were being reshaped through new fashions and distinct cultural and linguistic influences.

Such differences between speech forms can make it somewhat difficult for people to understand one another. Moreover, since Romani communities are always bilingual and accustomed to mixing languages in conversation, Roms from different countries who have other second languages will have difficulties following those phrases that their fellow Roms insert in a foreign language with which they are unfamiliar. But as long as communication is consistently in Romani and mixing is avoided, Romani people from different countries and regions are often able to understand one another rather well simply by adapting to the differences and reacting to their interlocutors with flexibility and patience. If we were to imagine a gradual trip from southern Greece all the way to Estonia, we would find that, as we move from one Romani community to another, the language varies only in tiny and hardly noticeable features from location to location. Romani dialects from the same or neighbouring regions tend to be on the whole mutually comprehensible. As in any other language, the further apart two communities are geographically the more distinct their dialects are from one another and the greater the difficulties their speakers will have in communicating with one another in Romani. But even if we continued the journey as far as Estonia, we would still be able to note overwhelming similarities with the Romani speech forms of the extreme south, and in all likelihood Roms from southern Greece and from Estonia could, with some degree of effort, have a conversation in their native language.

The dialects of Romani populations that have migrated to other locations following the formation period of the dialects in the sixteenth and seventeenth centuries are a notable exception to this language-geographical pattern. These include the dialects of the so-called Vlaxi, Olah or Laxi Roms of the Balkans, Ukraine and central Europe. As their name suggests, they are descendants of Romani migrants who had been settled in the Wallachian or southern Romanian principalities. A large-scale emigration of Roms from that area took place in the eighteenth century, when the region was troubled by war and political instability. Roms speaking Wallachian or Vlax Romani dialects moved westwards into Serbia, Bosnia and Croatia, and southwards into Bulgaria, Macedonia, Greece and Turkey. Some appear to have migrated into Hungarian territory as well. These Roms maintained their own communities alongside the settled Romani populations of the respective regions, also holding on to their distinct dialect. Other migrations include those of the German Roms or Sinte eastwards into Russia, Hungary and Romania, often following or joining German colonies in these countries during the eighteenth century. A significant migration wave brought Roms from Transylvania during the nineteenth century and perhaps even earlier into other areas of Europe. Groups such as the Kelderasha and Lovara settled throughout Europe, with large communities forming in Moscow, Stockholm, Frankfurt, Vienna, Paris and London. Descendants of this wave of migrants also make up the bulk of the Romani population in the cities of North and South America, led by groups such as the Machwaya and the Kelderasha. Their distinct Transylvanian Romani dialect has been retained and stands out wherever they have settled in proximity to other Romani populations.

Te Aves Baxtalo!:
LANGUAGE AND CULTURE

Romani is primarily, at least in historical perspective, a language of domestic interaction in the family domain. Conversation in Romani therefore tends to be spontaneous, familiar and informal. There are few scripted usages of the language and few contexts in which Romani is embedded into highly regulated institutional forms of discourse. There are, however, various formulaic expressions in the language. The most widespread greeting is *Te aves baxtalo!*, which literally means 'May you have good fortune!' A common greeting that is used to thank people or to celebrate companionship during a meal or a toast is *Aven saste!*, literally 'May you be healthy!' Upon arrival in a location, a person is greeted by those present with *Mišto aviljan!*, literally 'You have arrived well!' ('Welcome!'). This closely resembles the literal meaning and structure of corresponding greetings in languages of western Asia such as Kurdish, Persian and Turkish, and it is not unlikely that the expression was coined in Anatolia before the dispersion of the Roms across Europe. A similar case is the formula used to introduce traditional tales, the equivalent of English 'once upon a time'. The Romani phrase is *sas taj nas*, literally 'there was and there was not', which is the exact translation of the structure of corresponding phrases in Armenian, Kurdish, Georgian, Persian, Turkish, Azeri and Arabic.

The informal nature of Romani conversation is partly manifested in the fact that Roms virtually never use surnames when referring to one another. Actually, in many Romani communities people tend to have at least two forenames: the first is reserved for official use with outsiders, agencies and institutions and appears on the individual's birth certificate and other documents. It is usually a name that is common in the respective country or region of residence. The second is reserved for use by members of the family and fellow Roms. It may have a Romani sound to it, but Roms are generally fond of imaginative, original and fashionable names, and so Romani names are rather hard to predict. Formal forms of address are rare in Romani because the language is usually spoken among people who are personally acquainted with one another. However, older people are often addressed in the plural form of the pronoun 'you' (*tumen*) as a token of respect. In some Romani communities, more formal forms of speech can be heard when eulogies are made at funerals and when oaths are taken during proceedings of the Romani courts. Formulaic speech is also common among traditional Romani story-tellers or *paramičari* in central Europe. Story-telling is one of the oldest and most traditional forms of entertainment that is internal to the community. Traditional tales are often memorized and transmitted from generation to generation and they contain some very fixed opening and closing sequences.

Traditional Romani families usually insist on speaking Romani within the family and in all interactions with other Roms. However, foreign languages are considered a natural and necessary skill and Romani children are encouraged from a very young age to learn the languages of the surrounding populations. Both children and adults tend to switch back into Romani when addressing fellow Roms, whether family members or strangers. This has little to do with secrecy, which is often the outsiders' perception of such language preferences, and more to do with language acting as an emotional symbol of group identity. Nevertheless, in some communities Romani has been abandoned as the everyday language of the family as a result of pressure from the authorities and a policy of direct repression by imposing penalties on language use. This is thought to have been one of the main reasons for the decline in the use of Romani in Spain, Portugal, and partly in Hungary. In Britain and Scandinavia, linguistic assimilation was reinforced by intermarriage with indigenous populations of Travellers.

In these regions, Romani communities continue to use vocabulary derived from the Romani language, which they embed into conversations in the majority language (English, Portuguese and so on). In this way, language continues to serve as a boundary between insiders and outsiders and as an expression of family and community identity. Roms in Britain, Norway and Spain know on average around 200–300 words of Romani origin. They cover everyday concepts such as names for utensils, persons, food and drink and basic activities such as 'to come', 'to go', 'to run', 'to take', 'to give' and more. Roms in these countries use Romani vocabulary in much the same way as travelling populations use a camouflaged lexicon. Its main purpose is to emphasize a special emotional connection among speakers. Parents might use Romani words when encouraging their children to eat or instructing them to end their play and join the rest of the family. Adults use Romani words to indicate affection and friendship when discussing personal matters or when making emphatic calls such as warnings or exclamations. In the presence of non-Romani bystanders Romani vocabulary can be used for group insider communication to convey messages that strangers are not meant to understand. Romani traders may employ their knowledge of Romani words to coordinate a negotiation strategy in the presence of customers or to point out the merits or deficiencies of products to one another without revealing their true judgement to the buyer or seller. Roms who use Romani vocabulary primarily for such purposes tend to be creative and exploit the words that survive from the speech of their forefathers in order to invent new terms, putting together combinations of words and extending the meaning of existing ones. Technical or specialized concepts can be formed in this way in Romani by using 'iron-bird' for 'aeroplane', for example, or 'wood-tell-road' for 'signpost'.

Various features of the Romani language represent cultural notions that are specific to the Roms. Perhaps the most obvious is the absence of neutral words for 'man' and 'woman', 'boy' and 'girl', and 'husband' and 'wife'. When using any of these concepts speakers must specify whether the individual that is being referred to is an insider and part of the group or an outsider. Insiders are referred to as *rom* 'man' and *romni* 'woman', and these words are also used by Roms to denote 'husband' and 'wife'. Outsiders are *gadžo* 'man' or *gadži* 'woman'. The words for Romani children are *čhavo* 'boy' and *čhaj* 'girl', which are also used for 'son' and 'daughter'. Non-Romani children are referred to as *raklo* 'boy' and *rakli* 'girl'. This distinction in terminology is evidently symbolic of the social, cultural and spiritual demarcation that the Roms perceive between their own community and outsiders. But reality is often more complex, and language then sometimes gets in the way. One of my close Romani friends was married to a non-Romani woman of German background. When asked by fellow Roms whom he had recently met whether he was married – the literal expression is 'Do you have a *romni*?' (that is, a wife, a Romani woman) – he responded hesitantly: 'Yes, I do have a *romni*, a *gadži*' (that is, a non-Romani woman).

Another interesting feature of the language is the tendency to create new names for surrounding nations rather than simply adopt a word that is similar in sound to that nation's self-appellation. In the Balkans, Greeks are referred to by the Roms as *balame*, Turks and Muslims as *koraxane*, Orthodox Christians as *das* and Jews are called either *bibolde* meaning 'non-baptized' or *činde*, literally 'cut' ('circumcised'). Many Romani communities also create names for important towns in their regions, often using translations into Romani of the original place name or descriptions of a feature that is associated with the specific town such as a famous bridge, a cathedral, a river or the seaside.

Some ancient Indic terms are used for Christian concepts that have been acquired in all likelihood in Europe. They include *rašaj* 'priest' and *trušul* 'cross'. On the other hand, terms like *kris* 'court' and *magardo* 'defiled' are derived from Greek, though the associated concepts are often believed to be much more ancient. A further term for 'defiled' is *mahrimo*, one of the very few Romani words of Arabic origin. For this reason attempts to use the composition of Romani vocabulary to reconstruct the 'original' Romani culture or the social and physical environment that the ancestors of the Roms inhabited have usually proved futile. Some writers have nevertheless put forward such theories. The Hungarian philologist József Vekerdi claimed that Romani vocabulary testified to an origin in a population of nomads. The American linguist Ian Hancock, who claims British Romani descent, has argued quite the opposite. According to him, Romani vocabulary indicates that the ancestors of the Roms were professional warriors. Neither theory is particularly persuasive. Romani has Indian words for concepts such as 'song', 'dance', 'to beg' and 'to travel', for words like 'gold', 'iron' and 'silver', as well as for words like 'knife', 'quarrel' and 'shout'. None of these help us characterize ancient Romani culture and economy as specialized in music and dance, travel, metalwork or warfare. Nor does the presence of Greek or other European loanwords for concepts such as 'flower', 'grandfather', 'road' or the numbers 'seven' and 'eight' suggest in any way that these are concepts that were acquired only in Europe and were unknown to the Roms in their ancient Indian homeland. Vocabulary is volatile and languages adapt and adopt words for a variety of reasons, not just in order to fill conceptual gaps or to designate cultural innovations.

The influence of other languages on Romani has received much attention among linguists and students of the Romani language. In fact, for academics Romani provides a very interesting example of the extent to which bilingualism has a long-term impact on the vocabulary, grammar and pronunciation. The dialects of Romani show influences from a wide range of contact languages and linguists have been able to use these influences as a comparative sample in order to study general patterns in what is usually referred to as 'contact linguistics' – the study of the way the structures of languages change when speakers are multilingual and incorporate features of one of their languages into another.

A topic that has received less attention is the influence that Romani has had on other languages. We often take for granted that more powerful languages – those that have official status and are used in commerce, education and broadcasting – are more likely to exert an influence on minority languages, which are used primarily for face-to-face, oral and domestic communication usually by a smaller number of people. But Romani has had a considerable impact, especially on informal and slang vocabulary, in various languages. Although Roms have always had a lower social status as a marginalized minority population, they inspired certain sectors within the majority ethnic groups through their tight group solidarity and loyalty to one another, their economic and geographical flexibility and adaptability, their adherence to their own values and their seeming defiance of middle-class norms. Romani words were often picked up and used by groups who envied this resilience and the anti-establishment flair that was associated with the Roms. They entered the slang usage of young people in urban communities as tokens of an attitude of social rebellion, disobedience and freedom. From there they often spread into the general colloquial speech of both rural and urban populations. Popular English words such as 'pal' and 'chav' derive from Romani, as do British English regional colloquialisms like 'kushty' and 'minge'. Youth slang in the English border towns of Berwick-upon-Tweed and Hexham, just south of Scotland, where Romani families often sought refuge following expulsion across the political boundary, contains several dozen words of Romani origin, and teenagers can still be heard today announcing to one another: 'I'm ladjed to nash down the drom with my peeve', meaning 'I'm ashamed to walk down the road with my drink.' Slang expressions of Romani origin are abundant in many other European languages, including Romanian, Hungarian, Serbian, Russian, French, German and Swedish.

NEW TIMES, NEW CHALLENGES

Traditionally an oral language, Romani was first written down by outsiders – scholars seeking to document the language in order to study it and compare it with other speech forms, and later missionaries keen to translate the Gospels into Romani in order to convert the Roms to their faith. After the emergence of the Soviet Union, a liberal nationalities policy was introduced aiming to secure loyalty to and identification with the state by the country's numerous ethnic groups and nationalities. For the first time a centrally coordinated government effort was made to publish books in Romani. In the early 1920s Romani translations of monumental Russian literature such as the works of Pushkin emerged alongside numerous Romani editions of political and ideological pamphlets as well as original textbooks and children's literature in the language. But with the U-turn in nationalities policy under Stalin the efforts stopped and Romani-language publications were banned.

It wasn't until the late 1960s that new initiatives to write Romani emerged. During the Prague Spring of 1968 a circle of Romani intellectuals published guidelines for a Romani alphabet, while in London a group of pro-Romani activists began corresponding with Romani students and academics from around the world in an effort to establish an umbrella organization of Romani intellectuals. They founded the International Romani Union (IRU) and made the promotion of a written form of Romani a central item on its agenda. At the same time, in the early 1970s, Romani activists gathered in Finland together with academics and government officials to design a writing system for Finnish Romani, while in Macedonia a textbook for Romani grammar was published along with guidelines on proper usage and spelling. An international discussion emerged on how to create a standard Romani language. It was led primarily by members of the IRU and their supporters, and partly by Romani activists who were also working to develop literary forms of the language in their individual countries. The challenges were considerable. First, there is no central Romani government with the authority to impose a particular norm or with the resources to promote a standard variety of Romani either through the media or the education system. There is also no variety of Romani that would be accepted by all Roms as a standard, since there is no such thing as a Romani ruling class or a Romani capital city. Due to the geographical dispersion of the Roms the chances of reaching a significant number of communities and introducing them to a particular form of writing in Romani were weak from the beginning.

These challenges to a centralized standard remain today, though events have arguably surpassed the goals that had been set by earlier initiatives. The fall of the Iron Curtain in 1990 created opportunities for free association and expression of culture and ethnic affiliation across the countries of central and eastern Europe. Within months of the political changeover hundreds of Romani non-governmental organizations were formed and a demand emerged for printed material in Romani. Cultural magazines, political pamphlets, literary translations, newsletters, religious texts, dictionaries and children's books began to appear in various countries. Most were funded at first by charitable foundations, then by grants from the European Union and foreign governments and gradually drawing on sponsorship from local authorities and national governments. In almost all cases authors felt free to improvise with whatever form of Romani they felt more comfortable with, taking into consideration the needs and abilities of their target audiences. Almost all opted to write in their own local or regional variety of Romani. In most cases a writing system was designed that was based on some features of the alphabet of the state language, incorporating some symbols introduced by linguists, such as the use of *x* for the guttural sound (as in *loch*), or of the combinations *ph*, *th*, *kh* for the so-called 'aspirated' sounds, i.e. sounds that are followed by an *h*. A small group of activists advocated the use of a 'standard' alphabet with a number of custom-made symbols such as *ç*, *θ* and *ʒ*. These have remained an isolated minority among writers of Romani, although in Romania a government-backed initiative adopted this form of writing in the early 1990s and it has since been introduced into the school curriculum in dozens of schools around the country that have a large number of pupils of Romani background.

Instead of a uniform standard language, linguistic pluralism had gradually found its way into publications and local broadcasts in the Romani language towards the mid-1990s. At this time the community of Romani activists began embracing electronic communication via email and internet websites. With the freedom to improvise and reach distant audiences, online interactions proliferated. They typically feature a mixture of Romani dialects and spelling conventions. Pluralism continues to dominate the numerous electronic mailing lists, blogs and chat forums in Romani. The young generation of Romani language and culture enthusiasts, brought up with the norms of spelling shortcuts and other uninhibited creative approaches to communication common in text messages and blogs, seems completely undisturbed by the absence of central guidelines and rules, and the virtual world of spontaneous and improvised written communication in Romani is now flourishing.

Less advanced is the inclusion of Romani in the context of institutions, especially in education. Calls to promote awareness of Romani and even to include it in the teaching curriculum have been made on many occasions by international bodies such as the Council of Europe, UNESCO and the European Parliament. The European Charter for Regional or Minority Languages made provisions for the recognition of Romani as a minority language, and the governments of some seventeen European countries have followed the call and granted Romani official recognition. Yet the implementation of such commitments is difficult both politically and practically. The political will to tackle the issue of a Romani curriculum is often lacking. Teaching Romani at schools would require training teachers and spending considerable resources on the production of teaching materials. Such efforts have been underway in Romania, Sweden and Finland and in the form of pilot projects also in other countries, but they do not yet reach the majority of the Romani population of children. Many Romani parents are for their part hesitant to send their children to Romani-curriculum schools lest they should become stigmatized and segregated. After years of discrimination they view the acceptance of their children and their integration into mainstream school classes as an achievement that they do not wish to see shattered. Nor has serious broadcasting in Romani taken off quite yet, though a number of state-sponsored broadcasting stations produce weekly programmes in the language and some maintain websites with online broadcasting in Romani.

A further symbol of recognition of the language and the people who speak it is the inclusion of Romani on official websites of international organizations such as the Council of Europe and regular provision of interpreter services from and into Romani at international conferences. Research into the language has also expanded since the early 1990s, much of it supported by official research councils and carried out at leading universities in Europe and the United States. Romani language courses are offered regularly at universities in Toronto, Chicago, Austin, Paris, Manchester, Graz, Pécs, Bucharest, Helsinki and others. In 2008 the Council of Europe published a 'European

Language Curriculum Framework for Romani', with guidelines to assist governments in setting up teaching and learning programmes for the language. In 2012 a consortium of teachers and linguists created an online animated language course for Romani called 'RomaniNet'. The availability of Romani language materials and the accessibility of the language at conferences and on websites have inspired quite a number of non-Romani students and intellectuals to learn the language. More than ever before Romani is now on its way out of the private and isolated niche that it once occupied as the language of the Romani family. It is moving towards an entirely new kind of medium, one that is being shaped by transnational usage in a variety of forms backed by electronic media and the new technologies.

5

The Roms Among the Nations

MEDIEVAL ROOTS IN BYZANTIUM

Writing Romani history is a difficult task. To begin with, the Roms have never set down any accounts of their own lives and the events that shaped them. All the information that we have about earlier phases in the life of the Romani people is based on the accounts and impressions of outsiders. Romani history is therefore one-sided, reflecting the perspective of those who came into contact with the Roms but not of the Romani communities themselves. A further complication is the geographical dispersion of the Roms which means that each Romani community was necessarily affected by different events in different regions. The history of the Roms is therefore a history of several groups of people, at various times and in a variety of places. For this reason existing research by historians tends to focus on individual Romani groups in specific countries and in particular periods.

When we attempt to draw a synthesis of the research insights gained from such studies, we are assuming that different Romani populations share key features of their historical relations with the surrounding populations. These include the pattern of socio-economic organization of Romani communities, which determines their commercial relations with the majority, as well as the Romani system of beliefs and values, which contributes to defining their attitude to outsiders. These in turn influence majority society's own attitudes towards the Roms, which ultimately determines the way the Roms are treated by governments, religious institutions, and in everyday encounters with neighbouring populations. Romani history is therefore the story of the relations between the Roms and the surrounding nations.

No records exist of the pre-European history of the Romani people. In order to interpret their early origins and migration routes we rely almost exclusively on linguistic evidence, as discussed in the previous chapter. Some historical circumstances, the socio-economic profile of Romani communities, and the presence of other populations of Indian origin outside India lend themselves to a partial interpretation of the events that may have triggered the Roms' early migration out of India. The retention of an Indic language, the specialization in mobile service trades and a self-appellation derived from Indian caste-names such as Ḍom, Jat and Parya are shared by a number of populations of central and western Asia, among them the Dom of the Middle East, the Lom of the Caucasus, the Jat of Afghanistan and the Parya of Central Asia. This suggests that the early migration of the Roms was part of a steady movement of caste-like groups specializing in service trades who left India and migrated westwards. The linguistic evidence is supported by a series of genetic surveys of various Romani sample populations in Europe, including Bulgaria, Poland and Spain, which equally points to an origin in India. Attempts to relate the early migration of the Roms out of India to specific historical events, such as particular Muslim raids in northern India around the tenth century or the taking of a large number of prisoners by the Byzantines in Antioch in the ninth century, remain speculative. In the absence of concrete documentation we may never know the precise circumstances that led to the arrival of a population speaking an Indian language at Europe's doorstep.

The linguistic evidence, however, clearly points to a prolonged presence of the Roms in the Greek-speaking realm of the medieval Byzantine Empire. It is difficult to derive any direct conclusions about the Roms during this period from historical records. Some scholars have chosen to interpret various depictions of acrobats, jugglers and magicians as references to the Roms. Others believe that a description from 1322 of a nomadic group of tent-dwellers in Crete confirms the presence of a Romani population there. An isolated mention of the name 'Romiti' in connection with a group of destitute people living outside the town walls of Modon on the Greek Peloponnese is often brought in association with the Roms, although the self-appellation of the Romani people is not usually mentioned in historical records from this early period.

It can be assumed that the Roms in the Byzantine Empire were listed on a special register and that they paid a special tax. The Patriarch of Constantinople, Gregorios II Kyprios, is known to have issued an order sometime between 1283 and 1289 specifying taxes to be levied on the 'Athinganoi and Egyptians'. The latter name can be assumed to refer to the Roms. There is no known mention of the Roms in Byzantine tax registers. But the Ottoman rulers, who succeeded the Byzantines, continued to use the Greek name *Kibti* ('Egyptians') to refer to the Roms. This suggests that the Ottoman administrative policy towards the Roms continued the principles set by their Byzantine predecessors, and so it gives us an indirect insight into both the presence and the status of the Roms in Byzantium. The term Kibti (also spelled *Qipti*) was employed throughout the Ottoman period, and in 1668 it accompanies the writer Evliya Çelebi's citation of phrases in the Romani language, leaving no doubt that Kibti/Qipti referred to the Romani people.

Other sources from the fourteenth-century Balkans can also be interpreted as references to the Roms. A record from the Croatian town of Dubrovnik from 1362 mentions two 'Egyptians' involved in a dispute with a local jeweller over a number of silver coins. In 1378 groups of Agoupti or Gupti are described as living in a number of Bulgarian villages. Around the same time, the term Tsingan and similar variations begin to appear, evidently with reference to the same populations. In 1373 the Tsigani are first mentioned in Zagreb, with later records of court proceedings in connection with unpaid loans suggesting that there were several Romani families in the city between 1387 and 1397 who made a living as butchers and traders. In 1378 the Venetian governor of Nauplia in the Greek Peloponnese affirmed the settlement and trade privileges of the Acingani. A further Venetian document from Corfu dated 1386 mentions *feudum acinganorum*, a term that some scholars have interpreted as a reference to 'the territory of the Gypsies'.

Some of the earliest records describe the Roms as slaves in the Romanian territories of Wallachia and Moldavia. A letter written by *Voivode* ('Prince') Dan I in 1385 to the Monastery of the Virgin Mary in Tismana confirms a 'gift' of forty Gypsy families presented by his uncle, Prince Vladislav, to the Monastery of St Anthony at Vodiţa. The Gypsies of Tismana are mentioned in subsequent lists of the possessions of the monastery in 1387, 1391 and 1392. Another document from 1388 similarly describes a gift of 300 Romani families made by Prince Mircea to the Cozia Monastery. It is very difficult to pinpoint precisely when and how slavery began in the Romanian principalities but these descriptions show that it was firmly established by the late fourteenth century.

Although there is no direct attestation of Romani slavery in Bulgaria, Turkey or Serbia, it seems likely that the first Roms who crossed the Danube northwards into Wallachia and Moldavia were already slaves. Some scholars have suggested that Roms were captured by the Tatars and Ottomans during their raids on Byzantium and sold to Romanian princes, noblemen and monasteries already as early as the thirteenth century. The reason for enslavement was presumably the special artisan and craftsmen skills that the Roms had possessed for generations. The historian Viorel Achim assumes that the earliest arrival of the Roms in Romania coincided with the turmoil in the northern Balkans during the 1360s and early 1370s and the intensification of Hungarian–Bulgarian and Hungarian–Wallachian conflicts. Achim believes that the Roms crossed the Danube or were transferred from the south not in a single wave but over several decades in many different groups.

By the fifteenth century most Romanian monasteries owned Romani slaves. In 1428 Prince Alexander the Good donated thirty-one tents (i.e. families) of Tsigani to the monastery at Bistriţa in Moldavia, and a record from the following year reports that he made a gift of several Gypsy slaves to his wife, Princess Marena. Roms are also attested in subsequent years in the possession of the Romanian monasteries of Vişnevăţi (1429) and of Poiană and Moldoviţa (1434). A report from 1445 mentions that count Vlad Dracul, Prince of Wallachia, forcibly brought back 11,000–12,000 'Egyptians' from his successful campaigns in Bulgaria against the Turks and transferred them to the north of the Danube. In 1471 Prince Stephen the Great of Moldavia is reported to have returned from his campaign against the Ottomans with 17,000 captive Tsigani as slave labourers. Although these depictions are usually interpreted by historians as boastful exaggerations, at least as far as the numbers are concerned, they nevertheless convey a picture of the way Romani slaves were acquired by the Romanian princes during their military campaigns.

A distinction eventually emerged between three main categories of slaves: those owned by the state and its princes (or 'the Crown'), those owned by the monasteries, and those owned by the boyars or landowners. It seems that initially the princes were the only owners of slaves but that they made gifts of slaves to landowners and to the monasteries. Romani slaves were also sold at markets, a trade that continued well into the nineteenth century. Slavery drove many Roms to escape from the Romanian territories and to flee to neighbouring countries. The presence of Vlax or Wallachian Romani groups specializing in particular artisan trades in all countries of southeastern Europe and to the north of Romania, in Slovakia and Ukraine, testifies to recurring migrations of Roms away from the Romanian territories.

According to most records, Romani slaves were used either for agricultural labour or as craftsmen. Some slaves, called Vatraşi, worked for monasteries and princes and carried out domestic work and fieldwork. They had fixed dwellings and usually became linguistically assimilated. Others, called Lăieşi, lived on their master's estate during the winter but had freedom of movement and travelled in search of work opportunities during the summer. As slaves they were required to pay taxes to the Crown or the prince who owned them. Taxes were usually paid twice in a year, on the days of St George (24 April according to the Western Calendar) and St Archangel Michael (8 November). They were collected by Romani leaders and handed over to officials who were responsible for the supervision of slaves.

The nomadic slaves were primarily blacksmiths, but some also worked as stonemasons or comb-makers. Gradually, different clans became specialized in various trades, passing them on from one generation to another. This resulted in the formation of Romani groups who carried their trade designation as a group name. Among the specialized Romani groups were the coppersmiths (Căldarari) and sieve-makers (Ciurari). The Rudari and Aurari collected gold from riverbeds. The Ursari were bear-leaders, and the Lingurari made wooden spoons and other household utensils. Many of these and other titles remain as group designations today, more than a century after the range of trades has been extended considerably, and some traditional ones such as gold-washing or comb-making have been replaced completely by new occupations.

Romani slaves were in demand because of their skilled crafts and their importance to the economic market. With the growing dependency of landowners, monasteries and the Crown on Romani slaves, the Romanian term *Ţigan* came to be used synonymously with 'slave' and it still has a derogatory connotation in the Romanian language today.

Most references to the Roms in Romania during the century-long period of slavery describe them as living in tents and the statistics relating to them are based on a count of family tents. Some Romanian Roms have even maintained the group name Cerhari meaning 'tent-dwellers'. Each Romani group had a leader, called *jude* in Wallachia and Moldavia and *voivode* in Transylvania. Groups that were linked together by kinship and occupations appointed their own sheriff, whose task was to represent them in front of the authorities and to resolve disputes and conflicts between groups and individuals. Later on, in the eighteenth century, they became known as *bulibaşa* and were put in charge of a number of leaders from a particular region. These organizational structures were usually created by the state and their purpose was to help the state supervise the Roms and collect taxes from them.

Back in the southern Balkans, the Ottoman conquests were under-way during the fourteenth century and were concluded with the capture of Constantinople in 1453. Roms in the Ottoman Empire are first mentioned in tax documents. In 1430, 431 Romani households were counted in the Nikopol region in present-day Bulgaria. Ottoman statistics and tax registers frequently refer to 'Egyptians' (Kibti). They mention the number of households in each town, their religion and their occupation. Widespread professions among the Ottoman Gypsies were those of musician, blacksmith and iron-worker, leather-worker, horse-trader and dancer. Many Romani people converted to Islam and are mentioned in the registers with Muslim names such as Hussain, Dervish, Abdullah and Hamza.

In 1530 Sultan Suleiman I 'The Magnificent' issued a 'Law concerning the Egyptians in the province of Rumelia' (*Kanunname-i kibtiyan-i vilayet-i rumili*). It required the Roms of Istanbul, Edirne and other towns in Rumelia to pay specified taxes. The document details penalty taxes that are to be paid for undertaking work without permission, fees for marriage and fines for criminal offences. The law also required punishments to be inflicted upon Muslim Roms who nomadized together with non-Muslim Roms. The law illustrates that the Roms had a special position among the various ethnicities in the Ottoman Empire. They were subjected to a separate taxation regime and paid more than the majority of the Muslim population, and they were often governed in a unique way. For example, in 1574 Sultan Selim II ordered Gypsy miners in Banja Luka in Bosnia to elect representatives for every group of fifty, who negotiated taxation and other issues of status and privileges on their behalf.

'LORD ANDREAS, DUKE OF LITTLE EGYPT': THE MIGRATION WEST

Perhaps the most significant event that was to shape future relations between the Roms and the nations of Europe and later the New World was the wave of Romani migrants who left southeastern Europe at the time when the region was falling into the hands of the rising Ottoman powers. Roms arrived in Transylvania towards the end of the fourteenth century both via Wallachia and via Hungary. To this day there are two distinct Romani populations in Transylvania: the so-called Hungarian Roms or Romungri, whose dialect is strongly influenced by Hungarian, and the Wallachian Roms or Vlaxika Rom, whose dialect is influenced by Romanian. A source from 1388 mentions families using the surname Cigany or Cigan residing in a village called Ciganvaja in Szolnok county in Hungary, and tent-dwelling Cigans are reported as residents of various Transylvanian villages in the period between 1390 and 1406. A chronicle from 1416 also reports that the residents of the Transylvanian town of Braşov provided 'lord Emaus of Egypt and his 120 companions' with food and money.

This is the first of a long series of similar reports filed throughout the fifteenth century across the European continent. In 1417 the presence of newcomers was recorded in the Bavarian town of Augsburg.

According to the report they were being led by two 'dukes' and formed a group of fifty men accompanied by women and children. They had a dark complexion and were skilful in fortune-telling, and they presented themselves as exiles from 'Little Egypt'. In the same year similar encounters are mentioned in Lübeck and Rostock in northern Germany and in the following year in Colmar in Alsace. In 1419 it is reported that a group of Travellers whom the source refers to as 'Saracens' – a name given at the time to non-Christians and especially to Muslims – were refused entry to the town of Sisteron in the French Provence. Chronicles from the same year report the presence of 200 'baptized pagans' in the Swiss towns of Basel, Berne and Zurich.

A description from Deventer in the Netherlands mentions the arrival of 'Lord Andreas, Duke of Little Egypt' in 1420, accompanied by one hundred persons and around forty horses. He is said to have presented a letter from the 'King of the Romans' asking to provide his people with alms. The group claimed to have been persecuted and forced to leave their original homeland because of their Christian faith. A very similar description appears in an Italian chronicle from 1422. It describes the arrival in Bologna of a group of one hundred people led by 'Duke Andrea of Egypt', who carried a safe-passage note from King Sigismund of Hungary, the Holy Roman Emperor. The group included men, women and children, and they claimed to have adopted the Christian faith and were therefore unable to return to their country.

The arrival of strangers of a similar description is already recorded in Bruges in Flanders in 1421, and other sources place the Roms in Regensburg in Bavaria in 1424, in Paris in 1427, and in numerous other European towns including Tournai, Utrecht, Middelburg, Leiden and Frankfurt between 1424 and 1428. The records usually report a group of around one hundred people led by a person of noble title such as a 'duke' or 'count', with the newcomers usually claiming to be on a penance pilgrimage and producing safe-conduct letters allegedly issued by royalty or by the Pope. They are described as dark-skinned, wearing earrings and colourful though shabby clothing. It is stated that they engage in palm-reading and fortune-telling and that they claim to have originated in Egypt or 'Little Egypt'.

The historical records clearly connect the Gitanos of Spain with the same wave of migrants from the Balkans. In 1425 King Alfonso V of Aragón issued an order pertaining to the *Egipcianos* ('Egyptians'), instructing the people of the town of Alagón near Zaragoza to return two dogs that had been stolen to 'Count Thomas of Egypt'. In the same year a letter of safe-conduct was issued in Zaragoza to 'Don Johan of Little Egypt' (*Egipte Menor*). The 'Don' suggests that this person's noble status was taken for granted. The letter asks that the bearer be allowed to travel unmolested through the Kingdom of Aragón with those accompanying him and their possessions, which are said to include clothing, gold, silver, saddlebags and other items. The arrival of Tomas and Martin, two 'Counts of Little Egypt', was recorded in Castile in 1462 and it was reported that they headed a group of around one hundred men, women and children. Between 1462 and 1473 there are several other descriptions of this kind from various regions in Spain, all reporting that the Roms were welcomed and were provided with food and sometimes with shelter. More safe-conduct letters were issued in Seville in 1491 to the 'Egyptians' Jacomo, Felipo and Luis, stating that they were on their way on pilgrimage to Santiago de Compostela as a penance. According to the historian Richard Pym there are some thirty such safe-conduct letters in the Spanish archives, most of them referring to the Romani leaders as 'counts' or 'dukes' of 'Egypt' or 'Little Egypt'.

How can we make sense of these various chronicles? Although explicit identification of these migrants as Roms is lacking, the descriptions give a coherent picture that is easily reconcilable with the general appearance of the Romani people. They have a distinctive way of dressing, they speak a foreign language and they have dark complexions. They travel in extended families and specialize in entertainment and fortune-telling. Although there is some repetition of names such as Andrew and Michael in the references to their leaders, it is generally assumed that the reports relate to several groups and not just to one single travelling party. The subsequent settlement of Roms in conspicuous numbers all across Europe supports this assumption.

Some historians relate the use of the term 'Little Egypt' to the description from the port of Modon in the Peloponnese in 1384.

Modon was an important station on the sea route from Venice to Jaffa and was used as a stop by pilgrims on their way to the Holy Land. It might have therefore earned the title 'Little Egypt'. However, the reference might simply have been a fashionable explanation that the Roms used in order to satisfy others' curiosity about their eastern Mediterranean appearance and origins. The writer Angus Fraser offers a similar explanation for the safe-conduct letters and the story of being Christian pilgrims or refugees escaping persecution. He refers to these as the 'great trick', assuming that it was merely a device that proved useful in attracting local residents' trust and sympathy and in securing temporary shelter and income.

It appears that alongside the presentation of an Egyptian origin there was also some admission of an origin in Greece. A number of Spanish sources from the 1480s make reference to Greek merchants as well as to 'Bohemians' who were given safe-conduct passages. Some of these migrants were said to have called themselves 'Greeks' while others described themselves as 'Egyptians'. A document issued in 1476 in Barcelona orders the punishment of one Juan Fetó, who is referred to as originating from the land of 'Little Egypt' and was accused of stabbing another man, while a letter issued in Toledo in 1484 contains a pardon to one Givio, who is referred to as a native of the 'Kingdom of Greece'.

While many of these accounts describe the Roms as travellers who are only seeking temporary shelter, there are also indications that at least some Romani migrants were in search of opportunities to settle and that some communities were happy to grant them settlement privileges. In 1417 it is reported that Prince Alexander I of Moldavia gave Gypsies the right to settle and to seek employment in his province. Official registers document the presence of families carrying the surname Cygan or Czygan in a series of Polish cities including Trześniów, Królikoa, Berezówka and Świerczów between 1419 and 1436.

The Roms who had migrated to Transylvania were not slaves, as was the case in the neighbouring provinces of Wallachia and Moldavia, but free, settled and regulated by a tax regime. Records from the years 1476, 1487 and 1492 mention that Roms were granted permission to settle in the Transylvanian town of Sibiu and in the villages surrounding it. A German chronicle from 1524 refers to the outskirts of the

Transylvanian town of Braşov as *bei den Zyganen* meaning 'among the Gypsies', indicating the presence of a permanent Romani settlement there.

Early records also provide an attestation that Romani people gradually occupied particular economic niches, that they had a repertoire of highly specialized trades and that they received the protection and recognition of the ruling circles and state authorities. A series of chronicles from 1471 to 1516 and 1534 contains references to Gypsies who served in the armies of the Hungarian monarchs, to sedentary Romani settlers in Slovakia who served as castle musicians and metal-workers, and to Roms in Bohemia and in Transylvania who were metal-workers entrusted with making weapons and torture instruments. In 1489 Gypsies were paid to perform music for Queen Beatrix of Hungary. In 1500 King Vladislav II of Hungary ordered the Count of Transylvania to prevent his civil servants from arresting Gypsies – referred to as *certi Egiptii seu Cigani* meaning 'Egyptians, also called Gypsies' – who served in Castle Bran near Braşov. A record from 1525 documents a payment made to 'Pharaoneans' for performing music in the court of the Hungarian King Louis II at Csepel Island, and in a letter from 1543 Queen Isabella, ruler of Transylvania, praised the music of 'Egyptian musicians, descendants of the Pharaohs'. In 1564 a visitor to the Szekler region in Transylvania reported that a large number of Gypsies were working as agricultural labourers for the ethnic Hungarian Szeklers. In the same year, at the other end of the continent, Lithuania regulated the settlement of Gypsies, and Polish rulers allowed Gypsies to select their own leaders in order to simplify tax collection.

During the same period, however, the migration wave continued. A chronicle from Geneva dated 1477 notes the arrival of 'Saracens' who were driven out of the city. A later report from the city, from 1532, mentions a disturbance involving a group of 'Sarasins' who are said to refer to themselves as 'Bohemians' or 'Egyptians'. The Hungarian King Ulászló, who reigned from 1490 to 1516, stated that he granted a travel permit for twenty-five tents of Gypsy smiths to the 'Voivode of the Pharaonic people'. A letter issued by King James IV of Scotland to the King of Denmark in 1506 recommended the undisturbed passage from Scotland to Denmark of a group of 'Egyptian pilgrims' led by one 'Antonius Gawino, Earl of Little Egypt'. This is widely believed to be the very first mention of Roms in Britain, and it was promptly followed by others – Sir Thomas More wrote about an 'Egypcian' woman who told fortunes in Lambeth in 1514 and a report from 1530 mentions Egyptians who danced before King James V of Scotland. A record of the arrest of Gypsies for stealing horses in Huntingdon, England, is dated 1542, and in 1545 permission was granted for a group of Gypsies led by one Phillip Lazer to enter London. The arrival of Gypsies in Stockholm is already recorded in 1520, and from 1570 onwards there is evidence of Roms in Ukraine, apparently following migrations from Wallachia. By this time, Romani populations had established a presence throughout the entire European continent.

'OUTLANDISH PEOPLE': THE RISE OF PERSECUTION

While Roms successfully found a niche in the social, economic and political landscape of some European regions, their migration and settlement attempts were not free of friction and hurdles. The city of Milan was one of the first authorities to adopt strict legislation against Gypsies, making their presence in the town punishable by death in 1493. It seems that the hostile attitude of the authorities towards the Romani minorities was primarily an opportunistic attempt to identify scapegoats in light of a new tense political situation triggered by conflict and war. In 1496 the legislative council of the Holy Roman Empire, meeting in the Bavarian town of Lindau, declared Gypsies to be 'enemy agents'. In 1499 Ferdinand and Isabella, the new 'Catholic Monarchs' of Spain who led campaigns against Muslims, Jews and other minorities, enacted the first Spanish legislation placing restrictions on Gypsies. Their royal decree was addressed 'to you the Egyptians, who wander with your women and children'. The Roms were accused of having no way of supporting themselves apart from begging, stealing and deceiving, engaging in sorcery and fortune-telling and other 'activities that are not decent'. The law ordered Gypsies to take up permanent residence and recognized occupations and find a master to serve and to provide for them, or leave the kingdom. It gave them sixty days to comply and it detailed various punishments for those who failed to do so. The law also rendered invalid all letters of safe-conduct issued to Gypsies. The same ordinance was reiterated by Charles V of Spain in 1525, 1528 and again in 1534, suggesting that it was not implemented effectively.

The Turkish defeat of the Hungarians in 1526 and the resulting civil war in Hungary also led to strong anti-Gypsy sentiments. After the Ottoman conquest of central Hungary and the partition of the country, orders were given in the parts that remained under Habsburg control (now centred around Slovakia) to expel the Gypsies. However, only some local rulers chose to follow these orders, while others preferred to maintain the skills and services of the Roms. In 1541 a series of fires in Prague was blamed on the Roms. They were accused of being in the service of the Turks, and King Ferdinand I ordered their expulsion from the Czech lands. In 1548 the German Diet in Augsburg decided that the killing of Gypsies by civilians could go unpunished, thus declaring them 'fair game'. The wave of expulsions and bans spread across the continent. In 1530 King Henry VIII of England passed the Act concerning 'Egiptians' which targeted 'outlandish people calling themselves Egyptians' who were engaged in palm-reading and fortune-telling. The Act banned such people from entering the kingdom and ordered those who had already done so to leave within sixteen days or suffer imprisonment. The expulsion of Gypsies from Moravia was decreed in 1538.

The Spanish Inquisition began a campaign to investigate Gypsies in 1539. Roms were accused of superstition and sorcery. A report from that year, produced in Toledo, claimed that many foreign and indigenous vagabonds had begun to accompany Gypsies travelling through Castile and that these people had been adopting the Gypsies' language, dress and way of life. In response, Charles V once again reiterated the ordinance of 1499 and increased the penalties imposed on Gypsies for not complying with the law. Gypsy women would be flogged and Gypsy men would be condemned to serving in the galleys of the Spanish Mediterranean squadrons. This punishment was later to be imposed on all Gypsy men for a six-year period if they were found to be without a 'recognized occupation'. Increasing demand for oarsmen motivated the extension of this form of punishment at a later period, and in 1575 all vagrant Gypsies 'suitable to be arrested' were assigned to the galleys. Throughout the sixteenth and seventeenth centuries, Spanish archives document letters by individuals denouncing Gypsies for being untrustworthy and deceiving, and records of criminal investigations taken up by the Inquisition against Gypsies.

In 1551 the Advisory Council of Madrid petitioned the king to enforce existing legislation against Gypsies amid reports that they were still using letters of safe-conduct and committing various offences. In the second half of the sixteenth century Spain had found itself in a crisis following the demands of its wars in the Low Countries, its involvement in the French wars and its war with England. Insecurity and famine drove many to a life of wandering and criminality to survive. Gypsies were invariably associated with this image of non-sedentary travelling populations of vagabonds, and the demands for stricter crime prevention and a ban on travelling were equally directed towards the Gypsy minority. Valencia issued successive expulsion orders against Gypsies in 1564, 1585 and 1604, and Madrid banned Gypsies from entering and staying in the city in 1585.

The plague took a high toll at the end of the sixteenth century especially in Castile and Roms were motivated both to flee the disaster area and to escape persecution. During this period the southern province of Andalusia became an attractive region for the Roms. Its estates were larger, having been made up of lands confiscated from the Muslims and handed over to the Spanish nobility after the final phase of the Reconquista, the Christian conquest of the country, at the end of the fifteenth century. This meant less effective patrolling and so more opportunities to avoid being apprehended and expelled from the territory. Some families even granted protection to the Roms, in contradiction to the royal decrees of the time.

In England, an anti-Gypsy campaign began in 1549, when the Justice of Durham accused three 'Egiptians' of attempting to counterfeit the King's Great Seal. Under Queen Mary I, authorities in England introduced the Egyptians Act in 1554. It accused the Gypsies of 'devlish and naughty practices and devices' and introduced the death penalty for Gypsies who refused to leave the country. In 1562 the law was extended to those 'who accompany the Egyptians', indicating that the Romani community was attracting followers from among the indigenous English population. A series of police records from 1555–9 described the apprehension, imprisonment and in some cases expulsion of large groups of Roms in various parts of the country. In 1562 the English Parliament passed the Act for further Punishment of Vagabonds calling themselves Egyptians. It ordered Gypsies who had been arrested to leave the country within fourteen days of their release and imposed further penalties on those who had been in the company of Gypsies and 'imitated their Apparel, Speech, or other Behaviour'.

In 1569 the Privy Council of England ordered authorities in every county to capture, punish and send to their homes all vagrants, including Gypsies. In the following years it issued a series of anti-Gypsy orders pertaining to specific cases. In 1577 it called for the apprehension of eight persons who were tried at Aylesbury for feloni-ously keeping company with 'other vagabonds vulgarly called and calling themselves Egyptians'. They were accused of 'altering them-selves in dress, language, and behaviour', found guilty and hanged. In 1592 five men were convicted and executed in Durham for calling themselves Egyptians. In 1594 four people were hanged in London for 'consorting for a month with Egyptians', and in 1598 three men were convicted in Devonshire for 'wandering like Egyptians'. The fact that Roms and Romani values and customs were serving as role models for sectors of the population who were disenchanted with the ruling classes and the regime that they imposed was obviously of great concern to the authorities.

In Italy, Rome outlawed the presence of Gypsies in the city and its vicinity in 1557 and ordered Gypsies to leave the territory within two days. In the following year the Great Council of the Republic of Venice (the Council of the Pregadi) adopted a resolution 'Concerning the Cingani' in which it declared that the population was suffering annoyance, damages and manifold troubles from the Gypsies. It reiterated a call from 1549 to ban Gypsies from the Venetian territo-ries. The resolution offered rewards to citizens who apprehended Gypsies and handed them over to the authorities for expulsion, and it threatened to assign to the galleys any Gypsy who broke the law and returned to the Venetian territory. The Council reiterated the same resolutions again in 1588. The climate of expulsion and persecution now extended from the southern edge of the European continent through to the Baltic coast. Expulsion orders against Gypsies were issued in Warsaw in 1557 and in the town of Piotrków in western Poland in 1565, and in 1588 the Grand Duchy of Lithuania further tightened its regulations on Gypsies, threatening to punish peasants who offered them food and shelter.

UNDER THE PRESSURE OF EUROPEAN ABSOLUTISM

If European feudalism was an age of contradictory attitudes towards the Romani minorities on the part of majority society and its institutions, then the emergence of absolute and unrestrained monarchical power led to a centralization of state policies towards the Roms. The principal feature of these policies was an attempt to prevent the uncontrolled movement of the Romani minority population. In order to assert their control, authorities resorted to a combination of measures. On the one hand, they turned to expulsion as a way of removing those whose lives and routine they felt unable to control from their territories. On the other hand, governments attempted to force the Roms into permanent settlements and to impose on them tightly regulated routines.

In the Ottoman Empire, Roms became segregated and were viewed with suspicion for their nomadic way of life. The tax administration in particular complained about their movements, which made regular collection of taxes more difficult. Special decrees regulating the tax to be paid by the Kibtian were enacted in Rumelia in 1604 and in Sofia in 1610. Ottoman authorities attempted to settle travelling Roms in order to ensure regular tax payments. In 1630 Sultan Morad IV issued a decree that required Gypsies to reside in permanent settlements. Those who were settled were referred to as *yerli* or 'settled', and their descendants retain the group names Yerli, Erli or Arli throughout the southern Balkans today. Special penalty fees were imposed on nomadic Roms if they moved away without paying their taxes.

There was no violent persecution of Roms by the Ottomans, but they were generally viewed as untrustworthy and were regarded as the lowest social class in Ottoman society. Roms were often accused of not being true Muslims and they were referred to in many Ottoman administrative documents as 'those who hold Muslim names'. Many Roms were attracted to the Ottoman towns. Salonica and its surrounding villages, for example, had a population of around 4,000 Gypsies in 1706. They usually lived in huts and tents outside the town limits. Roms in what is today Bulgaria, Albania and the former republics of Yugoslavia were packed into their own neighbourhoods, residing in almost total segregation from the general population. In Bosnia, Roms were banned from residing in cities and only those who could prove to have a required skill or craft could dwell inside the city walls.

Gypsies were excluded from military service under the Ottomans. Nevertheless, some served in supporting services such as military bands and they were often recruited as executioners, smiths, ironworkers and entertainers. Music was among the main Romani occupations in the Balkans. Music and dance attracted audiences, but at the same time, they provided a justification for the segregation of the Kibtian based on accusations of immodest behaviour and loudness, which were said to constitute a danger to public order.

In Spain, Roms found themselves being accused of siding with the Moriscos, the descendants of Muslim converts, who were suffering increased persecution. In 1611 the Council of State in Madrid accused Gypsies of stealing and of pretending to be Christians and urged the king to expel them once the expulsion of the Moriscos was completed. Philip III of Spain issued an expulsion order against Gypsies in 1619, which also encouraged their sedentarization. Many Roms resisted sedentarization, however, fearing that registration and a fixed domicile would make them more vulnerable to persecution. Despite countless expulsion decrees, Romani populations remained in the whole of Spain. The local priesthood in many areas protected them and offered them sanctuary, defying instructions by the Inquisition. Various noblemen also granted them protection.

Part of the problem that authorities had come to face by this period was how precisely to define and recognize Gitanos. The term had come to denote all kinds of non-sedentary groups, including the Roms but also travelling hawkers and beggars of Spanish origin as well as foreigners. An ordinance that was issued in 1717 reiterating earlier expulsion orders had to be reissued periodically in subsequent years. It included a list of the towns in which Gypsies were allowed to settle if they wished to avoid expulsion and take on a sedentary life. But the edict triggered numerous petitions by Gypsies who had settled elsewhere and wished to remain there. Some of these petitioners produced letters of reference from noblemen and clergymen. The list was consequently extended on several occasions. In 1749, an order was issued to arrest all the Gypsies found in Spain. Thousands were detained but the action failed to eradicate the presence of Gypsies in the country. It appears that there were many mixed marriages of Gypsies with non-Gypsies, which made identification difficult. This trend of mixed marriages continued to increase during the eighteenth century.

Many Roms served in various armies during the Thirty Years' War (1618–48), including those of German principalities such as Brandenburg and the Palatinate. German archives from the period following the war contain numerous petitions from people identifying themselves as Gypsies, who asked to be granted passports and work permits in consideration of their service. While it is possible that in some cases fictitious military credentials were used to support these requests, sometimes they were accompanied by accurate information about the units in which the petitioners claimed to have served. (In some cases, Roms had even served as officers commanding entire units of Romani soldiers.) On the whole it appears that officials treated these petitions as credible and were often inclined to grant the request.

During the Thirty Years' War there appear to have been hardly any persecutions of Roms in the territories of the countries involved in the conflict (most of the countries of Europe, especially central Europe, where the war was being fought). This could have been due to the authorities' preoccupation with the war effort, but it may also have had to do with the fact that Roms served as soldiers and that their useful contribution was recognized and honoured. The motivation to serve in the military can be explained on economic grounds, as the army offered a salary equal to that of a labourer, as well as shelter, clothing and the opportunity to acquire weapons and horses and sometimes a share of bounties or enemy possessions confiscated in battle. Enlisting in the military for these reasons was of course widespread and not limited to the Romani population. But for the Roms, who lacked possessions, land and often a steady domicile, it was particularly attractive. Many Roms served in the armies of the Habsburg and Ottoman Empires as gunsmiths and specialized in the manufacturing and maintenance of weapons and ammunition. The war also opened up increased opportunities to Romani women to practise healing and fortune-telling among a distressed and disoriented client population, which was not only deeply superstitious but, at that time of uncertainty, also insecure and anxious and in need of comfort and reassurance. During this period the image of the Romani fortune-teller became a frequently depicted theme in the arts, especially among French and Flemish painters.

Following the Thirty Years' War, the second half of the seventeenth century saw a tightening of regulations against the Roms and, again, increasing discrimination. Records show that a large number of Roms were stripped of their military rank immediately after the war, suggesting that racial discrimination certainly played a role. Decrees were issued throughout the territories that had been involved in the war, banning Gypsies from settling and even from travelling through them and forbidding contacts and trade with Gypsies. Records from southern Germany show a growing number of expulsions of Romani families from the 1660s onwards. The Austrian authorities in Freiburg, for example, issued a decree in 1664 banning Zigeuner from their region. A court in Bavaria convicted a group of Gypsies of illegal entry from Bohemia in 1667, leading to a coordinated effort among the authorities to ban the passage of Gypsies through their borders. Conferences took place in the southwest German towns of Biberach in 1687 and Hechingen in 1707 in which officials representing principalities from various parts of the region came together to discuss measures to deny entry to Gypsies and to apprehend and deport those who were found in their territories. The documents issued in conclusion of these meetings adopted inciting wordings, referring to Gypsies as 'bands of harmful vermin'.

Expulsion policies became widespread in western Europe. In 1637 all Gypsies were declared outlaws in Sweden. In 1642 the law was modified to an instruction to deport all Gypsies from county to county towards the borders of the realm. Male Gypsies could be sentenced to death by beheading for any crime. In 1665 the Council of Geneva empowered citizens to apprehend and expel 'Saracens' from neighbouring villages and to use force if they offered resistance. In 1697 the Habsburg ruler Leopold I declared Gypsies to be outlaws and allowed their persecution. In 1710 a similar law was adopted by Joseph I and applied in Bohemia. The edict declared that Gypsies were to be hanged without trial and that Gypsy women and children were to have their ears cut off and be banished. In some areas of Austria Gypsies were branded on the back. The mutilations were intended to allow the authorities to recognize them as Gypsies who had already been banished from other parts of the country. Mass killings of Gypsies appear to have followed these laws. In 1717 Gypsies were banned from Bohemia and Silesia by a new decree and in 1721 that decree was amended to allow for the execution of Gypsy women.

In France, a series of edicts were enacted between 1634 and 1682 ordering the expulsion of Gypsies, though most of them appear not to have been implemented. In 1689, after a series of expulsion orders failed to achieve the desired results, King Louis XIV issued an expulsion decree against all 'Egyptians and Bohemians' and instructed that they be arrested, tortured and expelled if apprehended anywhere in the French territory. Initially, most edicts warned against the use of excessive force or firepower during expulsions. But in 1705 a decree was issued expelling Gypsies from the Swabian territories, which granted impunity to anyone who used force and violence to do so. In 1713 Emperor Charles VI of Bavaria declared that Gypsies could be shot to death with impunity. The law was amended in 1719 to allow both law-enforcement officers and citizens to 'massacre, or beat to death, or kill [Gypsies] in any other way'. In 1721, Count Georg Wilhelm of Bayreuth ordered that Gypsies be shot if they resisted arrest. In 1722 it is reported that troops in the Lower Rhine area successfully expelled a group of between 800 and 1,500 Gypsies who had been travelling through the forest of Thuringen.

In the 1720s and 30s Roms carried out a series of acts of violence in revenge for such repressive measures. The perpetrators were arrested and put on show trials in various central German towns, including Giessen (1726), Fulda (1727) and Darmstadt (1727). Their interrogations and subsequent punishments were widely publicized.

One of the factors that may have provoked repression against the Roms was the confidence they appeared to manifest in the period immediately following the war. According to the historian Thomas Fricke, records show that Roms who had served as officers in the military adopted a military style in their dealings with the sedentary population, now claiming authority by commanding their own clan and maintaining military titles and ranks, uniforms and decorations of various kinds. This triggered fear and resentment among peasants whom the Roms approached for food and supplies and jealousy among law-enforcement officers and army veterans.

Nevertheless, the principal cause of the increased repression was without a doubt the feeling of instability and insecurity that followed the war and the need to assert authority and control, and, not least, to find a convenient scapegoat. The task of apprehending and expelling Gypsies was often given to patrols made up of peasants and citizens. But increasingly, from the end of the seventeenth century, professional soldiers joined the patrols in order to increase their effectiveness. In southwest Germany during the eighteenth century, over 300 expulsions of Gypsies were recorded along with over 100 cases of imprisonment, 237 instances of the death penalty and many more of various forms of torture and punishment.

DARK TIMES IN
THE AGE OF ENLIGHTENMENT

The restrictions placed on Gypsies made it difficult for them to travel and to carry out their professions. Considering that even simple, innocent acts such as crossing territorial boundaries, selling goods or trading artefacts for food were illegal, clashes with the law could not be avoided. In the absence of any legal means of obtaining food and other basic supplies, many had to turn to theft from peasants in order to survive. For this, in turn, Gypsies were persecuted, arrested and punished through the strict enforcement of laws that banned them, expelled them and controlled their movements. The result was a long-lasting vicious circle of exclusion, criminalization and persecution.

The aftermath of the Thirty Years' War saw the emergence of travelling gangs of robbers in central Europe. These groups were often composed of displaced persons and soldiers returning from the war. They inflicted damage on the establishment and on the sedentary population. Police measures aimed at combating these gangs were often extended to include travelling Romani clans on a wholesale basis, targeting anyone identified as a Gypsy as a potential criminal. The threat perceived from travelling gangs led to wholesale incitement against all those lacking a fixed domicile and their criminalization. The scarcity of resources and extreme poverty in the wake of the war contributed to the emergence of other travelling populations such as itinerant bricklayers and smiths, couriers, musicians, seasonal workers, hawkers and peddlers and professional beggars. All these were increasingly associated with Gypsies. During the eighteenth century terms such as the German word Zigeuner and French Tsigane came to denote an itinerant lifestyle irrespective of the origin, culture or occupation of the individual group or family concerned.

Authorities' response to the growth of travelling populations was to increase their networking, surveillance and expulsion measures. Records were kept on travelling populations in an effort to understand their family structures, resources, hideouts and modes of operation, their customs and their language. In most cases information was extracted from Gypsies and Travellers who were arrested, interrogated and tortured. Roms were pressured to confess to their alleged crimes and to provide information about members of their family and their whereabouts, and about alleged crimes they had committed or were about to commit. The information obtained was logged and disseminated among law-enforcement officers in various territories and it later found its way into criminologist publications. Roms were also pressured to provide insights into their social and spiritual world and to reveal information about the Romani language, which the authorities considered to be a secret code that travelling people used to communicate among themselves without being understood by others. There is little doubt that this experience was responsible for the emergence of a strict protective attitude among the Roms in central and western Europe towards their culture, their social and family organization and especially their language, and the reluctance of the more traditional families among them to share information about themselves with outsiders.

One of the most famous cases is that of the Hannikel gang, whose members were arrested and tried in southern Germany in the 1780s. The records of the gang's interrogation formed the basis of the 'Sulz Gypsy List', published in the southwestern German town of Sulz by an inspector called Schäffer. The list details family connections, favourite targets and escape routes, weapon skills and more. It also contains a linguistic section, listing the translation of German phrases into Romani (referred to as the 'Gypsy language') and into the secret jargon that was widespread at the time among groups of indigenous Travellers or Jauner (and now known as Jenische, Yenish or Yeniche). The fact that Schäffer maintained consistent separation between Romani and Yenish phrases indicates that he was well aware of the distinction between the two groups, the Roms (Gypsies) and the Travellers. This was not the first publication that testified to such awareness. In 1755, a dictionary was published in Frankfurt that listed separately words in the so-called 'Thieves' Jargon' (referred to by the German name *Rotwelsch*), and words in Romani (referred to as the 'Gypsy language'). The book also contains the text of a letter from a Gypsy to his wife, the first ever attestation of a complete text written in Romani.

The emergence of a social welfare system in the eighteenth century made it the responsibility of municipalities to provide shelter for the poor. Local officials began to regard Travellers with suspicion, fearing that they would become a burden on the authorities. They responded by keeping strict records of their sedentary citizens and taking measures to prevent newcomers from settling within their jurisdiction. Irrespective of the practical challenges that the Travellers may have posed to the authorities, discrimination and persecution were not least motivated by the mere rejection among the majority of a nomadic lifestyle. Individuals lacking a steady domicile were thought of as rootless, lazy and work-shy and thus as predestined to carry out criminal acts. They were therefore viewed as a threat.

During this period, Roms favoured smaller territories in which they were able to establish closer contact with the majority population.

The Roms provided services and often controlled trade in certain products and tools. They were engaged in sharpening knives and supplied herbal medicines, and they provided various forms of entertainment such as music and dance. They sold glass items and practised woodcarving. They traded in horses and appeared at fairgrounds and in theatres. They performed healing ceremonies, told fortunes and gave advice. Their performance of magic exploited the superstitions of the majority population, who believed that the Roms, due to their foreign appearance, actually possessed supernatural powers. Roms were instrumental in communicating news and information from other territories. Some worked as seasonal labourers in agriculture, others made a living as hunters or foresters and a few were in the service of noblemen.

One of the ways in which Roms sought protection and stability was to approach noblemen such as counts and earls and ask them to stand as godfathers for their children. Regarded as a religious duty, such requests were seldom turned down. Once the relationship was documented, the Roms could claim protection and safe passage due to their alignment with a noble or reputable sedentary family. In many cases multiple godfathers are documented for a single child.

By and large, the Roms were a poor population who had to make do with simple clothing, makeshift accommodation and an irregular supply of food. They were therefore dependent on the economic activities of all members of the family, children as well as men and women. Reports from the seventeenth and eighteenth centuries indicate that for fear of persecution Roms in western Europe often resided in the forests and woods, to where they retreated once they had obtained a supply of food and water. Quite often their children were born in open spaces in fields and woods. They had no access to school or literacy. The Roms depended on the peasants for food and cash income and for tools and products that were manufactured in workshops.

Stopping in smaller areas provided greater security. Borders were a shorter distance away and could be reached and crossed more quickly. The strict partition of territories often meant that the authorities did not have the power to pursue the Roms once they crossed the border into a neighbouring jurisdiction. Many places forbade any contact with Gypsies, and Gypsies were prohibited to sell their services or products or to make purchases in markets and shops. The Roms depended on clandestine contacts in isolated farms and on theft for survival.

Nonetheless, an indication of the degree of integration of the Roms is provided in numerous eighteenth-century German sources, which list Roms with German surnames. Documentation of the Romani language in Germany from the early eighteenth century shows that the Romani dialect spoken there had already absorbed a very significant number of German loanwords and grammatical influence, indicating that the Roms had been fully bilingual for several generations. This in turn suggests that there were opportunities to interact with Germans. There is no doubt that it was in the Roms' interest to maintain stable relations of cooperation with the majority population while keeping their own family structures, traditions and spirituality. Such relations were often interrupted by suspicions on the part of the authorities who regarded the Roms as a foreign population that would not subject itself to the rule of the majority's institutions and regulations, and who were keen to find someone to blame for the misery and uncertainty of the period.

During the Habsburg Monarchy restrictions on Gypsies were relaxed for a short period in 1737 as a result of reforms led by Charles VI, and they were ordered to pay taxes. But under the reign of Maria Theresa (1740–80) harsh penalties for providing food or any other support to Gypsies were reintroduced, as were Gypsy deportation measures. A decree from 1749 banned 'vagrants and foreign beggars' and was used to expel Gypsies from Austria. But after a few years, the policy changed and a series of new laws was enacted. Gypsies were now referred to as 'New Citizens' and local councils became responsible for those in their area. Decrees were passed that forced the Roms to settle and assimilate. In 1758, Maria Theresa's first explicit edict on Gypsies ordered them to settle and pay taxes and to carry out mandatory services to churches and landowners. It also prohibited Gypsies from owning horses and wagons without special permits. Her second decree in 1761 made military service compulsory for Gypsies. In 1767, the wearing of traditional Gypsy dress and use of the Romani language were banned and recognition was withdrawn from Romani leaders. The final decree in 1774 forbade marriages between Gypsies and ordered that Romani children should be taken for adoption by state institutions or by non-Romani families, though there is little evidence that either of these measures was actually implemented.

Maria Theresa's son, Emperor Joseph II, continued these policies. In 1782 he issued the order known as *De regulatione Zingarorum,* 'A Regulation concerning the Gypsies'. It stated that Gypsy children must go to school and that Gypsies must attend church on Sundays and public holidays. Gypsies were banned from wearing long coats in which they might be able to hide stolen items. They were not allowed to own horses. They were required to work in agriculture and landowners were encouraged to provide them with land, and they were allowed to perform music only when there was no work in the fields. A further order from 1783 outlawed travelling and begging and banned Roms from taking part in fairs and public events. It also required officials to submit periodical reports on Roms in their jurisdiction. It limited the number of Romani musicians, ordered the destruction of Romani settlements and increased the surveillance on Romani communities. Use of the Romani language remained punishable, as did marriage between Gypsies. The regulations were only partially implemented and failed to achieve their goal of completely assimilating the Gypsies of the Habsburg Monarchy. However, many Hungarian Gypsies became sedentary and a large number lost their language as a result of the restrictions imposed on them.

The new assimilation policy pioneered by the Habsburg rulers was accompanied, and in part inspired, by discussions among writers, journalists and scholars about the customs, language and origins of the Romani people. In 1775 the Slovak Samuel Augustini ab Hortis published his influential article series on 'The Gypsies in Hungary'. Most of the text was devoted to the author's observations about the economic and social organization, dress, food and housing conditions of the Roms. He described their music, fortune-telling and magic and their service in the military. He listed words and phrases from their language. He reviewed various speculations about their origin and dwelt in particular on the theory that they had come from Egypt. He pointed out that there are Persian words in their language and reported the theory that they may have arrived in Europe with the Mongol invaders. Hortis appears to have been aware of William

Marsden's linguistic work and possibly also of discussions among a wider international circle of philologists who had taken a scientific interest in the Romani language. His was the first series of essays devoted to the Gypsies that claimed to be based on first-hand, empirical ethnographic observations. But it was his contemporary, the German Heinrich Grellmann, who gave Hortis's findings wide publicity, and above all academic credibility. Much of the text of Grellmann's 'Dissertation on the Gypsies' published in 1783 was based on Hortis's articles. Grellmann added not just a scientific presentation to the narrative, but also a political statement. He called on the authorities to turn the Gypsies into 'productive and useful citizens' by forcing them to abandon their own customs and to adopt the ways and habits of the majority. A son of the Age of Enlightenment, Grellmann regarded himself as a humanist and reformer whose task it was to stimulate an intellectual discussion and influence policy. His belief that both the Roms and society as a whole would benefit if Gypsies were forced from the margins into the mainstream would later find an echo in the attitudes of officials across the European continent. They would not only provide the scholarly justification for the policies pursued by the Hungarian Emperor Joseph II, but would also set the principles that would eventually inspire twentieth-century policies of forced settlement in countries such as Russia, Poland and Romania, and proposals to force Romani parents to give up their children for adoption by non-Romani families in countries such as Norway and Switzerland.

Although the measures adopted in Hungary and Austria remained an extreme attempt at forced assimilation during the eighteenth century, similar laws were being enacted in other countries as well. Sweden adopted a law calling for the sedentarization of Gypsies and their forced integration into the workforce in 1772. In Spain, Charles III issued a new ordinance in 1783, which changed the policy towards Gypsies in the spirit of many voices advocating their integration into Spanish society. The new law regarded them as Spanish citizens, not foreigners, and revoked many of the earlier repressive measures. In Russia, Gypsies had already been ordered to pay taxes by Empress Anna Ivanovna in 1733, and the Russian Senate allowed them to settle around St Petersburg and subsequently in a number of other provinces and to trade in horses. The breakthrough came, however, in

1783, when Catherine the Great granted the Roms the status of state peasants and allowed them freedom of movement and occupation. Her actions derived to a large extent from her personal romantic fascination with the Gypsies, whose image as a free, proud, artistically creative and spiritual people she admired. In Poland, the Seym or Parliament adopted a manifesto in 1791 granting Gypsies legal protection and freedom to settle and advising magistrates not to arrest them as tramps or vagabonds, with a view towards integrating them into settled society. A new chapter was being opened in the relations between the Roms and the rulers of the lands in which they resided, one in which the Roms were being offered protection in the name of humanism and equal opportunities but on the condition that they abandon their traditions and their separate identity.

6

Baptized Heathens: Between
Romanticism and Racism

THE GYPSY IMAGE IN THE ARTS
FROM RENAISSANCE TO MODERNITY

In 1788 an opera called *The Gypsy* was produced in Moscow in which Roms played the principal parts. It expressed growing fascination with the culture of the Roms, somewhat ironically perhaps, at a time when they were being encouraged to give up their traditions and integrate into mainstream, majority society. This contradiction constitutes a central theme in the preoccupation with images depicting Romani culture in the arts and literatures of European societies. The Roms offer majority society a kind of mirror. By contrasting itself with the Gypsies, majority society is able to cast a demarcation line around itself and its own identity, while at the same time expressing a yearning for forbidden values and norms.

By the eighteenth century, Romani populations had not only dispersed across the various countries of Europe, they had become permanent residents of them. In some places they acquired land, or had tight connections to local estates on which they served. For the most part, they provided mobile services, but their regions of settlement had become fixed and contained. They attended regular markets, and they cultivated regular client audiences. They adopted many of the customs of the regions they lived in and spoke the local languages fluently, to the extent that these had a considerable impact on their own Romani dialects. In many places they interacted with local institutions. They served local landowners, they performed for the nobility, and many served in the armies of the various European nations. State policies towards the Roms had fluctuated between tolerance and persecution. The majority of people among whom the

Roms lived probably continued to be unaware of the internal organization of Romani communities and of Romani values and traditions.

Yet gradually European societies began to develop their own image of the Roms – often based on superficial impressions of Romani appearance, dress and behaviour. These impressions were interpreted within the context of the beliefs, the values, the fears, the ambitions and the typical longings that mainstream European society cultivated, that is, within the context of Europeans' own understanding of themselves. In the arts, medieval inhibitions gradually gave way to more freedom to express longings and desires. The Roms became an object of fantasy and imagination. Art, literature and music embraced a romantic image of Gypsies while at the same time perpetuating the notion that they were outsiders who did not belong and who did not answer to society's moral code and behaviour norms.

The literary image of Gypsies was to become so powerful that it would dominate not only individuals' perception of the Roms, but also state policy towards them. As new forms of governance emerged and strived to consolidate their power, they turned to a public narrative that could unite their population and convince them to rally behind the rulers and the order they represented. Casting the Gypsies as outsiders who did not belong to that order became a regular and often integral part of that narrative. Measures to expel the Roms and to constrain their movement, to eradicate their culture and identity, and even to exterminate them physically were both inspired and legitimized by a vague and abstract notion of Gypsies as eternal wrongdoers who are so fundamentally different from mainstream society in their needs, desires, and habits that they can only be subjugated or even removed.

Understanding the literary images of Gypsies that the arts cultivated, and continue to cultivate, is therefore an essential key to understanding Romani history and the history of society's attitudes towards the Roms. To this day, most people in western society know more about the Roms from films and fiction than they know from everyday encounters. This is a vicious circle, since the image of the Roms that is broadcast through media and fiction often acts as a deterrent to seek opportunities to get to know the Roms through direct contacts. For the Roms, in turn, the knowledge that negative stereotypes of them prevail has often acted as a deterrent to approaching mainstream society and trying to explain who they really are. Invisibility is regarded instead as an important key to survival. I recall my Romani friend who drives from village to village to offer his services to potential clients and who claims, when asked about his origin, to be Irish or Italian. 'I make a living by denying who I am,' he says.

What is the role of literary images of Gypsies in shaping the course of history and attitudes towards the Roms? Where does the Gypsy image come from? How did it give rise to the Gypsy brand – the cultivation of an association between the Roms and fashion and individuality? And what use has been made of this image to propagate hostility towards the Roms and to try to justify some of the worst atrocities ever committed against a people on European soil?

The migration waves of Roms in the fifteenth century into central Europe had already inspired the imagination of artists and painters. One of the earliest depictions of Romani migrations is Diebold Schilling's painting of the arrival of Gypsies outside the city of Berne, from 1485. It shows a small crowd of men, women and children standing outside the city walls and indicating their destination by pointing towards the town. The description that accompanies the painting speaks of *getoufte Heiden*, 'baptized heathens'. It reveals precisely the fascination with the stranger-turned-neighbour, the foreigner who is also an integral part of society – a theme that will accompany artistic portrayals of Gypsies in centuries to come. The most common images that painters associated with Gypsies were female elegance (hinting at sexuality), magic and the supernatural, and crowds and gatherings (an appreciation of Romani life in extended family groups, representing an admiration of the values of loyalty and sharing). Typically, Gypsies were depicted against the background of an outdoor scene, an expression of the association of Roms with nature and landscapes. They were often shown together with horses and horse-drawn wagons, often in family groups accompanied by children. Prominent features in the pictures are their dark complexion and colourful dress. Romani women are commonly depicted in low-cut blouses, exposing their bosom in a deliberately suggestive manner.

Metaphorical use of the Gypsy image can also be found. Titian's *Gypsy Madonna* from *c.* 1510, one of the most famous Italian Renaissance artworks that relates to Gypsies, is in fact a portrayal of the Virgin Mary with Christ, and has nothing to do with an actual depiction of Gypsies. It is assumed that the title was chosen as a symbol of female beauty and elegance and perhaps of foreign exoticism. The Flemish Baroque painter Peter Paul Rubens included the image of a Gypsy woman playing castanets in his drawing of Turkish women (*c.* 1610), replicating sketches found in books and manuscripts in an attempt to convey an impression of the colourful ethnic diversity of the Ottoman Empire. The Dutch Golden Age painter Frans Hals the Elder gave the title *Gypsy Girl* to a painting from 1630 which portrays a young woman flaunting her breasts, widely believed to be a prostitute and not at all of Romani origin.

Later paintings, too, are often based more on artists' imagination or other real-life associations rather than on actual observations of Gypsy women. The French Impressionist Pierre-Auguste Renoir's 1868 work known as *In the Summer*, *The Bohemian Girl* or *Gypsy Girl* (*En été*, *La bohémienne*) is a painting of his mistress, and the French artist Jean-Baptiste-Camille Corot is reported to have used Italian models for his portrayal of the *Gypsy Girl at a Fountain* (*c.* 1865). The French Realist Gustave Courbet seems to have chosen the title *Gypsy in Reflection* for his 1869 painting of a young woman with an exposed bosom and loose hair to lend some legitimacy to the provocative presentation of sensuality. By contrast, Édouard Debat-Ponsan's *La Gitane à la toilette*, *Gypsy Woman at her Toilette*, from 1896, transmits a realistic view of a barefoot young woman with long dark hair in a long skirt and a loose top sitting outdoors on the riverbank against the background of a horse-drawn wagon. Realist Édouard Manet's *Gypsy with a Cigarette* from *c.* 1862 features a mature woman with a dark complexion and loose clothing with a white horse peeking behind her, and Pablo Picasso's *Gypsy in Front of Musca* (1900) shows the stereotypical image of a married Romani woman with a headscarf, dark hair, long skirt and apron and a colourful blouse staring at the seaside.

If the preoccupation with Romani women reflected an attempt to express majority society's issues with sexuality and sensuality, so the attraction to Romani gatherings might be seen as representing the fascination with a life in which solitude is supposedly unknown and the individual enjoys the perpetual and unconditional attention of a group. Artistic depictions of Romani gatherings are set invariably outdoors and usually on the road and around the caravan or in the woods. Famous and influential works include Jan Brueghel the Elder's *Gathering of Gypsies in the Wood* (early 1600s) and Vincent van Gogh's *The Caravans: Gypsy Camp near Arles* (1888). They are usually classified by critics as 'landscape' paintings, suggesting that the artists regarded the presence of Romani families on the roads and in the woods as an element of outdoor scenery as much as a cultural practice.

One of the central motifs in the artistic portrayal of Roms is their role in providing essential niche services to the majority. The principal focus is on the most exotic of professions, fortune-telling. Gypsies are associated with the supernatural, but the preoccupation with their assumed magical powers reveals majority society's need for, and dependency on, divination, superstition and charms of various kinds. Probably the most famous artwork in this connection is the painting *The Fortune Teller* (1594) by the Italian Baroque artist Michelangelo Merisi da Caravaggio, replicated again by the artist in a similar version in 1596. It depicts a rather pale-skinned woman, identifiable by her distinctive dress as a Gypsy, reading the palm of an elegantly dressed young European gentleman. While she touches his palm, the woman is gently removing a ring from his finger. This association of palm-reading with theft expresses the majority's ambivalence towards the Roms: they are needed and sometimes even admired and envied, but they are not trusted and are often feared. Caravaggio's *The Fortune Teller* sparked a trend. Many seventeenth-century artists followed in his footsteps, producing paintings of Gypsy fortune-tellers.

Over time, the image of Gypsies came to represent the quintessential in foreignness and exotic appearance. The German Expressionist Otto Müller devoted a whole series of works in the 1920s to Gypsies. His lithographs show Gypsies as dark-skinned figures sitting on the outdoor ground; bare-breasted, naked and dark-skinned Gypsy women with African features said to have been inspired by a series of ethnographic photographs taken in Africa; bare-breasted Gypsy girls in front of horse-drawn wagons; Gypsy women dancing to the accompaniment of a drummer; Gypsies in traditional headscarf and more.

The Gypsy image was embraced and promoted in other artistic media, too. Famous composers who took an intense interest in Romani music include the Hungarians Ferenc Liszt and Béla Bartók and the Czechs Antonín Dvořák, who composed his series of 'Gypsy Songs' in 1880, and Leoš Janáček, whose song cycle 'The Diary of One Who Disappeared', composed between 1917 and 1919, features a man who falls in love with a Romani girl and joins the Gypsies. The Gypsy musical motif had its debut as early as 1545 with Luigi Giancarli's musical production *La Zingana*, 'The Gypsy Woman'. Giuseppe Verdi's opera *Il Trovatore*, 'The Troubadour', first performed in 1853, is set in a Gypsy camp and is full of depictions of magic and curses performed by Gypsies. Johann Strauss's operetta *Der Zigeunerbaron*, 'The Gypsy Baron' (1855), is set in the Transylvanian town of Timişoara (Temesvár) and tells the story of a romance between a landowner and a Gypsy girl. This recurring theme in musical productions represents once again the imaginative association of Romani culture with unrestrained sensuality and individuality, which at the same time is viewed as forbidden. An essentially similar theme is contained in Georges Bizet's famous opera *Carmen*, first performed in 1875. Based on a novel by Prosper Mérimée from 1845, it is set in Seville and tells the story of a soldier who is seduced by a Gypsy woman. A significant precursor is Victor Hugo's Gypsy heroine Esméralda, depicted as a beautiful, exotic and passionate dancer admired by men in his novel *Notre-Dame de Paris*, 'The Hunchback of Notre Dame' (1831).

Perhaps the earliest literary work that has Gypsies as the main characters is the Portuguese dramatist Gil Vicente's *Farsa das Ciganas*, 'The Gypsy Comedy', written in Old Spanish in 1521. It tells the story of four Gypsy men who are horse traders and of four Gypsy women who engage in begging. William Shakespeare makes references to 'Egyptians' in his plays *Othello* (1604) and *Antony and Cleopatra* (1606). Particularly influential in shaping the literary image of Gypsies was Cervantes's novel *La Gitanilla*, 'The Little Gypsy Girl', published in 1613. Cervantes begins the book by stating that Gypsies come into the world solely to be thieves, that they are born to thieving parents, and that their destiny is to remain thieves. Their urge to steal, he said, is innate and is eradicated only when they go to the grave. Other plays by Cervantes depict Gypsies as baby-snatchers and beggars. These are without a doubt a reflection of contemporary stereotypes of the Roms, but the devotion of generations of audiences to these literary productions has equally contributed to cementing a very distinct negative picture of Gypsies, one which complements the romantic fascination with Romani culture.

In literature, Gypsies often symbolize an escape from the rules of mainstream society – especially in relation to sex, gender roles and the acquisition of possessions and capital. Gypsies are seemingly free of the constraints of civilization. They are portrayed as erotically charged and are therefore the subject of both envy and fear. Invariably, books depict Gypsy women as secretive and as passionate lovers of white European men. Erotic involvement with Gypsies is the realization of a fantasy but also a dangerous risk and an offence against the rules, creating inappropriate and forbidden relationships. Befriending Gypsies is therefore an act of defiance against the strict rules of society, whereas fantasizing about liaisons with Gypsies expresses a longing for freedom, excitement and adventure.

Gypsy men are described in literature as elegant and handsome. They too are often subjects of erotic fantasies as they are portrayed conquering innocent white girls and tempting them away from the chains of their middle-class lives. The desire to be in the company of Gypsies is often used as a metaphor for the desire to live out fantasies and break the rules. The adoption of the term 'Bohemian', previously used as a label for the Roms, to the lifestyle of artists in Paris of the 1840s demonstrates the association of Romani culture and lifestyle with romanticism, bright colours, performance, cosmopolitanism, passion and artistic creativity, as well as with a defiance of mainstream, bourgeois establishment and institutional constraints.

An early precursor of the Romantic depiction of Gypsies is Henry Fielding's *The History of Tom Jones, a Foundling*, published in 1749. It describes an encounter with the King of the Gypsies and his Egyptian people celebrating a wedding in a barn. Here too we find the seductive, passionate and uninhibited female Gypsy – in this case a married woman who immediately seeks the intimate company of Jones's companion, initially by pretending to tell his fortune. But the twist comes as she and her husband, who demands financial compensation from her outsider-lover, are punished by the Gypsy King, to the amazement of Jones, who remarks on how 'orderly governed' and disciplined the Gypsies are. Fielding has the king speaking in a heavily accented and grammatically broken English, a token of the foreignness of the Roms. But he shows some remarkable insights into the Romani notions of honour and solidarity, citing the king as saying that the difference between 'you and us' is that 'my people rob your people, and your people rob one another'.

While Gypsies became a favourite theme among artists already in the Renaissance and Baroque periods, a growing preoccupation with the Gypsy motif in literature is characteristic of European Romanticism. As scholarly interest in Romani culture and origins intensified, literary images of Gypsies entered into fashion. Johann Wolfgang von Goethe's novel *Götz von Berlichingen* (1773) describes a Gypsy camp in a forest and uses the attribute 'wild' in connection with their behaviour, while at the same time outlining the Gypsies' dependency on the local population.

The English poet John Clare relied very heavily on the image of Gypsies in a series of poems including 'The Gipsies Evening Blaze' (published in 1820 but written between 1807 and 1810), 'The Gipseys Camp' (1819–20), 'The Gipseys Song' (1825) and 'The Gipsy Camp' (1840–41). Clare's descriptions of Gypsies are more nuanced. He includes the typical picture of dark-skinned people gathered around a campfire, but he also describes in a very realistic way the relations between Gypsies and the settled population, challenging prevailing notions that Gypsies make a living through stealing and deception. Clare's principal interest was in life in the English countryside and he describes the presence of the Roms as an integral part of this life and the Roms as the carriers of many folk traditions. Villagers rely on Romani crafts, they are entertained by the music of Romani fiddlers and inspired by Romani dances, and their superstitious traditions create a demand for Romani fortune-tellers. At the same time they blame the Gypsies for misfortunes. Clare expresses his discontent with the way Roms were being criminalized by the authorities, and literary analyst Kristine Douaud describes how his journal entries testify to his fascination with Romani customs and social organization and how he recorded his impressions of Romani music and weddings.

Meanwhile, in Russia, Alexander Pushkin completed his lyric poem 'The Gypsies' in 1824. It is set among the Roms of Bessarabia, telling of a love story between the non-Romani man Aleko and the Romani woman Zemfira. In Pushkin's scenes, the Roms live outdoors, they wear bright colours and rags, their children are nude, and shouting and noise dominate their camp. The poem inspired a theatre production that first appeared on stage in 1832, and triggered a literary trend that included several works on Gypsies by famous Russian poets during the early 1830s.

In Victorian England a fascination with Gypsies allowed audiences an imaginary escape from the confines of bourgeois culture and was similarly associated with freedom, defiance of norms and sexual fantasies. Literature specialist Deborah Epstein Nord compares this fascination with Gypsies to Europeans' colonial fascination with the Orient, but notes that unlike the Orient, Gypsies are domestic and internal 'Others'. Their proximity and visibility and audiences' familiarity with them are crucial to the symbolic role that they play in literary productions. They are present but separate, familiar but exotic and alien. People depend on them for certain services and yet at the same time they distance themselves from them. They envy them for their freedom and assumed values of solidarity, loyalty and defiance of norms, yet at the same time they look down on them as lacking morality and spirituality.

This fascination is a leading theme in the works of some of the most influential nineteenth-century writers. In Jane Austen's *Emma* (1815), two young women encounter Gypsies begging on the road. They perceive them as frightening and need to be rescued from them. In Charlotte Brontë's *Jane Eyre* (1847), the character of Mr Rochester appears disguised as a Romani fortune-teller. George Eliot's novel *The Mill on the Floss* (1860) tells the story of a woman who runs off to join the Gypsies. This is just one of several works by George Eliot that contain references to Gypsies, emphazising their foreignness as well as their contrast with the prevailing notion of gender roles in Victorian England. A recurring theme in Eliot's work is the hint of the hidden Gypsy origin of family members and the kidnapping of children. Works such as her poem 'The Spanish Gypsy' (1868), which tells of a Spanish princess who discovers her Gypsy origins, offer a symbolic challenge to conceptions of boundaries between the genders and between population groups. Gypsies belong, but they are also foreign.

Victorian children's literature describes Gypsies as kidnappers, creating a fear of Gypsies as foreign and sinister and so serving to set boundaries and restrictions on contacts with them. Kate Wood's *Jack and the Gypsies* (1887) tells of a Romani woman who 'steals children', and Élie Sauvage's *The Little Gipsy* (1869) is the story of the forced kidnapping of an English girl by Gypsies. In M. E. Bewsher's *The Gipsy's Secret* (1871), a child's skin is blackened in order to disguise its non-Gypsy origins, and Emma Leslie's A *Gypsy Against Her Will* (1889) tells the tale of an innocent servant girl who is tempted by Gypsies to join them for a life of freedom and is then framed for a crime to prevent her from returning to her place of work and residence.

At the same time, the English author George Borrow (1803–1881) pioneered a new type of literary fascination with Romani culture and language. A missionary who made efforts to translate the Gospels into Romani and to document the vocabularies of English and Spanish Gypsies, Borrow came to be regarded as a major authority on Gypsies in Victorian Britain and inspired both the amateur and professional scholarly preoccupation with Romani culture, which eventually led to the founding in Liverpool of the Gypsy Lore Society and its journal in 1888. Borrow's books *The Zincali* (1841) and *The Bible in Spain* (1843) contain anecdotes of the author's encounters with Spanish Gypsies and a documentation of Romani vocabulary and cultural practices. His novels *Lavengro: The Scholar, the Gypsy, the Priest* (1851) and *The Romany Rye* (1857) continue to describe Gypsy life, culture and language in a manner that purports to possess scholarly authority.

Lavengro tells the story of the Gypsy man Jasper Petulengro. The name is an attempt to create an English Romani translation of 'Smith' and has since been adopted as a literary name by various enthusiasts of Romani culture as well as by Romani people presenting themselves to outsiders, for example in fortune-telling stalls in places like the

English sea resorts of Blackpool, Whitby and Scarborough and at the annual fair in Appleby in Cumbria. Borrow places a strong emphasis on the study of languages and the relevance of philology to the discovery of origins. Following in the footsteps of renowned philologists such as the German August Pott, who published a comparative grammar and dictionary of Romani dialects in 1843–4, Borrow emphasized the unity of the Romani people across Europe based on observations of their language. His final work, *Romano Lavo-Lil* (1874), was an attempt to deliver a comprehensive dictionary of Romani vocabulary.

Many Modernist representations of Gypsies in literature continued the theme of transcending boundaries set already during the late Romantic period. Prominent works include D. H. Lawrence's *The Virgin and the Gypsy* (1926), which tells the story of a young woman who rebels against the rigid rules of middle-class bourgeois family life and explores freedom and sexuality through her romantic encounter with a Gypsy man, and Virginia Woolf's *Orlando* (1928), which features a young girl who flees with a group of Gypsies who accept her as one of them because of her dark complexion. By the second half of the twentieth century, Gypsies were represented in virtually every literary and artistic genre, from Ian Fleming's description of women fighting over a man's affections at a Gypsy camp in *From Russia with Love*, released as the second James Bond film in 1963, to Martin Cruz Smith's Romani antique dealer hero in his crime novel *Gypsy in Amber* (1971).

Rather less noticed is the appearance of Romani participants in a number of comic adventures, intriguingly in roles that are quite untypical of Gypsies in other literary works. André Franquin's full-length comic book *Il y a un Sorcier à Champignac*, 'There's a Sorcerer in Champignac' (1951), based on a story by Henri Gillain, is part of the Franco-Belgian comic artist's series *Spirou et Fantasio*. It tells of mysterious magical occurrences in the little countryside village, which are blamed by its superstitious inhabitants on a Gypsy and his family who are camping nearby. A mob tries to drive them out, encouraged by the mayor, but this is stopped by the heroes, Spirou and Fantasio, who save the family, and it later transpires that the 'sorcerer' is an old scientist, the Count of Champignac, who has been conducting his experiments at the villagers' expense. Another Belgian artist, Hergé, world famous for his *Adventures of Tintin* series, follows a similar theme in at least two of his works. In *Le Testament de Monsieur Pump*, 'Mr Pump's Legacy' (1951), in the series *Jo, Zette et Jocko*, a minor scene has Jo, one of the main characters, stealing a Romani family's caravan in order to chase a gang of criminals. At the end of the story, which finishes in a second book, *Destination New York* (1951), Jo compensates the family by buying them a new, modern caravan.

Hergé's subtle insights into the relationship between Roms and Gadje are given more elaborate expression in *Les Bijoux de la Castafiore*, 'The Castafiore Emerald' (1963), in the Tintin series. Here too, suspicion falls on a Romani family camping near the mansion inhabited by the two main characters, when their celebrity guest's jewels disappear. But the two heroes, Tintin and Captain Haddock, refuse to believe the accusations and at the end they prove that the 'thief' was in fact a resident magpie. The portrayal of the Romani family is complete with a horse-drawn wagon, a grandmother wearing a headscarf and long golden earrings who tells fortunes, and a young man called Roman who plays the guitar by the campfire. The complexity of Rom–Gadje relationships enters centre stage when the benevolent attempts by Haddock and Tintin to offer the Roms a stopping place on their land and to bring home the young Romani girl Miarka, who had lost her way in the woods, are met with Roman's hostility and suspicion: 'I hate them,' he says. It appears that Hergé's biographers have so far overlooked the presence, apparently, of an unknown source of intimate impressions of Romani life. Centuries of suspicion and exclusion have made the Roms hesitant even towards offers of sympathy for fear that the hidden intention is to subjugate them and to force them to abandon who they are.

THE ROMS AND THE GROWTH
OF THE MODERN NATION STATE

The gradual emergence of a new social and political order in Europe accompanying the structure of the modern nation states gave rise to new attitudes towards the Roms that were no longer shaped primarily by spontaneous reactions to migrants, taxation needs or even an urge to control and subjugate populations, but increasingly by the power-ful force of literary and fantasy images associated with Gypsies. Though Gypsy was not yet a brand, it was becoming a leitmotif of imagination and popular culture. Strengthened by these images, poli-cies were further pursued that had their seeds already in earlier peri-ods. They included the idea of assimilating the Romani population, pioneered by the Habsburg monarchs in the second half of the eight-eenth century. An even older strategy was to place restrictions on the movements of the Roms and on their chances to earn a living. Mod-ern nationalism added new dimensions at several levels. Governments put forward coordinated policies towards the Roms that were said to be in the national interest. These often entailed restrictions on tradi-tional niche activities and travel and enforced settlement programmes, but also the protection, to some extent, of citizen rights. In response, Roms in many regions began to make use of the opportunity to par-ticipate in mainstream social and political life. The seeds of a Romani political elite could be detected, which identified with its respective nation state while also articulating for the first time its own aspira-tions as a nation. The changing political landscape opened up migra-tion opportunities, but these in turn triggered hostile reactions on the part of some governments, which now began to regard the exclusion of the Roms as an issue of national interest.

In Imperial Russia, an inclusion policy was adopted in the early nineteenth century, which would set the basis for an even more radi-cal integration strategy a century later, following the communist revo-lution. An initiative to settle Gypsies in villages was launched in 1803, followed by campaigns to register all Gypsies, ordered by the Russian Senate in 1811 and again by Czar Nicholas I in 1846. Elsewhere, attempts to eradicate a travelling lifestyle were more vigorous. In Sweden, Gypsies were subjected to compulsory recruitment into the public workforce from 1804 onwards. Under King George IV of England, the Vagrancy Act was amended in 1822 to include penalties on persons 'pretending to be Gypsies', telling fortunes, wandering, residing in tents or carts or setting up a camp by the side of the road. The Highway Act, which followed in 1835, continued to impose direct restrictions on Gypsies, making it an offence for Gypsies to pitch a tent or camp on a highway. During this period, merely being a

Gypsy gradually ceased to be an offence in England. Poland imposed identity cards on Roms, for which proof of permanent domicile was required. There is evidence of numerous instances between 1820 and 1862 of Roms being arrested for travelling or for not possessing documents. Norway, too, carried out a campaign during this period to settle travelling Romani families forcibly and to assimilate them. Documentation suggests that at least 256 children from families belonging to the groups known in Norway as Reisende or 'Travellers' were forcibly removed from their parents and placed in Norwegian foster homes between 1855 and 1863. These policies often aimed at replicating what was viewed as a partial 'success' in the Habsburg territories, especially in Hungary, where by 1893, over a century after the assimilationist policies of Maria Theresa and Joseph II were first enacted, some 30 per cent of Roms listed Hungarian as their native language in the population census, a figure that grew to nearly 70 per cent by 1910.

The disappearance of the remnants of feudalism from the European continent brought major changes to the Roms of Wallachia and Moldavia, a transformation that is viewed by many scholars as one of the most significant events in the history of the Roms. In 1831 the Wallachian Assembly passed a resolution calling on the improvement of the conditions of state Gypsies. In the same spirit that informed national policies in other countries, the initial aim was to eliminate nomadism. The new law now enabled landowners to acquire Gypsies from the government on condition that they allow them to settle on their estates and teach them to become farmers. A separate law adopted in the following year provided a new organizational framework for state Gypsies. It regulated their tax obligations and enabled the state to purchase Gypsies from private landowners. This allowed those Roms whose masters were reluctant to provide settlement incentives to escape private ownership and enter into the direct protection of the state.

But these reforms still failed to address the growing number of abolitionist voices who, between 1834 and 1842, inspired by the ethos of the French Revolution, intensified their campaign to put an end to Romani slavery in the country. The liberal writer Mihail Kogălniceanu estimated in 1837 that there were some 200,000

Romani slaves in the Romanian provinces. Mihail Sturdza, governor of Moldavia, responded in 1842 by emancipating the state slaves, an act that was soon followed by the liberation of church slaves. Wallachia freed its state slaves in the following year and continued to purchase slaves from private ownership, thus helping more and more people out of slavery. In 1848, nationalist revolutionaries in Wallachia and Transylvania demanded an end to Romani slavery as part of the modernization and national consolidation of the Romanian principalities. The process took several more years to complete. A decree prohibiting the separation of Romani families through the sale of slaves was adopted in Wallachia in 1850. The ownership of private slaves finally became illegal in Moldavia in 1855 and in Wallachia in 1856.

More than 50,000 Romani families were freed from slavery. Some remained on the estates in which they had worked and were granted better conditions. Many had trade specializations and experience in itinerant professions and turned to an itinerant lifestyle. The relaxation of slavery laws and the emancipation that followed triggered a wave of Romani migrations out of Romania. From as early as the 1830s and well into the 1860s the arrival of Vlax Romani clans belonging to the groups of the Kelderasha, Churara, Lovara and others was recorded in Poland, Russia, Austria, Germany, France and England, and from the 1880s also in the United States, Mexico, Venezuela and Brazil. Serbian independence in 1830 had already attracted a large population of Wallachian Roms into Serbia and many settled in the district of Belgrade.

Radical political changes appeared to have inspired a new sense of belonging among some Romani communities across the European continent. There is evidence to suggest that Roms joined the nationalist Sremska rebellion against Ottoman rule in Serbia as early as 1807. Many Roms are said to have fought alongside Hungarian nationalists in 1848–49 in the Hungarian war of independence, and in 1876 Roms participated in a Bulgarian nationalist armed uprising against the Ottomans in Koprivshtitsa. Conditions following Bulgarian independence in 1878 did not improve for the Roms, however. In 1888 laws were adopted to combat 'Gypsy nomadism' and to stop Romani immigration into Bulgaria from neighbouring countries, especially

Romania. In 1901 the Bulgarian state even considered suspending voting rights for nomadic and Muslim Roms.

The various national movements provided a model for imitation. In 1879 groups of Hungarian Roms held a conference devoted to the political and civil rights of Roms. Anti-Romani measures in Bulgaria triggered organized protests. Ramadan Ali, a self-appointed Romani spokesman who assumed the title of '*Czar-Bashi* of Bulgarian Gypsies', called a conference in the town of Vidin in 1901 and launched a campaign against the proposed legislation. A group of Roms submitted a petition to the Bulgarian National Assembly in 1906. The Romani political movement grew in subsequent years. Between 1923 and 1934 the Bulgarian Gypsy activist Shakir Pashov edited a publication called *Future*, which was banned by the government in 1925, and organized Romani participation in local council elections. A number of Romani cultural organizations were also formed during this period. One such, called Drustva Rom, was founded in Belgrade in 1930 but remained active only for a short period. In 1935 a Romani publication, *Romano Lil*, appeared in Serbia.

In Romania, Calinic I. Popp-Şerboiannu, a preacher of Romani origin, established the General Association of Gypsies in 1933. Its aims were to improve literacy rates among the Roms, to establish educational projects and a Romani museum, to publish books about Romani history and culture and to set up councils to solve disputes among the Roms and to represent them in dealings with the authorities. G. A. Lăzăreannu-Lăzurică, a journalist and writer of Romani origin, founded another Romani organization during the same period and took on the title of '*Voivode* of the Gypsies of Romania'. Many other regional associations were established in the 1930s, including the Association of Romanian Gypsies and the Union of Romanian Roma. Some of these groups published newsletters on Romani affairs and collections of Romani stories and songs. Their activities came to an end when all political parties were outlawed by the new Romanian regime in 1938.

Meanwhile, a phase of liberal policy towards the diversity of ethnicities and nationalities in the newly formed Soviet Union brought changes to the Romani minority there, too. In 1925, a Union of Gypsies was formed in Russia, acknowledging the Roms as a nationality. With government support it developed a standardized form of written Romani based on the North Russian dialect of the language and hundreds of Romani language publications appeared, including translations, political literature and children's books. A group of Romani families was settled in a collective farm near Rostov in Russia in 1926, and in 1931 the Romani theatre Romen was inaugurated in Moscow, which continues its performances today. Romani language publications were stopped in the Soviet Union as part of the tightening and centralization of the nationalities policy under Stalin in 1937. In a rather different kind of effort to assert Romani identity in public, Kelderash Roms in Poland sought to revive the old tradition of electing the King of the Gypsies. In 1928 members of the Kwiek family requested the authorities to grant formal recognition to one of their clan leaders as king. The Kwieks continued to represent the office and organize public coronations for almost a decade; that of Janusz Kwiek took place in July 1937.

While Romani participation in public life was on the increase in some regions of Europe, large populations of Romani immigrants were settling into a new life, largely undisturbed by any specific government policies, in the United States and the countries of Latin America. At the same time a new nationalist approach to a centralized anti-Romani policy was emerging. New measures were often justified with reference to growing immigration of Roms originally from the Romanian principalities. Already in 1849, the Polish police was being encouraged to initiate hunts against Gypsies for rewards. The purpose was to deport nomadic Roms.

In 1889 the state of Bavaria issued a decree warning local authorities that Romani immigrants were claiming to have lost their identity papers and requesting that new documents be issued to them to legitimize their status. Authorities were ordered not to issue such documents. In 1895, France carried out a national census of all 'nomads, bohemians and vagrants' and in 1912 introduced so-called 'anthropometric notebooks', which Gypsies were required to carry for identification.

In 1899, a Gypsy Information Service was established within the Imperial Police Headquarters in the Bavarian capital Munich, directed by Alfred Dillmann. It was entrusted with coordinating the surveillance and controlling the movements of Gypsies. Following a wave of Romani immigration via the Czech lands into Bavaria in 1905, Dillmann compiled an archive of Romani families, called the 'Gypsy Book', which contained the names of some 400 households and references to over 3,500 individuals. Anti-Gypsy measures continued to spread, with the German state of Hesse adopting legislation in that same year that prohibited Roms from camping on public roads and in open fields and forests and required them to deposit their documents with the local police whenever they left their place of residence. In the following year, Prussia introduced a law on the Struggle Against the Gypsy Menace and entered into special agreements with Russia and other countries to exchange information about Roms and to monitor and control their movements. Anti-Romani policy had been escalated to the international level.

With the outbreak of the First World War in 1914, the Prussian War Ministry authorized the Army Regional Command Headquarters to issue restrictions on Gypsies, limiting their freedom of movement in the areas adjacent to the French–German frontier or in proximity to military facilities and other strategically important sites. In 1916 a report by the German 8th Army Corps stationed in Koblenz accused Gypsies from Serbia of being spies collecting information on Russian prisoners of war. The German states continued to be at the forefront of anti-Romani measures in the aftermath of the war. In 1924 Bavaria introduced special identity cards for Gypsies, and by 1925 Dillmann's centre had compiled 14,000 files on Gypsies all over Germany. The following year Bavaria adopted a new law, against 'Gypsies, Travellers and the Work-shy', which in fact imposed further restrictions specifically on Gypsies.

A wave of new policies affected the Roms in other countries, too. A committee of the Swedish Parliament recommended in 1923 a ban on Gypsies entering the country. By contrast, in 1921 the Czechoslovak Republic had recognized the Roms as a minority, though requiring them to be registered and fingerprinted. However, in 1927 the state declared the Roms to be 'asocial'. They were forced to carry special identity cards and Romani children under the age of eighteen were ordered into special institutions. The new measures prevented Roms from entering certain regions and especially spa and holiday resorts.

Violent outbursts against Roms and even cases of murder were recorded in Slovakia. Hungary, too, adopted special regulations in 1928 that required the registration and fingerprinting of Roms.

PERSECUTION AND GENOCIDE IN THE SECOND WORLD WAR

The events of the Second World War were to bring unprecedented destruction and pain upon the Romani populations of Europe, who had already suffered generations and centuries of exclusion and persecution. One of the first laws passed by the Nazis in order to impose their race ideology was the Law for the Prevention of Offspring with Hereditary Disease, which was adopted in July 1933 and became effective in January 1934. It legalized the enforced sterilization of socially 'undesirable' persons and set in motion a series of measures that could be applied to Gypsies at the discretion of local authorities, though there is no evidence that it was actually used for racial persecution. The next piece of racist legislation that affected Roms was the so-called Nuremberg Laws of 1935, which forbade relations between Germans and 'members of alien races'. Although the Roms were not mentioned explicitly in the law, a leading legal commentary from 1936 specified that the only people in Europe who had always been considered racial aliens were the Jews and the Gypsies.

The new political climate led to aggressive restrictions on the freedom of movement of Roms. In 1935 numerous local authorities in Germany began to set up special encampments for Gypsies, usually surrounded by barbed wire and subject to intense surveillance and tight regulations on movement. The police in Berlin established a guarded site for Roms in Marzahn in the outskirts of Berlin in 1936, which eventually accommodated up to 800 Roms. Similarly, a camp for Roms in Cologne, surrounded by a two-metre fence with barbed wire, had been completed in April 1935, and by 1937 accommodated some 600 people.

Of the many hideous aspects of the persecution of Roms under the Nazis, one stands out in particular against all earlier types of oppression that had been inflicted on Romani populations – the attempt to legitimize persecution and eventually mass murder and genocide through pseudo-scientific arguments. In 1936, a psychiatrist from the University of Tübingen in southern Germany, Dr Robert Ritter, was appointed head of the Racial Hygiene and Population Biology Research Unit in Berlin, a section of the National Health Office. Ritter's 'research' aimed at mapping the genealogies of all German Roms and classifying their 'racial' affiliation.

Ritter's work followed from an ideological conviction that anti-social behaviour such as unemployment and criminality was hereditary and had to be eradicated by preventing the reproduction of the relevant population groups. Ritter used various classification categories, dividing individuals and their families into 'Pure Gypsies', 'Half-breeds with equal Gypsy and German blood', 'Half-breeds with predominantly Gypsy blood' and so on. Ritter and his team argued that criminality was stronger among those who were mixed, which for a while during 1942 led to suggestions that 'Pure Gypsies' should be exempted from persecution measures.

By 1941 Ritter's team had surveyed and registered some 40,000 persons. In a letter of May 1938 to the president of the Reich's Research Board, Ritter complained about the nature of anti-Gypsy policies to date, which, by forcing the Gypsies into settlement and assimilation, had in his view produced 'a most questionable and dubious mixed population'. On the basis of his surveys he promised to be able to provide very soon 'practical recommendations for a fundamentally new regulation of the Gypsy situation in Germany'. Ritter cooperated closely with the Reich's Criminal Police Office under the direction of Arthur Nebe, handing over lists of Roms to be arrested and deported. In December 1939 the Reich's Criminal Police Office wrote a letter of endorsement to the German Research Foundation, recommending that it should approve Ritter's request for funds to continue his research. Ritter himself stressed the urgency of his work, stating in his funding application from January 1940 that as a result of 'planned evacuation measures' the entire German Gypsy population would soon become 'inaccessible for research purposes'. Ritter's racial reports and genealogical charts on Romani families and individuals were to determine their fate in the Nazi concentration and later death camps.

Until 1937 it was the Gestapo that had the primary responsibility to arrest Roms and take them into 'protective custody' in concentration camps, as part of a campaign to improve the German gene pool. From 1937 it became the task of the Criminal Police to put Roms in 'preventive arrest' as part of a new campaign against criminality. These measures were accompanied by further restrictions and more intensive surveillance. In November 1937 the Nazi government excluded Gypsies from serving in the German military, though it was not until February 1941 that the Military High Command issued an order to discharge Gypsies from active service. In 1938 a central office for the 'Fight Against the Gypsy Menace' was established within the Reich Criminal Police, incorporating the centre that had operated in Munich. By that time it held over 18,000 files on more than 33,000 individuals in Germany.

In 1938 Heinrich Himmler, head of the SS, was put in charge of the 'Gypsy question' and issued a decree calling for the Regulation of the Gypsy Question with Reference to Their Racial Characteristics. Its implementation began with the incarceration of more than 2,000 German and Austrian Roms in the concentration camps Dachau, Buchenwald, Mauthausen and Sachsenhausen. In 1939 two detention camps for Gypsies were opened in the German Protectorate of Bohemia and Moravia, or the Czech lands, in Lety and in Hodonín. In 1942 both camps were formally transformed into concentration camps for Gypsy families. Entire families were incarcerated. Between August 1942 and April 1943, some 8,000 persons were sent to the camp at Lety and some 7,000 to that in Hodonín. From there they were later sent to the Gypsy camp at Auschwitz-Birkenau. Almost none survived; the Nazis annihilated nearly the whole Romani population of the Czech lands.

On 21 September 1939, only three weeks after the German invasion of Poland and while fighting was still continuing, the head of the Reich Central Security Office, Reinhard Heydrich, ordered the relocation of 30,000 German Gypsies to Poland. In anticipation of further wide-scale deportations, German Gypsies were prohibited to leave their places of residence in October 1939. By the end of the year, however, only some 3,000 people were deported under that order while others were kept in detention camps within Germany. But in January

1940, the Supreme Command of the German Wehrmacht requested that Himmler order a ban on Gypsies in the border area because they were considered 'unreliable' and posed a threat to the country's 'defence interests'. In response, a series of deportations of thousands of Roms was scheduled and carried out in mid-May 1940 from Hamburg, Cologne and Stuttgart. At the end of 1940 Gypsies were banned from working in factories run by the German military as they were regarded as a security risk.

In the summer of 1941, the German invasion of the Soviet Union known as Operation Barbarossa was under way and the German military began a campaign of executions of Roms in the Soviet Union. Hinrich Lohse, Reich Commissioner for the Baltic States and Belorussia, suggested that specific measures be taken against nomadic Gypsies, whom he accused of spreading diseases. In a memo to the SS in December 1941 he ordered that Gypsies be treated in the same way as Jews. Mass shootings of Roms subsequently took place in the German-occupied areas of eastern Europe. In some regions it was the Wehrmacht or regular army who shot them, in others the role was handed over to the Special Task Forces known as Einsatzgruppen. Despite Lohse's order it appears that the Einsatzgruppen operating in the Baltic areas did not search out Gypsies systematically. But they were nevertheless responsible for the murder of at least 3,500 Romani men, women and children. Reports by Einsatzgruppen operating in Ukraine and Belorussia testify to the executions of many hundreds of Roms. In the Crimean peninsula, the Einsatzgruppen were specifically ordered to target Gypsies and it is known from documentation that over 2,000 Roms were murdered there in 1941–2.

In Poland, mass executions of Roms took place in the vicinity of large cities. Romani families were rounded up and transported to concentration camps at Chełmno, Sobibór, Auschwitz, Treblinka and Bełżec, and it is possible that 20,000 were murdered. A part of the ghetto in Łódź, separated from the adjoining Jewish sector by a barbed-wire fence and a ditch filled with water, was prepared for a transport of Roms, and in November 1941 some 200 Romani families were brought to the camp from Austria, where they had been previously detained. Altogether six transports carried some 5,000 Romani prisoners, more than half of them children. Conditions in the camp led to a high mortality rate, and by December 1942 some 600 people had died. After two months all Romani prisoners were transported from the ghetto in Łódź to a death camp in Chełmno, where they were murdered.

The German military invasion of Serbia in the spring of 1941 was confronted with resistance from partisan groups. In reprisal against partisan operations, the Wehrmacht executed some 800 Jews and Roms who had previously been detained in a concentration camp near the town of Šabac. In October 1941, the German commander, General Harald Turner, reported that a further group of 200 Gypsies had been shot. He accused the Gypsies of providing intelligence to the partisans. The random killing of hundreds more Roms continued over the following weeks. In December 1941, several hundred Roms were deported to a concentration camp in Semlin. In August 1942, General Turner wrote to the regional Wehrmacht commander Alexander Löhr, reporting that Serbia was now the first country in which 'the Jewish question and the Gypsy question have been solved'. Estimates of the number of Romani victims vary but it appears that many thousands were murdered. Contrary to Turner's triumphant declaration, however, the great majority of Serbian Roms survived.

In November 1943, Hinrich Lohse initiated a new policy to deal with Gypsies under his jurisdiction. He instructed the German forces to regard sedentary Gypsies as citizens of the country but to deport nomadic Gypsies and part-Gypsies to concentration camps, where they were to be treated like Jews. The decision on who was to be considered a Gypsy was devolved to local police commanders. The policy led to the near-complete annihilation of the Roms of Lithuania and Estonia, and of a large part of the Roms of Poland and Latvia. During the same period the persecution was extended to German-occupied France, where some 3,000 Roms were incarcerated in detention camps under appalling conditions. The French police supervised the camps, under the instructions of the German occupying military forces.

Nevertheless, Nazi policy towards the Gypsies went through various contradictory phases. At an early stage the SS had already contemplated various extermination measures, including sinking Gypsies aboard ships in the Mediterranean Sea, sterilization and inclusion in the Nazis' euthanasia programme for the mentally disabled. Many thousands of Romani men and women who survived the camps had been forcibly sterilized. Hitler himself is quoted as having said in 1941 that 'the Gypsies are romantic only in the bars of Budapest' and describing them in terms of the typical stereotypes as thieves and as a public nuisance.

Historians continue to argue over the significance of a diary entry written by Heinrich Himmler on 20 April 1942 following a telephone conversation with Reinhard Heydrich. The note says 'no extermination of Gypsies'. It is known that Himmler had entertained the idea of preserving so-called 'pure-blooded' German Gypsies as a kind of sample of a primordial population and that he even issued a decree to this effect in October 1942. Via its organization Ahnenerbe, which was devoted to the ideology of racial purity and worked closely with Ritter's team, the SS also commissioned an Austrian doctoral student in linguistics, Johann Knobloch, to carry out a study of the Romani language among Romani prisoners at Lackenbach concentration camp near Vienna. The SS wanted to know whether, if the Roms were isolated from other populations, their language would revert to its original 'Aryan' character. After the war, Knobloch became an influential linguistics professor at the University of Bonn in Germany, where he headed the institute of linguistics until his retirement in 1985. Texts collected as part of his doctoral thesis were published as a book in 1953.

The head of Hitler's Chancellery, Martin Bormann, opposed Himmler's ideas about the 'preservation' of German Gypsies, and on Hitler's authority he instructed Himmler on 6 December 1942 to call off the plan. Ten days later, on the 16th, Himmler issued his notorious so-called 'Auschwitz decree', ordering the deportation of German Gypsies to the death camp at Auschwitz-Birkenau. Some groups of Roms were exempted but were subjected to forced sterilization that took place in the concentration camps. They included Romani soldiers who had not yet been discharged and Sinte of the Lallere clans who were considered by Robert Ritter to be 'racially pure'.

The Gypsy camp in Auschwitz had been set up in 1941. Himmler's 'Auschwitz decree' ordered the deportation directly to Auschwitz of some 10,000 Roms who had remained in the Reich. In March 1943 Himmler ordered the deportation of all Dutch Roms to Auschwitz, and between February 1943 and the summer of 1944 deportations of

Gypsies to Auschwitz continued from Germany, Austria, the Czech lands, Poland, the Netherlands, northern France, the Soviet Union and the Baltic countries. Many Romani prisoners at Auschwitz were subjected to the medical experiments of Josef Mengele and his collaborators.

In the spring of 1943, Rudolf Höss, the commander of Auschwitz, set up a special Gypsy family camp at Auschwitz II (Birkenau), consisting of some forty wooden barracks. Höss was later to write in his memoirs that the Gypsies had been his 'favourite prisoners'. Altogether around 22,600 individuals were incarcerated there during 1943–4, two-thirds of them from Germany and Austria. Records show that more than 19,300 were murdered. On 2–3 August 1944, some 2,900 Roms who had remained in the Gypsy family camp were murdered in the gas chambers in order to make space for Hungarian Jews who had been rounded up and were being transported to Auschwitz. Romani associations today commemorate this mass murder on 2 August. Mass executions and deportations of Roms from Slovakia and Hungary to German concentration camps continued until 1945.

Purges extended not just to the German-occupied areas of Europe but also to the satellite countries that were strongly influenced by Nazi ideology. Restrictions on Gypsies in Slovakia had already been introduced in 1939. Gypsies were banned from trading in horses and they were allowed to keep their citizenship only if they could demonstrate that they had permanent residence and employment. In June 1940, Gypsies were banned from entering parks, cafés and restaurants and from using public transport. In 1941, many Gypsies were forced into seasonal labour camps, and nomadic Roms were ordered to return to their homes and were placed under police surveillance. Romani houses situated along public roads were torn down and their inhabitants relocated. In late 1944, many Roms participated in the armed insurrection against the German occupation of Slovakia. In retaliation the German forces and their collaborators inflicted yet more atrocities on the local Romani population – on 14 November 1944 a group of sixty-five Roms were massacred in Čierny Balog by German soldiers, who burned them alive in two huts. Slovak police murdered 111 Roms, an entire community, in Ilija on 21 November 1944, and pogroms continued in Slatina and Neresnice. Detention camps for Gypsies were opened in Dubnica and Vahom in November 1944 and entire Romani families including children were incarcerated there.

In Romania, restrictions had previously been placed on nomadic Roms in February 1937. The Romanian Ministry of Internal Affairs claimed that the Roms constituted a risk to public health by spreading typhus and other diseases. The measures were tightened with the establishment of the royal dictatorship in 1938, and nomadic Roms were now prohibited entrance into villages and towns. Soon after he assumed the political leadership of the nation, Ion Antonescu advocated the expulsion of Roms from Bucharest and discussed the possibility of deporting all Roms into labour camps within the country. On Antonescu's orders the Ministry of Internal Affairs decreed on 17 May 1942 that a census of the Romani population should be quickly undertaken. Roms were required to register and were subsequently not allowed to leave their county of residence.

A decision was then taken to deport the Romani population from Romania into the occupied areas of Transnistria in Ukraine. The deportations began in June 1942 and targeted at first some 11,000 nomadic Roms. In September they were extended to some 13,000 settled Roms and a few hundred more were deported in 1943. Altogether Antonescu's regime deported approximately 26,000 Roms. They were settled in the vicinity of Ukrainian villages in huts that had been dug into the earth. The aim was to organize them under supervision for work in agriculture and industry. Conditions were poor and there was a shortage of food and healthcare. Diseases broke out. Many perished of hunger, cold and illness. The precise number of victims remains unknown but some historians estimate that half of those deported to Transnistria died there.

In Bulgaria, the Nazi-inspired authorities issued a decree in 1942 allowing them to recruit Gypsies for compulsory labour in public works and later in agriculture. Marriage between Gypsies and Bulgarians was outlawed from 26 August 1942. The following year the Bulgarian authorities began to allocate smaller food rations to Gypsies than to Bulgarians, and a campaign was launched to expel Roms from the capital city, Sofia. In Hungary, some Romani families had already been transported to Auschwitz in 1943 as part of the deportations of the Austrian Roms. Beginning in the autumn of 1944, a more systematic effort was made to deport Hungarian Gypsies, and it is estimated that around 28,000 were sent to concentration camps. Only 3,000 survived. The independent state of Croatia also adopted Nazi-like policies in 1941. Roms were forbidden to use pavements and were required to register with the police. Many were arrested and transported to concentration camps run by the Ustaša, the fascist Croatian militia. Some were sent to death camps, often in Sardinia, or executed.

The wave of persecution inspired by race ideology extended beyond the direct reach of the German occupiers and their allies. In 1941 Sweden extended a sterilization law from 1934 targeting 'psychologically inferior' persons to include so-called social indicators, leading to the forced sterilizations of over 1,000 members of the population of Zigenare or Swedish Gypsies (also called Tattare). A systematic registration of travelling Gypsies was undertaken, justified by the threat of war. In Norway, the Mission for the Homeless carried out forced sterilizations of some 300 Romani and Traveller women during the 1930s and 40s, and around 1,700 children were taken away from their parents and adopted by Norwegian families or placed in children's homes. This process continued until the 1970s. Norway's Lutheran Church issued an apology for its role in the campaign in 2000. The Norwegian Roms of eastern European origin (the Vlax Roms) had fled the country when this persecution began. In the early 1930s they attempted to return, but were denied re-entry into Norway. Many perished as a result in Nazi concentration camps.

The horrendous events of the Second World War and the atrocities committed against the Roms during this period had a devastating impact on Europe's Romani population, one that is often compared to the fate of eastern European Jews. In 1972, amateur historians Donald Kenrick and Grattan Puxon estimated that the Nazis and their collaborators murdered some 219,000 Roms. The late historian Michael Zimmermann, whose research on the Romani genocide is the most comprehensive to date, has suggested that the number of documented victims is around 94,000. His research showed that there is clear evidence of the murder of at least 50,000 Roms within Germany and the territories that it occupied between 1938 and 1945.

Zimmermann estimated that in the satellite countries Croatia and Romania at least 25,000 were murdered by Croat militias and German forces, and that around 19,000 of those deported to Transnistria by the Romanian authorities lost their lives as a result of poverty and disease. The actual number could be higher, since not all executions carried out by the German Wehrmacht in the Soviet Union and the Baltic lands were documented.

In Germany, media and politicians tend to cite the number of 500,000 victims claimed by some of the German Romani associations, while some Romani activists have suggested that the number of Roms murdered by the Nazis was as high as one or even two million, though so far these figures have not been verified by any research. None of those involved in the genocide of the Roms under the Nazis were brought to justice after the war. Many complaints were made by representatives of the victims against individuals including, among others: Robert Ritter, head of the Race Hygiene Research Unit, and his associates, Adolph Würth, Eva Justin and Ruth Kellermann; Leo Karsten, who headed the Unit for Gypsy Affairs in the Criminal Police; and Paul Werner, who coordinated the deportations of Roms on behalf of the Reich Central Security Office. Investigations took place after the war but no criminal charges were brought against any of the suspects by the German authorities.

7

Romani Identity in the
Twenty-first Century

THE SCARS OF WAR

Romani survivors of the genocide and persecutions faced the immense challenge of rebuilding their lives in the aftermath of the Second World War. Entire families, and in many areas entire communities, had been completely destroyed and annihilated. Those who were fortunate to survive had lost relatives and friends. As with other victims of Nazi persecution, many looked for ways to return to some kind of daily routine through which they could put the horrors behind them, but naturally the scars would remain. This was especially harrowing for Romani survivors, whose lives had revolved around the extended family. Those who found themselves on their own had few resources on which they could draw in order to build a new life. Many thousands of Romani women and men who survived the concentration and death camps had been forcibly sterilized by the Nazis and were unable to start families of their own. The majority returned to the places in which they had lived before the war in the hope of finding some kind of lifeline in the form of residence and work opportunities. But, tragically, those who faced the biggest obstacles in the way of reintegration in their pre-war neighbourhoods were those who had been targeted most ruthlessly by the Nazis for extermination: the Romani clans of Germany.

Inspired by a growing number of associations and support groups of former political prisoners and Jewish survivors, Roms began filing claims for compensation for their suffering, assisted by their own community leaders and activists. The claims had both an immediate practical purpose and a symbolic function. On the practical side, survivors had almost invariably lost all their pre-war possessions and, crucially for the Roms, their family support networks. Material compensation in the form of financial aid and a basic income allowance were a necessary precondition to try to regain some form of normality. At the emotional level, the survivors were traumatized and insecure as a result of the persecution they had suffered. Recognition of the injustice inflicted upon them was a first and fundamental step towards regaining confidence in order to continue their lives now that the horror had ended.

A proposal for a compensation law was first accepted by the Allied military government in 1948 and came into effect in Germany in 1949. Its core task was to separate the claims of specific victims of Nazi crimes from claims for general damages caused by war. The victims were limited to those who experienced racial, political or religious persecution. The authorities that ruled on compensation claims therefore had to judge whether the crimes had been committed on racial, political or religious grounds. In the immediate post-war period, some Roms did succeed in obtaining compensation and restitution. But these individual cases did not lead to a general recognition of the Roms as victims.

Rather than protect the Romani survivors and support them, the new German administration and its justice system put obstacles in their way. While Jewish victims were granted *prima facie* recognition as victims of racial persecution, Roms were denied such recognition. A history of prejudices that depicted the Roms as engaged in 'criminal' and 'asocial' activities gave rise to the view that their incarceration by the Nazis might have been justified for reasons of security and to maintain the social order. Claims for compensation for physical damage through sterilization and for psychological damage through incarceration were not recognized for this reason. Claims for lost possessions were rejected on the basis of a wholesale prejudice that Gypsies did not own possessions. Claims for compensation for lost income on the basis of a reduction of earning capacity (as a result of physical and psychological damage and years lost due to imprisonment) were rejected on the grounds that Gypsies were unlikely to have sought employment even under other more favourable circumstances.

Like the German Jews, the Roms had been stripped of their citizenship rights by the Nazi regime's racist legislation. Post-war West

Germany introduced into its constitution Article 116-2, which reinstated the citizenship rights of those who had lost their German nationality 'for political, racial or religious reasons' in the period between 1933 and 1945. The overwhelming majority of Roms had not taken up clandestine political activities against the Nazis nor were they members of a recognized religious minority. Their persecution had been based entirely on their Romani ethnicity, which the Nazis had defined as a 'racial' trait. While the Nazis presented their views of the 'racial' characteristics of the Jewish population in the form of intense political propaganda, the supposedly 'racial' features of Gypsies were formulated largely in pseudo-scientific research reports by Robert Ritter and his team of 'racial hygienists', complete with body measurements, detailed genealogical charts and a 'sociobiological' assessment of what they defined as 'hereditary asocial behaviour'. There was every proof that the persecution and genocide against Romani minorities had been carried out on the basis of a racial ideology. Nevertheless, many Roms encountered difficulties reclaiming their German citizenship. As a result they were also considered to be ineligible for compensation payments, which according to the West German compensation law could be made only to German citizens. By the time their citizenship was reinstated and compensation claims were filed again, claimants were often informed that the deadline for submitting claims had passed.

One of the key problems was the continuity of attitudes towards Roms in Germany in the period immediately following the war. In the state of Hesse, for example, the 1929 law for Combating the Gypsy Menace remained in force until 1957. In Cologne, the authorities confirmed the validity of Himmler's decree from 1938 on the Regulation of the Gypsy Question in March 1949. In Bavaria, the Central Agency for Vagrants continued the work of the Gypsy Police and extended its archive of photos, personal data and fingerprints of German Roms. A statute that imposed restrictions on the movement of Roms (now simply relabelled Landfahrer, 'Vagrants' or 'Travellers') remained in force until 1970. Sophie Ehrhardt, who had served as assistant to Robert Ritter in the Racial Hygiene Research Unit, continued to work at the prestigious University of Tübingen in southwest Germany until her retirement in 1982. Her professorial thesis, submitted to the university in 1950, was devoted to 'The role of epidermal systems in criminological and race-genetic expert reports'. It detailed how Ritter and his colleagues made use of body tissue samples and measurements collected from Gypsies in the 'racial assessments' they wrote for the benefit of the Nazi criminal police. In 1974, Ehrhardt published two academic articles on 'Palmar flexion creases of Gypsies' and on 'Gypsy skulls', and in 1980 she completed a manuscript on 'Anthropometrical and dactyloscopic studies of German Gypsies: A comparison with non-Gypsies and other Gypsy groups'. Ehrhardt was asked to retire only after Romani activists occupied the research laboratories of Tübingen University in protest against her work.

In 1956, the German Federal Supreme Court ruled that the resettlement of Roms from Germany and Austria to Poland in a series of deportations between January and April 1940 had been an illegal military act but not one that was racially motivated. On this basis it denied the survivors' claims for compensation. In 1959, the same court decided even more specifically that it was not until Himmler's 'Auschwitz decree' of December 1942 that Nazi policy was directed towards the annihilation of the Gypsies. The court further stated that the comparison with the Jews was not valid because the Jews did not possess the kind of properties that had made the 'Gypsy lifestyle' a 'national plague' even before National Socialism.

This view began to be challenged by the courts soon afterwards, however. In 1961, a court in Frankfurt ruled on the basis of various SS decrees that the persecution of Roms had been prepared and planned by the Nazis in a way that was quite similar to the persecution of Jews. In 1962, this view was adopted by the Federal Supreme Court, which conceded that the collection of material by Robert Ritter was racially motivated and that therefore individuals who were imprisoned as a result of his assessment had been subjected to racial persecution. A year later, the same court ruled that deportations carried out in 1940 were, in part, racially motivated.

From that moment onwards, Roms who had received compensation only for the period following the 'Auschwitz decree' of 1942 but had been deported earlier were entitled to have their cases reopened and considered for compensation for the entire incarceration period. In many cases, however, deadlines had passed and witness testimonies were no longer available as ever more of the frail survivors passed away. It was not until 1982 that the German government formally acknowledged that Sinti and Roma, now the official German term for the Romani minority, had been victims of racial persecution by the Nazis. This followed a series of campaigns by Romani associations in protest against the continuing denial of the extent of Romani suffering under the Nazis. Chancellor Helmut Schmidt granted recognition to the Central Council of German Sinti and Roma, an umbrella organization representing Romani associations in different parts of the country, and compensation funds were set up in several German states to which Romani survivors could apply. The government also funded and continues to support a documentation centre, operated by the Central Council, which is devoted to the study of the genocide on Roms during the Second World War.

In other western countries, post-war policy towards the Roms tended to focus on their status as a socially deprived group and on their itinerant lifestyle. In Sweden, recommendations to improve the housing, health and education situation of Roms were adopted in 1956. The Romani activist Katarina Taikon (1932–95), whose family arrived in the country as part of a wave of Kelderash Romani immigrants from Russia between 1885 and 1914, played a key role in the public campaign to improve the living conditions, level of education and social inclusion of the Roms. In 1973 the Nordic Gypsy Council was established to represent Roms in Sweden originating from eastern Europe and Finland. It was later expanded to become the Roma National Federation.

In France, authorities continued their practice of forcing Roms to register and to carry special identification cards. In 1969 the anthropometric notebooks were replaced by a new form of registration and the old official label 'Nomads' was replaced by the new administrative term Gens du voyage, 'Travellers'. Nonetheless, French Roms complained of continuing surveillance. England attempted to restrict the movements of travelling Romani families through the Caravan Act of 1960. The law prohibited the use of land as a caravan site without a licence and planning permission. This made it impossible for Gypsies to continue a century-old tradition of stopping on open fields or paying farmers a small fee for using their land as a stopping place.

The Caravan Act was modified in 1968 to allow county councils to provide accommodation for travelling Gypsies in their areas, and Gypsies were allowed to stop only at these designated sites.

The issue of travelling lifestyles and the need to find stopping opportunities for Travellers in various European countries was brought to the attention of the Council of Europe, representing at the time only around a dozen western European countries. The Council's Recommendation 563 on the Situation of Gypsies and other Travellers in Europe from 1969 called for the creation of designated caravan sites for Gypsies by local authorities, for special education provisions for travelling Gypsy children, and for a guarantee of equal rights for Gypsies. This was the first in what was to become a series of interventions on the part of the European governing bodies on behalf of the Romani nation.

Across the Iron Curtain that was now dividing Europe, debates were underway in the ruling communist parties on whether the Roms constituted a national or ethnic minority. The discussions were inspired in part by the liberal nationalities policies of the early days of the Soviet Union and the continuing ideological commitment, at least officially, to combat any form of racism and discrimination on the basis of ethnic origin. However, at the same time, the policy of strict centralization of all social, political and economic affairs and tight control of the population in virtually all domains of everyday life led to a view of the Roms as 'deviant' from majority society. Measures were considered, and in some countries implemented, to restrict the growth of the Romani population and to assimilate the Roms into mainstream society. Nomadism was banned, as were many traditional occupations and separate settlements, and an effort was made to integrate the Roms into the urban workforce.

In many regions throughout central and eastern Europe Romani shanty settlements were destroyed and their inhabitants were moved into apartment blocks in urban areas. As a result Roms obtained access to education, healthcare and jobs. Romani men found employment as unskilled labourers in industrial production and construction, and, as a result, their traditional skills and family-based economic organization were lost, though this transformation brought with it many benefits for the Romani population. Literacy rates rose among the Roms. Although they remained on average poor and less educated, for the first time a small population of Romani professionals emerged. In Bulgaria and Yugoslavia Roms participated in political activities of the ruling party and were trained and served as teachers, and groups of Romani intellectuals, professionals and writers emerged in Hungary, Yugoslavia and Czechoslovakia.

On the whole, however, deprivation continued, not least because of prevailing prejudice and social exclusion. The new measures were often contradictory and aimed not just at integrating the Roms but also at controlling them and destroying their traditional social structures. They were thus unable to eradicate the consequences of century-old marginalization. Literacy rates and life expectancy among the Roms remained lower than average and poverty remained higher. In addition, many Roms refused to cooperate with the new policy. Some sold the apartments allocated to them and moved back to the shantytowns where their traditional family structures and social organization in extended families could be better preserved.

Some governments adopted explicit Romani-related measures and set up bodies to draft them and to monitor and support their implementation. Poland offered nomadic Gypsies housing and employment in 1950 and established an Office for Gypsy Affairs in 1952. The Bulgarian authorities began to implement a programme to settle nomadic Gypsies in 1953. Segregated Romani quarters were set up in dozens of Bulgarian cities and villages and a segregated Romani school system was established in order to educate Romani children. In 1956 the Bulgarian government banned Roms from travelling, and in 1958 it announced that all Gypsies without regular jobs would be forced to work in the state industrial and agricultural sectors. Restrictions were imposed on Romani cultural activities and a Romani theatre in Sofia was closed down. The Bulgarian authorities expressed suspicion of the tendency among Muslim Gypsies to associate with the Turkish minority, and in 1964 special boarding schools were opened for Roms in order to combat their preference to attend Turkish schools. This followed an effort in the early 1950s to push Muslim Roms to emigrate to Turkey. The restrictions on Muslim Roms continued as part of Bulgaria's policy to suppress expressions of Turkish ethnicity and culture. In 1984 the government forced Muslims to adopt Slavic-Bulgarian names and imposed restrictions on the performance of Romani music in public as part of the campaign against Turkish culture.

Restrictive measures were adopted against the Romani population in other Soviet bloc countries, too. Hungary began issuing special black identity cards to Roms in 1954, which were distinct from the red identity cards issued to all other citizens and were intended to allow officials to identify the Roms more easily. Even so, a Hungarian Gypsy Cultural Association was established in 1957 at the initiative of a Romani woman named Máriá László. It received backing from the Ministry of Culture and offered support to Roms working in cooperatives. But soon after, in 1961, the Hungarian communist party adopted a policy of assimilation towards the Roms. It declared that Roms did not constitute a nationality and branded Romani schools, cooperatives and the promotion of the Romani language as harmful because they 'perpetuated the separate position of Gypsies and slowed down their adaptation to society'. Measures were decided on to move Romani families from poor housing into new homes in cities and villages, thereby encouraging cultural assimilation.

Authorities in Czechoslovakia declared a 'Gypsy crisis' in 1956, which they linked to the nomadism of many Roms. In 1958 the Czechoslovak communist party adopted a resolution calling for an 'unconditional solution to the Gypsy question'. It banned the designation Cigan, 'Gypsy', and replaced it by the phrase 'citizens of Gypsy origin'. Gypsies were divided into three categories – nomads, semi-nomads and sedentary – and efforts were made to force nomadic Roms to settle. In 1963 an influential study commissioned by the party described the Roms as an undesirable and underdeveloped class and their language and culture as unworthy of preservation, and called for their geographical dispersal and assimilation. In response, the Czechoslovak communist party produced an 'assimilation plan' for Gypsies in 1965, introducing resettlement and employment opportunities for Gypsies, especially in Slovakia. Several hundred Romani settlements were destroyed and their inhabitants were moved to the Czech regions Bohemia and Moravia. A special council was set up to coordinate Gypsy policy.

The USSR ordered nomadic Romani groups to settle in 1956, and Poland launched an assimilation campaign in 1964, imposing restrictions on travelling and on Romani gatherings and requiring Roms to register with local authorities. In the early 1970s the Romanian communist party introduced a similar policy. An assimilation campaign was initiated and traditional Romani gatherings were prohibited. The government issued a confiscation order for gold coins, which Romani families used as investment, and Roms were assigned to factory work.

In contrast to these restrictive policies of assimilation, there were also occasional moves in some communist countries to recognize Romani identity officially. The Prague Spring of 1968 enabled Romani writers to establish an association in Czechoslovakia, which drafted an alphabet for the Romani language and began to promote publications in the regional Romani dialect. Several other Romani cultural associations and musical groups were also set up and Romani intellectuals were invited to join a Romani language commission at the Oriental Institute of the Czech Academy of Sciences. But recognition and freedom were shortlived, and within three or four years most of these new initiatives were banned. The government resumed efforts to displace Romani families from their shanty settlements into accommodation in urban areas, and Romani children were prohibited from using the Romani language on school grounds. In 1972, the Czechoslovak government issued a decree that encouraged the sterilization of Romani women. Health officers began to pressure Romani women to undergo sterilization in return for financial incentives, with the aim of reducing the birth rate among the Romani population. The rules were redrafted in 1986, extending the programme to younger women from the age of eighteen.

In Hungary, a new constitution drafted in the early 1970s recognized the right of ethnic minorities to maintain their own language. In 1984 the Hungarian communist party adopted a resolution that supported the promotion of Romani culture and called for the establishment of appropriate institutions for its dissemination. Two new organizations were set up in the following years: the National Gypsy Council and the Hungarian National Gypsy Cultural Association. They too became active in developing a written form of the Romani language and promoting publications mainly in the Lovari dialect, alongside other cultural and information activities. Yugoslavia allowed Roms to establish and maintain a number of cultural organizations in the early 1970s. The Yugoslav Republic of Macedonia recognized the Roms as an ethnic group in 1971. Discussions about the status of the Romani minority continued in the other republics during the 1970s until finally the Roms were officially granted nationality status in 1981, though only Bosnia-Herzegovina and Montenegro actually adopted an amendment to this effect into their constitutions. The designation Cigan was banned from official documentation as derogatory and replaced by the term Rom, which was adopted as the official name of the Romani minority. Romani-language publications were launched in Macedonia and in Serbia, and in 1978 the official biography of President Tito of Yugoslavia was translated into Romani.

'THE ROMA COMMUNITY NEED TO KNOW THAT UNFOUNDED ASYLUM SEEKERS WILL BE RETURNED IMMEDIATELY': MODERN EUROPEAN POLITICS

The collapse of the communist regimes in central and eastern European countries during 1989 opened up new opportunities for the expression of Romani identity. Countless Romani cultural associations sprang up and international networking among them led to a thriving exchange of ideas and to the production of Romani-language books and magazines, websites, online social forums, conferences and cultural festivals. Opportunities for political participation at various levels also emerged and a new era opened in the history of Romani representation and leadership. The process of European integration set in motion in the aftermath of the transition to democracy in central and eastern Europe facilitated the movement of Romani individuals and the migration of families and contributed to an increase in public awareness of the Romani population among the majority society. Yet the new political order also posed challenges to the Roms, who have since had to face new threats and new forms of exclusion and marginalization.

In several ex-communist countries, Roms became actively involved in the democratization process from the very beginning. In Hungary, Romani intellectuals formed the association Phralipe, 'Brotherhood', in 1989. In an alliance with the Association of Free Democrats, which emerged as the second most important party in the elections of March 1990, Phralipe was able to send two Romani representatives into the new Hungarian parliament: Antonia Haga and Aladár Horváth. Other Romani political associations were formed and some of them forged alliances with Hungarian political parties. Following the Velvet Revolution in Czechoslovakia in 1989, hundreds of new Romani associations were created. The Romani Civic Initiative (ROI) became one of the largest and held a national meeting in Prague in the spring of 1990. In Bulgaria, Manush Romanov won a seat in parliament in 1990 as a representative of the Romani minority. Several political groups were established, including the Democratic Union of Gypsies–Roma.

These and many other Romani organizations became part of a growing landscape of Romani civil society initiatives: a loose network of associations and individual activists who took on the challenge of raising pride and confidence among members of the Romani minorities and opening up new opportunities for Roms through educational and cultural activities as well as through the dissemination of information and political lobbying. In the early 1990s much of the financial and logistic support for these was provided by European schemes as well as by charitable foundations. Initiatives such as the European Union's PHARE programme, originally launched to promote economic and social cohesion in preparation for the extension of the EU to include new member states in central Europe, made a substantial contribution. Within a few years, a dedicated scheme within the PHARE programme was launched to support Romani initiatives, increasing its annual budget from around €12 million in 1999 and €13 million in 2000, to over €30 million in 2001. This was used to finance the work of Romani non-governmental organizations in Bulgaria, the Czech Republic, Hungary, Romania and Slovakia, including support for the education of Romani children and for the preparation of social inclusion strategies for the Romani minority in the domains of employment, infrastructure and living conditions.

A major contributor to Romani civil society activities has been the Open Society Institute (OSI), part of a network of charitable foundations established and financed by the Hungarian-American businessman George Soros. The OSI set up a number of Romani programmes including a Culture Initiative, a Media Initiative, a Research Scheme and various other projects to support Romani education and advocacy work. It is estimated that in its first ten years of work for the Romani minorities, between 1992 and 2002, the OSI invested more than $30 million in these programmes. Many of the schemes recruited Roms into managerial positions, and funding was awarded to hundreds of Romani individuals, groups and associations to support Romani media and publications, training and education, culture and advocacy activities that directly engaged thousands of young Romani community activists and had a direct impact on tens of thousands of individuals and their families.

Other, independent schemes to which OSI has been a major contributor include the European Roma Rights Centre (ERRC), an advocacy and legal advice initiative active in defence of Romani human rights; the Next Page Foundation, which awarded some $120,000 between 2002 and 2007 to fund Romani language publications of several kinds (electronic and printed) and of various content types (folklore, dictionaries, teaching materials and media) in eleven countries; and the Roma Education Fund, launched in 2005, which by 2012 supported over 300 projects with a total budget of more than €250,000, all in the field of advancing school and pre-school inclusion of Romani children.

Increasingly, governments began to take on direct responsibility for programmes in support of the Romani population. This was facilitated through ever greater political pressure for the formal recognition of the Romani population as an ethnic and linguistic minority. Legislation adopted in Hungary and the Czech Republic in 1993 recognized the Romani minorities there, and Slovakia followed in 1998. Provisions for the recognition of Romani minorities were adopted in other countries, including Romania and Macedonia, and during the 1990s, Romani minorities were also officially recognized for the first time in a number of western European countries, including Austria, Sweden and Finland.

Despite these many manifestations of progress, Romani minorities have suffered some extreme setbacks in the aftermath of the democratization process in central and eastern Europe. The collapse of the state economic sector in the former communist countries resulted in high unemployment rates among the unskilled, to which the Roms generally belonged. Roms have found it particularly difficult to gain alternative employment due to increasingly overt discrimination. The political changes also unleashed xenophobic sentiments that had existed for centuries and generations but were suppressed under the strict control of the communist police states. Once the tight public order policy was relaxed, extremist groups came to the fore, which not only propagated hatred against the Romani minority but also took to outright racist violence. In the Czech Republic, more than 1,200 violent attacks against Roms by skinhead gangs were registered between 1990 and 1997. In Romania, ethnic tensions arose in the spring of 1990 and led to a series of violent acts against Romani neighbourhoods in Bucharest. The violence spread to other areas of the country and continued for several years. One event that received considerable media attention was the attack perpetrated in September 1993 by a mob of hundreds of ethnic Hungarians and Romanians against Roms in the Transylvanian village of Hădăreni. They burned down houses and murdered seven people, and some 130 Roms were driven from their homes.

In the southern Polish town of Mława, several dozen Romani homes were burned down by a mob chanting racist slogans in June 1991. The victims were reported to be economically well off, a fact that was said to have provoked the envy of extremists among the local population who had been badly affected by the economic changes in the country. In August 1992, a mob in the eastern German city of Rostock attacked Romani residents of a hostel for asylum seekers with firebombs. These are just isolated examples of thousands of acts of violence that targeted members of the Romani minority, who on the whole remained defenceless and in numerous cases unassisted by the local police authorities. Most of these attacks were perpetrated by spontaneous mobs, but in a number of cases Roms were singled out as targets of preplanned acts of violence. In February 1995 several Austrian Roms died in the town of Oberwart when a bomb exploded as they were trying to remove the hostile graffiti message 'Gypsies back to India' from a commemoration plaque for the victims of the Nazi genocide. In Italy Romani children became the victims of bomb attacks in the towns of Florence and Pisa in January and March of the same year.

Although the anti-Romani violence was the work of extremists, many Romani activists and human rights advocacy groups have blamed an aggressive mood in mainstream public opinion and inflammatory statements by politicians for the climate that helped incite such animosity. In Bulgaria, Hungary, Romania, the Czech Republic and Slovakia, press reports published after 1991 repeatedly blamed the Romani minority for an increase in criminality. Local authorities and national politicians often made public gestures that were hostile to the Roms. In the Czech Republic, the municipality of Ústí nad Labem erected a wall to separate a Romani estate from neighbouring housing in 1998. In Slovakia, Vladimir Mečiar, who served several terms as prime minister between 1990 and 1998, was particularly vocal in attacking the Romani minority, referring to the Roms in his public speeches as a 'mentally backward' population. Roms in former Yugoslavia were caught between the fighting parties in the conflicts of the 1990s. In the Bosnian war of 1992–5, the Romani minority was not formally allied with any side, but Roms were nevertheless targeted and suffered detentions, expulsions and massacres at the hands of both Serbian and Croatian militias. During the Kosovo war of 1998–9, Roms were accused of siding with the Serbs and were often attacked by ethnic Albanians. Many thousands of Romani families from both regions have had to leave their homes and seek refuge abroad, often in western Europe.

Some Romani migrants had already arrived in western Europe before the fall of the Iron Curtain. Many Roms from Yugoslavia, the only eastern bloc country with open borders, had established themselves in northern European countries such as Germany, Belgium, France and the Netherlands as part of the labour migration from southeastern Europe in the 1960s. When this was halted in the early 1970s, applications for political asylum became the only legal immigration opportunity. Polish Romani families joined Yugoslav Roms applying for asylum in the West in the 1980s. Most applications were rejected, however, and the immigrants found themselves facing compulsory expulsions. In Germany, and to some extent in other countries too, Romani immigrants were supported by some of the local Romani associations as well as by human rights groups, churches and trade unions, and in a number of isolated cases groups of Romani immigrants in Germany, the Netherlands and Sweden were granted special residence permits.

Soon after the fall of communism, in the summer of 1990, Romani immigrants from Romania became more visible on the streets of major western European cities. Their presence triggered a wave of hostile reactions in the press and among many conservative and right-wing politicians, who called on the authorities to expel them. In Germany, shop owners in the small town of Lebach and neighbouring villages went on strike in protest against the arrival of over 1,000 Romani asylum seekers from Romania, who had been referred to the town by the authorities in Berlin in August 1990. Because many refugees claimed not to be in possession of any identity documents, Germany signed a readmission accord with Romania in November 1992, which granted German authorities the right to send Romani immigrants to Romania even in the absence of proof of their Romanian nationality. In return, Germany offered the Romanian government a generous package of development aid.

In the autumn of 1997, the arrival of several hundred Romani families from the Czech and Slovak Republics in the British port of Dover was accompanied by an extremely hostile wave of reports in the British press. In response, UK immigration officers were stationed at Czech and Slovak airports to check the ethnicity of passengers heading to the UK. These measures continued for quite some time. The British prime minister, Tony Blair, even sent a personal letter to his Czech counterpart, Vladimír Špidla, on 4 July 2002, in which he wrote:

> I am very grateful for the help we have had over pre-clearance at Prague airport. While the scheme has undoubtedly helped, claimants have started to get round it by travelling overland to Dover and other UK ports. At present the bulk of the claimants are from the Roma community, arriving in the UK on long-haul coach services. They are clearly

well organised and being assisted in taking advantage of our immigration laws. That is unacceptable. So I hope that you will take whatever action is necessary against the coach drivers, to stop this abuse now. In addition the Roma community need to know that unfounded asylum seekers will be returned immediately.

The fear of Romani migrations was one of the principal factors that motivated some countries to restrict the movement of Romanian and Bulgarian citizens after these nations joined the European Union in 2007. This fear was amplified by a lack of understanding of the causes of Romani migrations. Politicians and civil servants alike regarded Romani migrants as vagrants or nomads. In Italy, police raids on the makeshift settlements of Romani immigrants from Romania and former Yugoslavia, referred to in the public discourse as 'nomad camps', became a common occurrence. In March 2000 some 400 police officers used excessive force against a group of several hundred Romani immigrants at a site on the outskirts of Rome, aiming to send out a public message that the authorities were heavy-handed against Gypsy migrants. Three similar operations followed two months later targeting Romani encampments in other parts of the city. In the summer of 2010, the French president, Nicolas Sarkozy, ordered the evacuation of some 300 settlements of Romani immigrants from Romania and Bulgaria. The camps were declared illegal and destroyed and entire families were taken into police custody and expelled from the country. This triggered a series of international protests from human rights organizations as well as from the European Commission, which condemned France for acting in violation of the European treaties that grant freedom of movement to citizens of the European Union.

Both the rising number of violent attacks against Romani minorities and the arrival in the West of Romani immigrants from central and eastern European countries led international and European political institutions to take an interest in the situation of the Roms as early as 1990. In July of that year, the summit meeting of the Conference on Security and Co-operation in Europe (CSCE, later to be renamed Organization for Security and Co-operation in Europe, OSCE), held in Copenhagen, recognized the special problems facing the Romani population of Europe. In 1992, the Council of Europe adopted a recommendation on the 'Roma (Gypsies) in Europe', which called for support for social inclusion, education and political participation, and the United Nations Commission on Human Rights adopted a resolution for the 'Protection of Roma'. In the following year the United Nations High Commissioner on Refugees (UNHCR) issued an official report on the situation of Romani refugees and migrants, and the CSCE High Commissioner on National Minorities published a report on the 'Roma (Gypsies) in the CSCE Region'. Both the Council of Europe and the OSCE set up offices devoted to monitoring the Romani situation and providing support in a variety of fields. The European Parliament also adopted a series of resolutions in support of the rights and protection of Romani minorities, which accompanied various documents produced by the European Commission and its Fundamental Rights Agency on Romani inclusion and participation.

A body of expert recommendations thus emerged that led to a growing political consensus that transnational action was required on the part of governments and multilateral organizations in order to protect the Romani population from hostility in the short term, and to help it overcome, in the long term, its historical position as a marginalized group suffering from poverty, poor housing and health, restricted access to education and inability to participate in the decisions that affect its destiny. In June 2003, the businessman and philanthropist George Soros convened a conference in Budapest, attended by the political leaders of eight central and eastern European countries alongside representatives of Romani communities from across Europe. It launched the Decade of Roma Inclusion, an initiative planned for the period between 2005 and 2015 during which the participating states would make a special coordinated effort to improve the situation of their Romani minorities. The World Bank and other organizations pledged their support.

Mass expulsion of eastern European Romani migrants from France in the summer of 2010 triggered intensified debates in the European press and political institutions about the Romani situation. As a consequence, in the spring of 2011 the European Commission instructed all member states of the European Union to submit 'national strategies' specifying their plans to promote the inclusion of Romani minorities in the domains of housing, employment, education and healthcare. This initiative came amid a new wave of violence and incitement of hatred directed against the Roms. Especially affected were the Romani communities in the Czech Republic, Bulgaria and Hungary, but also in Italy and to a lesser extent in a number of other countries. Violent attacks against Roms have been on the increase again. Reports filed since 2006 have shown a rise in the number of arson attacks on Romani houses, physical assaults on Romani individuals, destruction of property and police brutality. Sometimes entire Romani families were attacked in their homes, and on some occasions the assaults targeted entire Romani communities. A number of incidents resulted in deaths, and in quite a few cases violence motivated Roms to flee from their homes and to seek refuge elsewhere, often in other countries.

Most of the incidents were attributed to Neo-Nazis and other right-wing extremists, but some of the assailants seemed to lack any clear political affiliation. Italy witnessed a series of arson attacks in Milan, Naples, Rome and in Sicily against Romani immigrants from Romania and former Yugoslavia between 2006 and 2009. Mobs vandalized Romani homes and set them on fire. In December 2011 a vigilante mob in Turin burned down a Romani camp. The trigger for the attack was the claim made by an Italian teenager that two Romani men had raped her; later she confessed that she had invented the entire story. In Bulgaria crowds marched in the streets carrying banners and wearing T-shirts with the slogan 'I don't want to live in a Gypsy country'. Between 2008 and 2012 mobs took to the street on numerous occasions in Hungary and the Czech Republic chanting anti-Gypsy slogans, and attacked Romani neighbourhoods with Molotov cocktails and on some occasions with firearms. The European Roma Rights Centre based in Budapest has published a detailed online database in which hundreds of incidents have been recorded. In an isolated incident in the summer of 2009, the residence of Romani immigrants from Romania was fire bombed in Belfast in Northern Ireland.

Romani and human rights associations also reported their concern about police activities during this period. Police in the Czech Republic, Slovakia and Bulgaria have been accused of abusing Roms in custody, both verbally and physically. Special forces of the Macedonian police clashed with Romani residents of Šuto Orizari after a customs inspection in April 2010, injuring several dozen people. In Britain, the London Metropolitan Police led a campaign called 'Operation Golf' in 2009–10, which carried out surveillance of Romani immigrants suspected of trafficking children. After the investigation was concluded, the officer in charge, Superintendent Bernie Gravett, boasted on BBC television that over seventy suspects had been arrested for a variety of offences – but none has actually been charged with human trafficking. In 2011, riots broke out in connection with the enforced eviction of caravans of Romani Gypsies and Irish Travellers from the Dale Farm site in Essex. Families had lived for many years there, on land they legally owned, but the local council had denied them planning permission and so their caravan settlement was deemed illegal. In October 2010 it was revealed that the French authorities maintained a database, created in 1997, on 'non-sedentary ethnic minorities', which included personal data on Romani and Traveller families and was used for the purposes of targeted police surveillance.

Activists and analysts alike have tended to attribute the escalation in anti-Romani violence after 2006 to intensifying political incitement against the Romani minority. In Hungary, the right-wing Movement for a Better Hungary, also known as Jobbik, launched a campaign against the Romani minority in 2008. In the same year, the Italian prime minister, Silvio Berlusconi, signed a decree declaring a state of emergency in relation to the 'settlements of nomads', a term used for the makeshift quarters of Romani immigrants. The government subsequently began to collect personal data, including fingerprints, of the Romani residents of so-called 'nomad camps'. Politicians at national and local levels supported anti-Romani campaigns in Bulgaria, and in the Czech Republic the Autonomous Nationalists were just one of several movements that posted calls on the internet urging crowds to attack Romani homes.

The reasons behind the rise in public expressions of anti-Romani hatred are complex. Following the enlargement of the European Union and the growing relevance of European institutions, many political circles in the new member states embarked on an ideological search for a new national identity. Some perceived the introduction of European norms and regulations as an imposition of foreign political correctness. In many places there was resentment, for example, against the policy of desegregation applied in the education system to ensure that Romani children had full and fair access to schooling. The deterioration of the economic and social welfare of many Roms following the decline of the centralized economy, and their subsequent depiction as a criminal class, coupled with the growing assertiveness of a young Romani intellectual elite, have also triggered hostility. Politicians relying on right-wing populism have been exploiting this climate for their own ends. The anti-Romani mood has been further fuelled by the historical and embedded image of the Roms as work-shy, still prevalent in many countries. In western Europe it has been strengthened by growing criticism of immigration and opposition to the presence especially of large Muslim minorities, whose culture, like that of the Roms, is regarded as foreign, and by a perception of the Roms as nomads and illegal vagrants.

An interesting lesson can be learned from the experience of local authorities and services in Manchester, England, who, in 2010, began to engage actively with a small population of Romani immigrants from Romania who had settled in the city following Romania's accession to EU membership in 2007. A group of several dozen families, altogether around 500–600 people, took up residence in rented accommodation in a deprived area of the city. Tensions arose in the neighbourhood, and a series of complaints were made to the local municipality. The authorities put together a Roma Strategy Group consisting of representatives of various local services, including schools and the police. They also organized a series of residents' meetings in which they gave neighbours an opportunity to put forward their complaints and concerns. A long list of problems allegedly triggered by the presence of the Roms was compiled. It included complaints that Romani parents refused to send their children to school, that they violated hygiene rules by disposing of rubbish on the pavements and in back alleys, that they had no meaningful source of income, and even that they formed part of criminal gangs engaged in human trafficking.

The city authorities were persuaded, however, by a coalition of local schools, charity organizations and academics to listen to the needs of the Romani community. One of the schools pioneered a mentoring scheme in which several Romani adults from the community were hired to give support to Romani children, now making up around a third of the entire school population. A local charity provided funds to set up a one-year training programme in basic skills for a dozen young Roms, and the police, social services and schools began employing these young people as part-time interpreters and mediators in their interactions with Romani residents. Three years on, in the spring of 2013, Manchester City Council published a document outlining its 'Roma Strategy'. It emphasized the enormous gap between outsider perception and the reality of Romani life. School attendance, it reported, was purely a problem of the availability of school places. Once barriers were broken down and schools were persuaded to take on Romani children, the attendance rates of Romani children began to outstrip those of non-Romani children. Work was a problem of legal constraints that denied Romanian citizens the right to find paid employment and forced them into dependency on housing and child benefits. Once individuals were granted work permits on the basis of the skills they possessed and the interest of institutions in employing them, they became role models for the entire community, especially the young children. A close scrutiny by the municipality of residents' waste-disposal habits revealed that the Roms observed the same standards as other residents in the neighbourhood. Tellingly, the document emphasized that no evidence whatsoever was found of organized crime among the Roms, and indeed that the allegations of criminality distracted the local authorities from engaging with the community and delayed the process of social inclusion considerably. The Manchester experience shows just how important it is to break down the barriers of perception and prejudice.

FINDING A VOICE

Political movements that represent the interests of national or ethnic groups are invariably associated with aspirations for some kind of regional autonomy or even territorial independence. For this reason, many are puzzled by the fact that Romani activists have formed both local and regional organizations and have put forward proposals for political participation and for programmes in the fields of education, culture and social welfare. Some writers have even expressed their scepticism towards these efforts, claiming that the very notion of political activity or nationalism is alien to Romani culture. The Roms, they say, are kinship-based family groups and have no tradition of viewing themselves as a nation. It is certainly true that family-based ties are very important to the social organization of Romani communities. At the same time, solidarity among Romani communities has always existed. Moreover, as times change and more and more young Roms are obtaining an education, many have had the chance to reflect on the situation of their people and to develop a vision for the future. An ever-growing number of educated Roms are forming links with Roms in other regions and countries, facilitated by travel opportunities, conferences and electronic media. Romani society has entered a new era in its history.

Attempts to form local Romani associations that would promote Romani culture and represent the interests of local Romani communities go back to initiatives of Roms in Russia in the 1920s and in Romania in the 1930s. These were all discontinued as a result of restrictions imposed by the authorities. The post-war period saw contradictory tendencies in the countries of the Soviet bloc, with initiatives such as the Cultural Alliance of Hungarian Gypsies being granted permission to operate for a short time (in this case between 1957 and 1961) under the tight supervision of the ruling communist party, only to be dismantled when the party decided to change its policy towards the Romani minority. Such was also the fate of the Union of the Gypsies–Roma of the Czech Republic and the Union of the Gypsies–Roma of Slovakia, which operated between 1969 and 1973, of the Gypsy Alliance, set up in Hungary in 1974, and numerous others.

Even in western countries, where freedom of association generally provided more generous opportunities, Roms sometimes encountered difficulties setting up political groups. In 1959, Ionel Rotaru, an Ursari Rom from Romania, founded an organization in Paris called *Communauté Mondiale Gitane*, 'International Gypsy Community', but it was banned by the French government in 1965. The group subsequently re-established itself under the name Comité Internationale Tzigane. In 1966, English Gypsies founded the Gypsy Council to promote awareness of their community, to fight discrimination and to promote access to education and other services. It still exists today. Over the past decades it has been especially active in campaigning for the extension of caravan site provisions for Gypsies and Travellers in Britain.

Soon after its establishment, the Gypsy Council forged links with Romani activists in other countries, including Romani intellectuals in Czechoslovakia, Yugoslavia and other eastern bloc countries who, during the late 1960s, enjoyed temporary freedom of association and cultural activism. These were invited to a World Romany Congress held in London in 1971. A second World Congress was held in Geneva in 1978. Over one hundred delegates from twenty different countries participated and they decided to launch the International Romani Union (IRU), an organization that would represent Romani people worldwide. The IRU committed itself to the idea of a Romani nation and made efforts to create all the symbols of nationhood. It adopted a flag and a national anthem and its key members began working to create a standard written Romani language with up-to-date terminology. Some also attempted to rewrite Romani history, promoting the idea that the Roms once had a kingdom of their own in India that was destroyed by invaders and its population exiled. High on the agenda of the IRU was the commemoration of the Romani victims of the Nazi genocide during the Second World War, and IRU members began to make representations to the German government and to international bodies seeking compensation payments and formal recognition of the IRU.

While European institutions and governments remained hesitant in granting the IRU such recognition, support came from the government of India under Prime Minister Indira Gandhi, who agreed to grant official recognition to the Romani people as an 'Indian diaspora nation'. The initiative came from a retired Indian diplomat, W. R. Rishi, who developed a passion for the Romani people and their history, language and culture. In 1977, the Indian government filed a motion at the United Nations Economic and Social Council Sub-Commission on the 'Promotion and Protection of Human Rights', which was adopted as an official resolution. The text recognized that the Romani people had 'historic, cultural and linguistic ties of Indian origin'. In 1979 the same body granted the IRU consultative status.

This was probably the IRU's most significant achievement. Despite the impression it tried to communicate to outside bodies, the IRU remained a very loose framework of activists and lacked both a clear strategy and transparency. Its leadership consisted of a number of Romani intellectuals, including, among others: the medical doctor Jan Cibula, a Czech Rom residing in Switzerland, the engineer Sait Balić and the academic Rajko Djurić from Serbia, all of whom served as presidents of the organization; and the American academic Ian Hancock of British Romani background, who was IRU liaison officer with the United Nations. But their activity was not always well coordinated. Representations were often made on 'official' IRU letterheads by various people, all claiming to be speaking on behalf of the organization. The political scientist Ilona Klimová-Alexander, who studied the IRU's work closely, pointed out that its isolated efforts at the United Nations had actually proven to be quite successful but that subsequent opportunities to follow up on this work had not been taken up by the IRU activists.

In Germany, the campaign by Romani survivors to gain recognition and compensation as victims of Nazi persecutions had turned by the late 1970s into a public protest movement, led by a small circle of Romani activists with the support of several established German non-governmental organizations, the most prominent of which was the Society for Endangered Peoples. The campaigns targeted the German press and institutions such as churches, trade unions, universities and political parties. They included protest marches to the sites of former concentration camps, flagging what the activists provocatively presented as the continuity of persecution since the Nazi period. The principal motor behind the campaign was the *Verband Deutscher Sinti*, 'Association of German Sinti'. In 1980 it was renamed Central Council of German Sinti and Roma and, in 1981, assisted by the Society for Endangered Peoples, it hosted the third World Romany Congress in the German town of Göttingen.

In the following year the Central Council was recognized by the German federal government as the official representation of the Romani people in Germany. The government made a commitment to support it financially and to consult it on all matters relating to the Romani minority. Under the leadership of its chairman of many years, Romani Rose, the Central Council of German Sinti and Roma remains one of the most powerful and best resourced of all Romani associations and probably the only one that has this kind of official status in any country. Modelled in part on the representation structure of the Jewish minority, the Central Council presents itself as an umbrella organization that is mandated by associations based in the individual federal states. Each of these functions as a registered society and has registered members. The federal executive is not elected directly by the membership but by a coalition of associations. Membership of the associations is in turn voluntary and individual, and so technically the organization represents its members, not necessarily all Roms in the country.

In the late 1980s a growing number of Romani immigrants from eastern Europe confronted Romani associations in Germany with a new challenge. After labour immigration from southern Europe was halted in 1973, the only prospect of immigration was via the political asylum route. While some Romani families from Poland had been able to complete the procedure successfully in the late 1970s, the authorities reacted to a growing wave of immigrants with a wholesale rejection of applications. Once legal proceedings had been exhausted, many thousands were threatened with expulsion back to Poland and Yugoslavia. The Central Council of German Sinti and Roma instructed its branches not to support Romani immigrants, arguing that its duty of representation was limited to German citizens. It also expressed a fear that the achievements of German Roms during their campaign for restitution would be diminished if they were to be associated with the negative images that immigrants triggered in German public opinion.

However, other Romani associations in Germany did agree to support the Romani immigrants. They included initiatives in Cologne, Frankfurt and Berlin. The Rom and Cinti Union (RCU), an organization based in Hamburg that had broken away from the Central Council, led the campaign under the leadership of its chairman, Rudko Kawczynski, a Rom who was born in Poland and raised in Sweden and in Germany. The strategy adopted by the Romani movement in the 1970s came back to life as the RCU lobbied for support from churches, trade unions and other civil society initiatives, and added a commitment towards Europe-wide solidarity with all Romani people. The RCU introduced a new type of political activism that differed from the more intellectual character of the activities of the IRU. It blocked motorways and border crossings and asked for asylum for its members in local parish churches in order to draw attention to its demands. It argued that the Roms were de facto stateless since they had no country of their own, and therefore required protection. An ideological split emerged among the Romani associations in Germany between those who regarded themselves as speaking strictly on behalf of the Romani citizens of Germany, and those who saw themselves as part of a European Romani nation. Provoked by the growing prominence of European-level political initiatives in respect to the Romani minorities, the Central Council of German Sinti and Roma released a political identity manifesto in 1993 that defined the German Sinti and Roma as an ethnic-German minority, using the term *volksdeutsche Minderheit* that was usually reserved in German political discourse for ethnic-German minorities in post-war eastern bloc countries.

A major turning point in the development of the Romani political movement was of course the fall of communism and the establishment of countless Romani associations in 1989–90. There had been some increase in the activities of Romani groups in some countries prior to the political transition. Between 1985 and 1989 National Gypsy Councils had been set up in Hungary as political advisory bodies at local level, appointed by the communist party, and in 1986, the Cultural Alliance of Hungarian Gypsies was revived in order to distribute public funding for Romani cultural events. The Union of Roma in Czechoslovakia was formed in 1987 and demanded that the communist party address the problems of Romani citizens. In addition, many Roms throughout the eastern bloc countries had joined the ranks of the communist party and some achieved party positions at various levels, hoping to be able to influence decisions and promote issues that were in the interest of the Romani minorities.

The Romani political parties formed when the democratization process began broadly failed to attract a sufficient number of votes in order to gain representation in legislative assemblies even in countries with a proportionally large Romani population. Nevertheless, a number of Roms were elected to national parliaments as part of special agreements or coalitions with mainstream parties. Romania introduced a regulation in 1990 according to which a seat was reserved in the Lower Chamber for the Romani party that received the largest number of votes. Romani representatives were elected in the 1990 Czechoslovak elections as part of the Civic Forum coalition, and in Hungary two representatives of Phralipe were elected in 1990, and three Romani members were elected in 2002 as part of the Fidesz party (a coalition of the Hungarian Civic Party with the Hungarian Democratic Forum). Many Roms have since served as local councillors and mayors in almost all eastern European countries. Hungarian Romani activists established the Roma Parliament in 1990 as an independent representation of Romani interests, while in Romania, the Romani Center for Social Intervention and Studies (CRISS) led by Nicolae Gheorghe and the *Aven Amentza* Foundation formed a coalition in 1999 to cooperate with the Romanian Ministry of National Minorities. Juan de Dios Ramírez Heredia, a Spanish Gitano, served as a member of the European Parliament between 1994 and 1999, and Lívia Járóka, a Hungarian Romani politician, was elected to the European Parliament in 2004.

In April 1990 the IRU held its fourth World Romany Congress in Warsaw, the first after the fall of communism. The assembly appointed several working groups that went on to obtain financial support from the European Commission for the creation of a standard Romani alphabet and a Romani encyclopaedia and for a research group on Romani history. Several publications arose from this work, and lobbying aimed at the European Commission and the Council of Europe intensified. However, the pace of changes meant that the IRU had now become just one of many Romani political associations. In November 1990, the Rom and Cinti Union based in Germany, which was operating internationally under the label Roma National Congress (RNC), organized an international conference of delegates representing Romani associations from around a dozen European countries. The conference called for the establishment of a constituency-based, elected European representation of the Roms called EUROM. A follow-up meeting took place in Budapest several months later but the idea failed to gain wide support at that stage.

Other initiatives in support of Romani self-government and political participation emerged in various countries. In Sweden, where a national framework for the representation of ethnic and immigrant minorities had been in place for some time, representatives of the various Romani communities, including Romani immigrants from Finland and from the Balkans, were invited to participate in a National Romani Council. In Hungary, a model for 'Self-Government' was introduced in 1994. In districts known to have a Romani population of significant size, citizens were allowed to vote for a minority self-government council. This body had consultative status and was entitled to express opinions on minority acts, statutes and decrees. It was also invited to participate in the professional supervision of minority education and to help establish educational and cultural institutions. Several hundred Romani self-government forums have since been elected at local level throughout the country.

European bodies have often noted the absence of a legitimate, constituency-based Romani representation at European level. The Council of Europe's Parliamentary Assembly in its Resolution 1203 (February 1993) 'On Gypsies in Europe' called on the Council to grant consultative status to 'representative international Gypsy organisations'. However, the Council was unable to identify such an organization. From 1993 onwards, regular meetings were held with Romani activists who were involved in lobbying international institutions. The forum was referred to as the Standing Conference of Roma Associations in Europe and included individuals who identified with the International Romani Union, the Roma National Congress and others. But these organizations also continued their independent activities. After a gap of a whole decade, the IRU convened again in Prague in 2000 for its fifth World Romany Congress, with sponsorship from the Czech government, and elected the Czech Romani lawyer Emil Ščuka as president. It resumed a routine of issuing press releases and setting up working parties, and its meetings took on a somewhat more regular pace. The sixth congress took place in Lanciano in Italy in 2004. Once again it elected a president, Stanisław (Stahiro) Stankiewicz from Poland, and launched a new IRU World Parliament, headed by Dragan Jevremović, a Serbian Rom residing in Austria. A seventh congress followed in Zagreb in 2008.

The issue of a genuinely mandated European representation of the Romani people remained on the table. It had been raised in 2001, when the president of Finland, Tarja Holonen, addressed the Council of Europe and called for the establishment of a consultative Romani body. Discussions took place with a number of prominent Romani activists, and in 2004 the Council of Europe entered into a formal agreement with a new body called the European Roma and Traveller Forum (ERTF), led by Rudko Kawczynski as president of the board. The ERTF was to serve as a pan-European umbrella organization that would eventually seek a direct mandate from Romani constituents across Europe. In the meantime, it holds consultative status at the Council of Europe and is involved in discussions of policy measures and documents that relate to the Romani minorities.

There are other Romani associations functioning at the international level, among them the European Roma Information Office (ERIO), a lobby group operating at the European Commission in Brussels that is led by Ivan Ivanov, a Bulgarian Rom, and several email discussion lists of Romani activists, such as the Roma Virtual Network, *Romano Liloro* and *Romane Nevipena*. In 2011, the European Commission and the Council of Europe jointly launched a European Academic Network on Romani Studies, which is not intended to represent the Romani minority but rather to offer an academic perspective on issues of policy.

It is obvious that the Romani minority in Europe now has a voice, or perhaps many voices, in the processes that shape European policy, and to some extent also the policies of national governments, towards the Roms. But the issue of representation continues to pose some serious challenges. First, none of the Romani associations has a clearly defined constituency or a well-formulated and transparent political mandate. Many Romani non-governmental organizations tend to be led and run by small circles of friends or even family members. Participation is voluntary and often irregular. Though some associations may have hundreds of followers at the local or regional level, they usually lack a formal election procedure for officers and committees and many do not even offer their members a regular forum in which to hold political debates. Given the nature of the campaigns to which Romani associations have usually devoted most of their energy and attention, discussions have focused on tactical decisions aimed at resolving immediate local crisis situations. Debates on long-term strategies have been reserved for occasional conferences and congresses where Romani delegates from several countries have the opportunity to share experiences and articulate their vision for the future.

There are different perspectives and viewpoints about the future. The Central Council of German Sinti and Roma, for example, sees itself as representing members of a minority who are German citizens and have their roots and point of orientation in Germany. Its spokesmen acknowledge a historical affinity with the Romani populations of other European regions and a common cause in the struggle against prejudice and discrimination, but they tend to resist the drafting of strategies at the European level, partly, perhaps, because they cherish their political achievements over the past decades on behalf of their own community in Germany and would not wish to jeopardize those by renegotiating the terms and mandates of representation. They also resist any suggestion of state sponsorship of or support for Romani language and culture, insisting that these are private matters that must remain the sole responsibility of Romani families and confined to the home setting. They therefore oppose Romani schools, Romani language broadcasting and theatre and publications in the Romani language. The Central Council has also opposed the label 'non-territorial' in respect of the Roms, because it fears that this questions the connection between the Roms and their country of residence and ignores the fact that many Romani minorities feel that their roots are in the region in which their families have lived for many generations.

Romani activists Nicolae Gheorghe from Romania and Andrzej Mirga from Poland have presented their own view in a unique policy paper published in 1997. Both men have an academic background in the social sciences and both were recruited and sponsored in the early 1990s by the Project on Ethnic Relations (PER), an initiative with close links to the United States government which worked to build bridges between Romani political initiatives and administrations in central and eastern Europe. Both men also served as Senior Advisers on Romani Affairs to the OSCE's Office for Democratic Institutions and Human Rights. In their manifesto, Gheorghe and Mirga emphasized the role of Romani 'elites' in changing the status of the European Romani populations and in promoting their social inclusion. In a subtle way they distanced themselves from the preoccupation with national symbolism among bodies such as the IRU and even from demands for Romani cultural autonomy, and argued instead for a process of integration that should enable individuals of Romani descent to pursue whichever career paths they chose without having to suffer discrimination due to their background.

At its World Congress in Prague in 2000, the IRU issued a communiqué calling for recognition of the Romani people as an 'a-territorial European nation'. This attracted criticism from many activists and observers who were sympathetic to the cause of Romani rights but argued that the concept of 'non-territorial' risked implying that individual states could deny responsibility for the well-being of the Romani minorities within their territories. Of course, this was not the intention of the declaration's authors. The aim was to emphasize that the Roms do not have a country of their own and that there is therefore a need for a Romani voice to speak on their behalf, irrespective of their country of residence. Such a voice might find more resonance in a united Europe, where European institutions have growing influence on various aspects of policy. This view was echoed by the ERTF. In its 'Charter on the Rights of the Roma', first published in 2010, the ERTF avoided the term 'non-territorial', perhaps in order not to offend some of its potential member associations. Instead it defined the Roms as a 'European national minority', as a 'national minority without a state or a claim to a state' and as a 'pan-European national minority'. It placed the emphasis on shared origin and shared language and on the right to 'cultural autonomy'.

WHO SPEAKS FOR THE ROMS?

Romani political organizations are seeking to redefine the relationship between Romani communities and majority society. Their agenda is to grant the Roms a voice in managing their affairs and in pushing forward with social inclusion and political participation, to change outsiders' perception and fight prejudice and discrimination, and to empower members of their own communities to articulate their needs, fend off prejudice and pursue new ambitions. Providing the Roms with a voice means asking governments at various levels to take into consideration the demands and proposals made by Romani representatives to be allowed to have a say in managing their affairs. To this end, Romani activists try to work together with authorities to set up mechanisms for consultation with the Romani community. This requires setting up a leadership and representation structure that would have the trust of both Romani communities and the authorities that hold the key to delivering support. Quite often, the path to achieving such trust involves the creation of political symbols of nationhood and gestures of political organization, such as the appointment of officers whose powers are primarily emblematic and the publication of manifestos calling for social and political change, the implementation of which is usually entirely dependent on outside support.

Removing the barriers preventing social inclusion requires a change in outsiders' attitudes towards and perception of the Roms. Romani activists work hard to eradicate the stereotypical image of Gypsies as lawless and uneducated social outcasts and of Gypsy culture as the choice of a joyous lifestyle, and to replace them with a notion of nationhood that is much closer to majority society's image of itself: a complex society, consisting of various social layers and occupation groups including professionals, with its own traditions and values, history and community institutions. This often leads activists to invent a new narrative of Romani history, one that can also be used to inspire young members of the Romani community to develop self-confidence and to empower them to articulate their needs and seek ways to take their destiny and that of their families and communities into their own hands.

Sometimes activists get carried away in constructing such historical narratives. Understandably, they wish to remove barriers by emphasizing the similarities between the Roms and other nations. But numerous websites and the writings of Romani intellectuals show that this is often achieved through an interpretation of history that is based on imagination and fantasy rather than on a scholarly scrutiny of the evidence. The geographical dispersion of the Roms as a nation without a territory and the historical specialization in service trades are both explained in these narratives as an anomaly that came about as a result of outside oppression and subjugation. The Roms are described as the victims of conquerors who took over their lands in India and forced them into exile, condemning them to becoming an underclass permanently in search of handouts and dependent on majority society. Ironically, such depictions bear certain similarities to the traditional tales that one finds in some Romani (as well as Traveller) communities, which describe the destiny of the Roms as wanderers as a punishment inflicted upon them for an ancient sin. In reality, such narratives can cause much confusion as they are pitched to compete with scholarly interpretations of the origin of the Roms and the historical events that led to their present-day situation. As part of their quest for self-representation, however legitimate, Romani activist-intellectuals often take steps to try to diminish confidence in mainstream scholarship in order to fortify their own position as true representatives of the Roms towards the authorities and as indisputable role models who seek to inspire their own people. They sometimes attack university researchers specializing in Romani studies as biased and portray their own historiographical narratives as authentic and genuine simply on the grounds that they are put forward by people who claim Romani family background.

Changing attitudes and perceptions is of course not an easy task. To begin with, traditional images are, as we've already seen, very deeply entrenched. On many occasions I was shocked at the way even civil servants and professionals who work with Romani people on a daily basis are caught in a whirlpool of prejudice. I once attended a meeting along with English Romani friends at the office of the Traveller Education Service in the north of England. We were there to plan activities to support Romani children. We had never visited the area before, and at the end of the meeting my friends asked for directions on how to leave the town centre by car. The unit's manager, an educated woman who had been directing the Traveller Education Service and working with the community for many years, provided a short explanation and then, in front of my Romani friends, turned to me with a smile: 'They'll find their way, they know how to get around everywhere.' She probably did not realize how offensive her words could be. Another time, at the headquarters of the European Commission in Brussels, I took part in a meeting with senior European officials who asked academics to advise them on various aspects of Romani society and current political aspirations. When my academic colleagues and I emphasized that one must distinguish between Romani people, Travellers and various other minority groups, the reply from one of the division heads present was: 'To us they are all the same.'

Romani activists must struggle against a fortress of biased and patronizing attitudes even in their dealings with those who are supposedly entrusted with helping them improve their people's situation and support their social inclusion. They also struggle to bridge the enormous gap between what people know or think they know about the Roms, and what the activists would like them to think. Most traditional Roms accept that the non-Roms are generally ignorant about Romani culture. Some even cultivate this ignorance; old professions such as fortune-telling are examples of how they capitalize on the fact that non-Roms believe Roms have supernatural powers. Others simply seek satisfaction in their own conviction that they are fortunate to have the support of their families and the freedom to organize their work around their family life, to share and to be there for one another, and they pity non-Roms for their strictly hierarchical and impersonal work environments and for what they perceive as the absence of generosity and spontaneity in their society. It is therefore also difficult to motivate many Roms to take action to approach mainstream society and to ask for more understanding of their ways and for respect towards their community.

Inevitably, those engaged in Romani politics tend to be individuals who are, to some extent at least, caught between two cultures. Many Romani activists are in fact of mixed parentage. They are often individuals who grew up within the mainstream culture, ashamed of, or afraid to acknowledge, their Romani family connections. Others are persons of Romani background who acquired an education and spent the early years of their careers capitalizing on their Romani connections by engaging in academic research on Romani culture or providing expertise to public services and institutions on Romani society. They feel a strong commitment to challenging prejudice and to improving the destiny of their people. But many years of their lives have been spent struggling for recognition and acknowledgement among their non-Romani colleagues and peers.

Paradoxically, many activists of mixed background try to strengthen their status as recognized experts on Romani affairs by emphasizing how authentic their narrative is. I recall the perplexed reactions of a Romani family in Germany that was once visited by an American academic who claimed Romani descent. He had learned to speak Romani as an adult, but had a strong American accent and had great difficulties following the flow of casual conversation in the language. He came to Germany to deliver a lecture at a local university, and I invited him to meet some of my Romani friends. He arrived at the family home wearing a necktie in the colours of the Romani flag, his jacket decorated with over a dozen badges and emblems that commemorated various conferences of Romani political activists. He showed everyone his passport, into which he himself had inserted a stamp that said 'Romanestan' – a reference to a fantasy Romani homeland. Sitting on the sofa opposite the television in the family's living room, he demonstrated his dismay at an advertisement for Levi's jeans that depicted a bare-chested young man by spitting on the floor and uttering in disgust: 'Gadje!' And he lectured the family's father on how 'we Roms' must 'continue to fight for our culture'. The reply he received showed just how his attempts to mimic authenticity went down with his hosts: 'Everyone has to fight for the things they don't possess,' they said. 'We fight for human rights, you fight for culture.'

Alongside countless Roms who are sincerely committed to serving the interests of their people, the Romani activist scene seems also to offer a platform for a kind of modernized, politically correct version of the old Gypsy brand. At one of the academic events devoted to Romani studies, a workshop held in Budapest some years ago, I met a Polish artist who was living in Berlin with her husband, a photographer. She was interested in Romani culture and had visited Romani communities in several countries. We had long and interesting conversations about Romani history, art, music and politics. Our paths crossed again a couple of years later, at a similar event. This time she seemed more emotionally engaged, and she took a special interest in the stories of Romani survivors of Nazi concentration camps and particularly of Romani orphans. She explained that she had a somewhat intriguing family background herself. She had never met her father, and her mother told her very little about him. It seemed that the mother was very keen to avoid the topic of her grandmother's background – the lost father's mother. Apparently, she had died in unknown circumstances. The artist, we can call her 'Agnieszka', was unable to explain why her mother withheld the full story from her. Could it be that her grandmother had been a Romani woman who perished in a Nazi concentration camp? Is it possible that her father was of Romani descent – a Romani orphan?

Our third and (so far) last encounter was at a conference on Romani history, culture and politics in Istanbul, to which various academics and Romani activists were invited. Agnieszka had since been to India, in search of her cultural roots. She had been very productive in her work, and she gave a presentation in which she discussed slides of her recent paintings. She explained how her choice of colours and patterns reflected her Romani identity. She admitted that this identity was spiritual, not a product of her upbringing but rather a genetic trait that was deeply embedded in her soul. 'I inherited, on a non-verbal basis, my father's Holocaust identity, which is apparent in my life and in my art,' she declared. She reported on her experiences 'as a Romani artist' visiting India, which she called 'the home country of my ancestors'. And she ended her presentation with an emotional appeal: 'We Roma should try to rediscover and reacquire the visual tradition that we lost when we lost India.'

Agnieszka's rediscovery of a supposedly Romani identity was, by her own admission, a kind of escape route from a situation of emotional distress and a personal identity vacuum, anchored in her early childhood, which she described as a 'post-traumatic experience'. She was not the first person I met who had 'transformed' into a Rom. I had been acquainted with a German social worker, we'll call her 'Kerstin', who had spent many years supporting a Romani community. One of her jobs was with a local Romani non-governmental organization, and she lost it when the director needed the position for one of his family members and forced her to resign. Frustrated, she sought support from a trade union and started legal proceedings. This, however, backfired and she was confronted in court with a series of allegations of professional negligence and incompetence, to which she struggled to respond. Emotionally hurt by what she perceived as unjust treatment after years of dedicated service, she embarked on a path of soul-searching. It was during a yoga seminar in Switzerland that Kerstin was suddenly overcome by a deep conviction that her grandmother must have been a Romni, and that she therefore had just as strong a claim to the job she had lost as any member of a Romani family.

Some years ago I was invited to spend several months as a visiting researcher at a university in Australia. Just a week or two before my journey, a number of postings on an online discussion forum of Romani activists caught my attention. They were written by a woman, we can call her 'Sandra', who identified herself as the leader of an Australian Romani organization. She described her association's efforts to lobby the authorities to give support to an exhibition on Romani Australians, which they were hoping to launch at the Immigration Museum in Melbourne. A few days after I arrived in Melbourne I made contact with Sandra and expressed my interest in hearing more about her work. She invited me to her home in a small settlement about an hour's train ride away. A man who identified himself as Sandra's husband met me at the station. Tall and blond, in his late thirties, accompanied by two small children and driving a van, he had the appearance of the prototype Anglo-Australian.

The family home was a small wooden cottage. Some of the walls were decorated with prints of cliché Gypsy caravans. There was an old and dusty computer in a corner, which obviously served as Sandra's portal to the online Romani discussion forum, and on the single bookshelf I spotted activist Ian Hancock's manifesto book *We Are the Romani People*, and activist Ron Lee's *Learn Romani*, alongside a German–English dictionary. Sandra herself was preoccupied in the kitchen (which doubled as entrance hall, dining room and sitting room, and held the computer as well, so apparently it also served as the Romani organization's headquarters) and she announced proudly that her Hungarian Gypsy goulash would be ready in just a few minutes.

Sandra, in her mid-thirties, was wearing a mid-long skirt and a plain sleeveless blouse, and had decorated her thick long blonde hair with red ribbons. She spoke perfect English but with a slight German accent, and as we shared the goulash she told me her story. She grew up in southern Germany. Her grandmother, she said, had been a Sinta

– a Romani woman of the Sinti group. She didn't get to know her much, because the grandmother did not visit often and passed away when Sandra was young. Sandra had been a rebellious child. She ran away from home at the age of sixteen, on her own. She had many adventures travelling across Europe, hitching rides, sleeping rough – 'like a Gypsy'. At the tender age of twenty-two she wrote a novel that described the sexual escapades of a young girl, possibly containing some autobiographical elements. She met her Australian husband in England and together they moved first to Queensland, and then on and on, from one town to another, changing jobs, renting whatever small houses were affordable, moving the kids from one pre-school to another – 'like Gypsies'.

I was curious about her Romani organization and whom it represented. Perhaps I could meet some of the other members? 'Not quite yet,' was the reply. So far, Sandra and her husband were not aware of any other Romani people in the area. For that reason, it was proving difficult to collect artefacts and personal testimonies from Romani Australians, which the Immigration Museum had set as a condition before it would consider opening an exhibition on the local Romani community. But there was a website. Despite the fact that the computer equipment at her disposal was old and unreliable, Sandra put much time and effort into her Romani website. It included photos of her children alongside pictures of Romani caravans and the Indian gods Ganesh and Lakshmi. There was an introductory text, where Sandra described how she had grown up in a 'rather dysfunctional family' and had a 'rough childhood and teenage life'. There was a big banner with the motto: 'Proud to be Romani, proud to be me, my people are Gypsy and Gypsy is me'. And there was a whole page entitled 'My Gypsy Tattoos', which displayed photographs of Sandra's bare legs and feet ornamented with the Romani flag and other insignia. Apparently she was totally unaware of the Romani taboo on exposing the lower body.

These three women – Agnieszka, Kerstin and Sandra – have embraced the Gypsy brand of individuality and rebellion as an escape from situations of emotional despair where they felt desolate, abandoned and excluded. They put their feelings, fears and passions through a kind of intellectual recycling process that enabled them to develop a symbiosis of their life experiences and the ideals and principles of the Romani political movement. They have rationalized their emotional anxieties by attributing them to a Romani ancestry, whether real or imagined, and declaring the destiny of the Romani people to be their own.

These are, of course, marginal players within the broader scene of Roms who are actively engaged in promoting Romani participation in public, political and intellectual discourse. But they are illustrative of the complex relations between Romani society and the outside world that surrounds it. Romani culture continues to be seen, even and especially by those outsiders who embrace it, as an escape route from daily routines and sometimes even from reality. A kind of virgin no-man's land exists between traditional Romani communities and their codes of behaviour and values, and mainstream society and its institutions and public discourses. This unexplored territory attracts Roms who seek to build bridges between their own society and the world around them. It also attracts individuals who seek an outlet for their hidden passions.

For Romani political activists, this means that there is a continuous need to establish credibility and to flag authenticity. In the absence of any clear mechanism, in most places, through which Romani representatives can be elected by Romani constituents to speak on their behalf, activists need to convince officials that they have the trust of their people and the authority to put forward proposals for measures and policies that affect the Roms. This often entails challenging the legitimacy of others who come forward as experts on Romani affairs. The Gypsy Lore Society has found itself caught in debates about what is and what is not legitimate behaviour in regard to Romani culture. The society, founded in Britain as a scholarly circle in 1888, does not pretend to represent the Roms or even to advise officials in political matters. Instead, its focus remains academic. It organizes annual meetings of scholars who lecture on a range of topics, from history to ethno-musicology, and it supports an academic journal – *Romani Studies* – that offers a forum for scholarly discussions of Romani society and culture, as well as Romani history and politics.

In 2012 the society held its annual conference in Istanbul. Its hosts were the local municipality and the Turkish government. The programme included a number of talks by Romani teachers and young Romani scholars. Turkish officials and Romani political figures made opening speeches and a large crowd from the local Romani community joined an open-air concert that accompanied the conference, cheering the video clip of the Turkish prime minister saying to a Romani audience: 'You are our brothers and sisters.' It was a model of partnership, celebrated by an enthusiastic group of international participants.

Yet behind the scenes, tensions emerged. A young group of human rights activists from the United States accused the organizing committee of giving legitimacy to the policy of local authorities, who were evicting Romani families from their ancient homes as part of a large-scale neighbourhood regeneration programme. Others demanded that the society issue a public apology for statements about 'Gypsy genes' that had appeared in its newsletter in the 1950s. A Romani activist from eastern Turkey expressed his disappointment that, while money was being spent to hold an international event, the magazine he wanted to publish, with pictures and short reports from his community, had no funding. Two or three people who attended the conference banquet complained that no Romani musicians were included in the local band hired to entertain the guests. The Romani flower sellers whom I met at the street corner close to the conference hotel told me that they were unaware of the event but were glad to hear that a group of distinguished international guests was taking an interest in their culture.

'Who speaks for the Roms?' is now the title of a number of articles, conference talks and even books. They wonder whether there is any reliable way to tell what a majority of the Romani population really wants, but, more importantly, they ask who is authorized to contribute to shaping policies designed to help the Roms out of their historical marginalization, protect their dignity and their self-confidence and ensure their children enjoy access to education and career opportunities. They also ask who is authorized to describe to others what Romani culture is and who the Roms are. Recently, the European Commission and the Council of Europe launched a European Academic Network on Romani Studies. They invited specialists in Romani history, language, culture and politics to engage in discussions with officials and policy-makers and to provide their expert opinion about what governments should do to foster Romani social inclusion. The Network elected a committee, but debates erupted when none of the nominees who had declared they were of Romani descent managed to obtain the required number of votes. Could expertise on Romani affairs be provided without the voice of the Roms? Conversely, does descent always grant a person the professional tools or even the critical perspective needed in order to understand relations between the Roms and the majority society among whom they live? The Romani political movement has set new challenges to the process of reshaping the public image of the Roms and negotiating relations between Roms and non-Roms, but tensions and mutual suspicion continue to accompany these relations.

8

Conclusion

In the introductory remarks to this book, I mentioned the magnitude of the responsibility and difficulty in writing and informing about the Romani people. While being an academic who has spent much of my career investigating the Romani language and Romani culture and history may possibly lend my narrative greater credibility, it also entails risks. Academic work is about scientific discovery and about communicating discoveries to an audience. In studying cultures, the way we communicate our observations inevitably contains an element of interpretation. Whether we want to or not, we assume the task of creating and propagating images of others. When it comes to marginalized and vulnerable communities such as the Roms, academics face special challenges. Most of the images people have of the Roms are based not on face-to-face encounters but on fiction and fantasy that have dominated the depiction of Gypsies in the arts and literatures for many centuries. As academics we are often in a position to provide more accurate information, but first inevitable preconceptions must be tackled. When telling people who the Roms are, we must often begin by telling them who they are not.

The social demarcation lines that still exist between the majority population and the Romani minority mean that, in many societies, people have few opportunities to make direct contact with the Roms. Instead, they rely on information from books and media and often from hearsay and myths. As academics and journalists who research Romani communities, or teachers and social workers who engage with them, we are often regarded as alternative sources of information. Our encounters with Roms can lead us to new insights and new conclusions. Audiences who wish to know more about the Roms often approach us and ask us to provide such information. This puts us potentially in a position to be able to help revise attitudes. But it also gives us considerable power to shape attitudes towards the Roms in a new way.

Romani representatives are often rightly concerned that this power could at times be abused, if not with malicious intent or out of ignorance, then simply because the perspective and the priorities of outsiders who work with the Roms or who study their culture are not necessarily identical to those of the Roms themselves, or to those who engage in advocacy on their behalf. This difference in perspective sometimes leads to tension and friction. Such tensions are amplified by the fact that, for historical reasons, the Roms have had limited access to education and professional careers. Romani presence in leading professions, in government, media and academia is therefore still marginal. When outsiders take the initiative to inform about the Roms, this can easily be misinterpreted as an attempt to negotiate the destiny of the Roms without consulting them.

Some people have suggested that all public dissemination of information about the Roms should be subject to censorship by Romani representatives. But there is an obvious danger that freedom of information and freedom of debate might be curtailed by considerations that might serve the short-term interests of individual persons or sectors rather than the greater good of all. Another proposed approach calls for the narratives of individuals who claim Romani descent to be ranked higher than those of outsiders who write about Romani culture. Advocates of this position claim that having a Romani perspective, however defined, makes one's narrative on Romani issues more accurate and more reliable. In my opinion, there is no proof for this assumption. Surely, researchers of Romani background may have the advantage of introspection when it comes to gaining access to cultural practices such as customs and language in their own community. But merely associating one's destiny with that of the Roms does not automatically grant one a sharper insight or an intellectual advantage when it comes to what researchers are trained to do: analyse events and practices and draw general conclusions from them.

The question seems to be not who should have the monopoly on information, but rather how information can contribute towards establishing a new kind of relationship between the Roms and the people among whom they live. Many years ago I felt very inspired when I read Tzvetan Todorov's account of the debates that surrounded the Spanish Conquest of America. Todorov described how the explorer Cristóbal Colón, more widely known as Christopher Columbus, the Spanish Conquistador Hernán Cortés, and the Bishop Bartolomé de las Casas (the 'Protector of the Indians') argued whether the native Americans had souls, whether they were to be enslaved or converted to be 'good Christians', whether they should be forced into permanent submission or even possible annihilation or whether they might become partners in a new society. Todorov's narrative revolves around the realization that there is no predetermined link between knowledge and appreciation. Information is not a guarantee for tolerance, nor is it a prerequisite for affection. The difficult relationship that has existed for centuries between majority society and the Romani people proves Todorov's point. Many are attracted to a romantic fantasy image of Gypsies without actually knowing much about the Romani people, their values and daily lives. Others throughout the ages have studied their habits and recorded them in order to subjugate them and control their destiny. The Roms have often reacted by cultivating the romantic image, however inaccurate and unrealistic, in order to sustain expressions of sympathy, while trying to maintain invisibility and avoid exposure of their internal customs and view of the world in order to try to escape subjugation. Neither strategy, understandable as it may be in the historical circumstances, has helped outsiders gain a better familiarity with their Romani neighbours.

The principal challenge that I faced when writing about the Roms was to find a way in which information can contribute to understanding and towards shaping a relationship based on respect and tolerance. The Roms are often depicted as a group that likes to isolate itself from the mainstream. While it is of course true that many Romani people are protective of their culture and values, they are also a model of cultural tolerance and flexibility. They are traditionalists who maintain ancient customs. Yet at the same time they are reformers who do not resist ideas and practices simply because they were introduced by others, but embrace them and integrate them into their lives. The fact is that we have a lot to learn from the Romani people, not least in regard to resolving conflicts and disputes: they are the only nation in Europe and western Asia that has never declared war on another nation and that has never tried to subjugate others into adopting its ways.

The problem we have in understanding the Roms is not just a problem of information and knowledge, but a fundamental issue of conceptualization. The Roms are a nation without a territory, without a state, without a written history, without a religion regulated within a social framework through formal clergy or institutions of worship. Their traditional work profile is also distinct, with a preference towards service occupations rather than agriculture and manufacturing and towards flexible self-employment rather than office work in large organizations with strict hierarchies and promotional and disciplinary procedures. For all these reasons, we have come to associate the Romani people with a caste, a lifestyle. Captivated by the differences between our own society and the Roms', we project our fantasy images onto their culture. We think of them as free, sensual and uninhibited, but at the same time as lawless, unrestrained and undisciplined.

Over the past centuries, the world has become divided into nation states where territory, institutional hierarchies, social practices and everyday customs pretend to merge into an integrated whole. In this world there seemed to be no place for a people that cultivated a sense of self-identity that was not strictly bound to these structures, norms and domains. Their skills were granted appreciation and their distinctiveness inspired our imagination, but otherwise they were regarded as inherently alien, a nuisance at best, an object to be restrained and controlled at worst.

But as travel becomes easier, as trade is globalized, fashions are shared, communications are intensified, and the exchange of values and ideas is less and less regulated, we have begun to embrace a greater degree of pluralism in our understanding of ourselves and of others. Many of us and many around us are, ever more, becoming citizens of the world. The coffee we drink and the books we read may come from opposite ends of the globe; we travel around the world for holidays and education; many leave their original homes to take up a job elsewhere; and some find partners from other backgrounds, raise children who are multilingual, and have friends and relatives of different cultures and on different continents.

In trading one space for another because it brings us comfort and prosperity and perhaps even mere excitement, in adopting the ways of others selectively without giving up our own sense of self, we, society in general, have now started to adopt practices that the Roms have been engaging in for many centuries. The Roms, for their part, are demanding access to education and institutions and are taking up a variety of professions. Their culture is becoming more and more visible to outsiders through websites, books and festivals, their language is being written down, and their leaders are being elected to public offices and speak at international forums where they interact with elected officials, ministers and civil servants. In embracing global, transnational and cosmopolitan attitudes, we are becoming in some ways more like the Roms, while the Roms are adopting some of our ways in organizing their own communities and individual careers.

I started this book by asking: 'Who are the Gypsies?' The answer is obvious to every Rom. And yet in the context of political activities and the wording of charters, manifestos and other programmatic declarations, the question of how precisely to define Romani identity assumes a new twist. Ironically, numerous European writers, artists and scholars and countless American songwriters, fashion designers and bloggers have developed and nourished an image of Gypsy culture as representing a kind of primordial society, one that predates modern ideologies of nationalism and the statutes and institutions that accompany them. In today's globalized world, places of residence, social networks, and cultural tastes and preferences are all floating dimensions that can be sampled and shaped in an almost infinite number of combinations. Not just the products we use and the information networks we tap into are global and non-territorial, but we are also increasingly subjected to transnational decision-making processes. Cosmopolitanism – the experience of being a citizen of the world – is becoming a norm rather than the exception. In this context, negotiating a modern Romani identity does not at all seem like rummaging in the primordial. It looks much more like venturing into a post-modernist future, where individuals are free to pick who they are and where they live, what fashions they follow and what blend of customs and values they decide to call their own.

Appendix:
The Mosaic of Romani Groups

A Romani person might ask another 'What Rom do you belong to?', expecting as an answer the name of a group that is well known and usually associated with certain customs and trade specializations, a particular Romani dialect, and sometimes also a specific region of origin. Most Romani populations have their own group names, though members of the group will often refer to one another as *amare roma* – 'our kind of Roms' or 'our people'.

Probably the oldest Romani settlements are found in Greece. Many of the Roms in this country have been sedentary for many centuries and only some continue to practise specific service occupations such as musical entertainment or seasonal labour. The settled Greek Roms refer to themselves as *roma* or, in some areas, as *romacil*. The latter appears to be one of the older group names and can also be found among some of the Roms of western Europe, such as the *Romnichals* of England, the *Romanichel* of France, the *Errumantchel* of the Basque Country and the *Romachel* of Finland. Many of the Greek Roms are Orthodox Christians who immigrated to the country from Turkey in the aftermath of the Greek–Turkish war in the early 1920s. Their ancestors migrated from Romania and Bulgaria during the Ottoman period and usually belong to one of the *Vlax* Romani nations.

Throughout the southern Balkans, including the northern regions of Greece, we find Romani populations known as *Yerli*, *Erli* or *Arli*. The term means 'local' or 'settled' in Turkish. It indicates that these groups had been granted settlement rights within the towns or in their immediate vicinity and had become sedentary already during the

Ottoman period, from the fifteenth century onwards and perhaps even earlier, under Byzantine rule. They engage in a range of trades, from shopkeeping to seasonal work, and they speak closely related dialects of the Romani language. Other Romani groups of the southern Balkans were nomadic until the first part of the twentieth century and some even later. Their group names usually derive from Turkish or from one of the Slavic languages of the region and usually reflect the group's earlier specialization in certain crafts. Among the larger Romani groups in Turkey, Bulgaria, Macedonia and Albania we find *Kalajdži* and *Kovački*, 'tinners', *Burgudži*, 'drill-makers', *Kalburdžu*, 'sieve-makers', *Muzikanti*, 'musicians' and *Sepetči* 'basket-weavers'.

A large population of Roms in Bulgaria, Serbia, Montenegro, Macedonia, Albania, Greece and Turkey originates in Romani groups that immigrated from the Wallachian regions north of the Danube during the eighteenth and nineteenth centuries. Reminiscent of their areas of origin in Wallachia is the cover name *Vlaho* or *Laho*, which many retain alongside more specific group appellations such as *Mečkari*, *Rešitari*, *Čergari*, *Džambazi*, *Košničari* and others. They speak a cluster of Romani dialects that contain many words from Romanian. These groups are sometimes referred to by scholars as the early *Vlax* migrants and their dialect is usually labelled southern *Vlax* Romani.

In the southern Balkans, Muslim Roms who live among Turkish and other Muslim minorities often refer to themselves as *Koraxane* (pronounced 'koh-ra-ha-neh') or *Xoraxane* ('hoh-ra-ha-neh') meaning 'Turkish'. The term derives from the name of the medieval central Asian *Karakhanid* Turkish Empire. Those who live among the Slavic-speaking Orthodox Christians are called *Das* or *Dasikane Rom*. The word *das* is an Indic word for 'slave'. The association with the Slavs is based on a word play inspired in all likelihood by the similarity between the Greek words *slavi* 'Slavs' and *sklavi* 'slaves'. Some Roms who gained a privileged position and received protection from the local sedentary population were seen as tightly affiliated with the majority population and earned the title *Gadžikane Rom* – literally 'non-Romani Roms'. This seems to be a very old designation and is used not just in the Balkans but also among some of the Romani groups in Germany, who refer to themselves as *Gatchkene Sinte*.

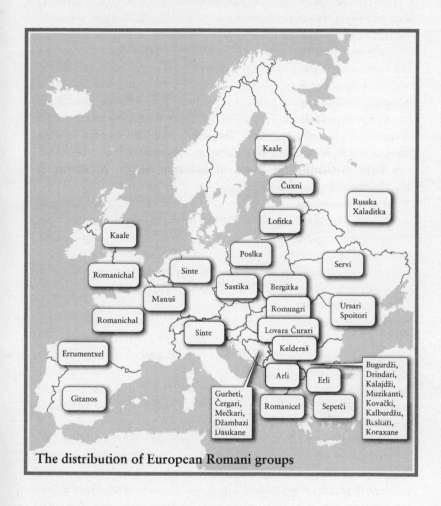

The distribution of European Romani groups

Roms have formed part of the ethnically diverse population of the southern Balkans for more than 800 years. Romani neighbourhoods are usually known in the Balkans as *mahala*, a Turkish word for 'quarter'. Different Romani groups often mix within a Romani *mahala* but related families will tend to inhabit a cluster of houses, and so the neighbourhood will typically show geographical divisions among Romani groups and family clans. One of the most populous Romani quarters in the Balkans is Šuto Orizari or Šutka, a district of Skopje in Macedonia. It is home to a diverse Romani population and has its own municipality, which for many years had a serving Romani mayor. Local radio and television stations broadcast in Romani and Romani teachers in local primary schools occasionally use Romani as an informal language of instruction.

In Romania, Romani populations tend to have occupation-based names that derive from the Romanian language, such as *Spoitori*, 'tinners, smiths', *Ursari*, 'bear-leaders', *Čurari*, 'sieve-makers', *Kelderari*, 'kettle-makers', *Korturari*, 'tent-dwellers', *Lautari*, 'musicians' and *Laješi*, 'nomads, camp-dwellers'. Some names, like *Vurdonara*, 'caravan-dwellers', are Romani-derived. The *Spoitori* live mainly in the southeastern parts of Romania, while the *Ursari* are widespread in the south but have also migrated northwards along the Black Sea coast as far as Ukraine. Both groups appear to have migrated into Romania from Bulgaria and do not form part of the *Vlax* Romani population.

The *Kelderari*, *Lovara*, *Čurari* and *Vurdonara* are *Vlax* Roms and share similar customs and dialects. They seem to have formed as groups in the Banat and Transylvanian regions of the country. Many left the area during the nineteenth century. Some moved to the southern Balkans, where they are sometimes known as the later *Vlax* migrants. Linguists call the dialects they speak northern *Vlax* Romani, with reference to their formation in the northern provinces of Romania. *Vlax* Romani communities are found all across Europe in urban centres such as Moscow, Paris, Stockholm, Berlin, Hamburg and Vienna, as well as in North and South America. The *Lovara* or 'horse-dealers' are a closely related group whose name derives from Hungarian. The largest community of *Lovara* is found in Hungary, where they live in small towns and rural communities. The *Lovara* were part of the large nineteenth-century migration of *Vlax* Romani groups from Romania and Transylvania and *Lovara* communities now exist all over central and eastern Europe.

Romani settlements in Romania are typically segregated from the villages of ethnic Romanians and Hungarians. In some districts, almost every other town and village has a Romani quarter on its outskirts. When I visited a Romani family in a small picturesque village in the Transylvanian hills, I asked the boys to show me around. We walked down the main road past a row of around a dozen houses when the boys stopped right in the middle of the village and said that we had now seen everything. I glanced down the road at the remaining two-thirds of the built-up area and gave them a puzzled look. 'Oh,' they said, 'that's where the *Gadje* live.' The other side of the village included the school and the only shop. Yet the boys did not consider those to be part of their own local community.

Romani populations from Wallachia also settled in Moldavia, Ukraine and Slovakia. In the latter two countries, *Vlax* Roms are often known as *Servi* or 'Serbians', indicating either confusion about their place of origin or quite possibly a migration route that took them first to Serbia, which still has a large *Vlax* Romani population today. A group of Muslim Roms in the Crimean Peninsula have a unique set of customs and their own Romani dialect, which is closely related to that of some of the Roms in the southern Balkans. Some Crimean Roms migrated from Ukraine into neighbouring Russia, while others migrated south during the Ottoman period into the Dobruja region in southeastern Romania.

In the heart of Europe we find a territory in which Roms have been living in permanent settlements for many centuries. This region corresponds roughly to the historical Habsburg Monarchy or Austro-Hungarian Empire and it includes parts of Croatia, Hungary, Slovakia, Ukraine and Austria. The sedentary Roms in these regions usually live in small settlements on the outskirts of towns and villages. In the past they specialized in seasonal labour and in providing other services to the farmers. Some Roms are performers and others are waste-collectors and traders. Their dialects form a continuum that is known in Romani linguistics as the group of 'Central dialects'. Some of the Romani clans in this region, but not all, view themselves as belonging to the *Romungri* or 'Hungarian Roms'. In Hungary itself, many *Romungri* have abandoned their language and they now usually refer to themselves in Hungarian as *Cigány* or 'Gypsies'. *Vlax* Romani groups such as the *Lovara* have been providing itinerant services to farmers and towndwellers in the same areas, trading livestock, tools and utensils.

In Poland there is a division between the *Bergitka Roma* or 'Mountain Roms' of the southern highlands, whose customs and dialects are very similar to those of the Roms in neighbouring eastern Slovakia, and the Roms of central Poland, who call themselves *Polska Roma* or 'Polish Roms'. The Polish Roms used to travel but became sedentary as a result of government pressure during the 1950s and 60s. Many maintain close ties with the Romani communities of Lithuania, Belarus and Russia, with whom they share many customs and among whom they often have family relations. The *Sasitka Roma* of Poland, literally the 'German Roms', are named after the *Saxons* of central-eastern Germany and contemporary western Poland, among whom they have lived for many generations.

In the Baltic lands, three of the major Romani communities are the *Loftika Rom* or 'Lithuanian Roms', the *Čuxny* of Latvia and Estonia and the *Xaladitka* (pronounced 'ha-la-dit-ka'), also referred to as *Russka Roma* or 'Russian Roms'. There are indications that some of the clans of the *Russka Roma* had served as bodyguards and militias for Russian noblemen and landowners in the eighteenth century, hence their group name *Xaladitka*, which means 'uniformed'. Russian Roms spread throughout the Russian Empire during the nineteenth century. Many were nomadic until the beginning of the twentieth century, selling horses and livestock as well as household goods at markets. Following the communist revolution many were persuaded or forced to settle, some in collective farms created specifically for Roms. During a brief period in the late 1920s the Russian Roms were recognized as an ethnic minority. The Soviet government established Romani schools and hundreds of books were printed in the Russian Romani dialect. Although this modest form of cultural autonomy was abolished by the mid-1930s, education levels among the Russian Roms remain among the highest of all Romani populations and Russian Roms have had access to a variety of professions in urban centres.

The Romani population of Germany and neighbouring regions in the Netherlands, Belgium, Austria, northeast France and northern Italy stands out in several ways. It has its own dialect of Romani, which is strongly influenced by German, and a very strict moral code. German Roms usually refer to themselves as *Sinte* rather than *Rom* but they continue to call their language *Romnes*. Many popular depictions draw a connection between the name *Sinte* and *Sindh*, the former Indian province now in southeastern Pakistan. But this connection is purely impressionistic and is based on nothing but a coincidental sound similarity. Documents from the eighteenth and early nineteenth centuries mention two group names that were used as self-appellations by the Romani population of Germany. The first is *Kaale* meaning 'black' or 'dark-skinned', which is also a common self-appellation among Romani groups in Spain, Wales and Finland. The second is *Manuš* meaning 'people'. The term *Manouche* is still used by closely related Romani clans in northeast France. It is also used by the *Jenisch* community of Travellers in Germany to refer to Gypsies – *Manisch*.

The feminine singular form of *Sinte* is *Sinta* or *Sintitsa* – typical of European loanword formations and quite distinct from the way Indic words inflect in the language. The word therefore appears to be a rather late acquisition, not one inherited from Indian times. It is only attested as the self-appellation of German Romani clans in written descriptions from the nineteenth century onwards. The earliest mention of the term is in late eighteenth-century documents that describe police interrogations of members of travelling gangs of outlaws, referred to in the German sources as *Jauner* ('tricksters'). The *Jauner* had a secret jargon that they used to conceal messages from outsiders and law-enforcement officers in particular. They also had secret names for other populations. They called the Jews *Kaimer* and they called the Gypsies *Sinte*. It appears that this nickname coined by non-Gypsies was adopted sometime in the early nineteenth century as a self-appellation by some Romani clans, perhaps in much the same way as some African-Americans use the term 'nigger' with a humorous rather than derogatory meaning when talking among themselves. The fact that the *Sinte* continue to call their language *Romnes* and use the terms *rom* and *romni* for 'husband' and 'wife' just like all other Roms confirms that they are historically part of the very same Romani population and that their feeling of distinctness and the label that they now use for themselves emerged only in the not too distant past.

The *Sinte* were a travelling community, though most of their clans have had connections with a fixed settlement area for many generations. Until the Second World War they lived largely in caravans and travelled for work within their immediate region as well as to more remote areas on a seasonal basis. Most *Sinte* now live permanently in apartments, often in council-provided housing on the fringe of urban settlements. But seasonal travelling is still very common among them. The *Sinte* are extremely protective of their cultural customs and especially their language. Traditional *Sinte* are usually very reluctant to share information about their language and culture with outsiders and they stand out among modern Romani communities in resisting the introduction of books or websites in their language. However, *Sinte* belonging to evangelical missionary movements have been engaged in translating the Gospels and producing religious literature for children in a written form of their language, and young *Sinte* engage quite passionately in their own online chat rooms where they often use an improvised written version of *Sinte* Romani.

Italy has a diverse Romani population, reflecting its geographical position and shape. The Romani clans of Veneto, South Tirol, Lombardia and Piemonte in the north are *Sinte* and many have close connections to the *Sinte* of Germany and Austria. The Roms in Molise, Abruzzo and Calabria in the south appear to be of Balkan origin and have historical connections to the various Romani populations of Serbia, Croatia and Albania. They arrived as part of a multi-ethnic immigration that brought Croatian, Albanian and Greek settlers from the Balkans into southern Italy in the seventeenth century. They maintain their Romani dialects, which show close connections with those of the Balkans, but also a strong influence from the local Italian speech forms. Until recently, the Roms of Molise and Abruzzo were semi-nomadic, based in villages and making a living by selling horses, mules and other livestock to peasants. Over the past few generations their families settled in the local towns where they tend to occupy specific blocks of flats or conjoined houses known as Gypsy quarters. Many Italian Roms are immigrants who arrived in recent decades from Slovenia, Croatia, Montenegro and Serbia. They usually settled in segregated encampments on the outskirts of major Italian cities, which are known publicly as nomad camps.

The Gypsies of Spain and Portugal are known as *Gitanos/Ciganos*, the former deriving from the term *Egiptanos* 'Egyptians'. The *Gitanos* no longer speak Romani, but documents indicate that the language was still used in Spain and Catalonia until the early eighteenth century. Their internal name for themselves is *Caló* or *Calé*, which derives from Romani and means 'black' or 'dark-skinned'. This term is also used to designate a Romani-derived vocabulary that is still used by many *Gitanos* and *Ciganos* when speaking their own dialects of Spanish, Portuguese and Catalan. Spain has one of the largest Romani populations in Europe. A large community lives in Andalusia and is often associated with Flamenco dancing and singing. The *Gitanos* of Andalusia usually live in semi-permanent quarters on the fringes of villages and towns and in segregated areas in the larger cities. Many specialize in trading at market stalls but have little or no recent tradition of travelling in caravans.

In England and Wales, Romani Gypsies use this term when referring to themselves in everyday conversations, while reserving the word *Roma* for recent Romani immigrants from continental Europe. Some English Gypsies used the self-appellation *Romnichals*, which is now more widespread among those who emigrated to the United States, while Welsh Gypsies called themselves *Kaale*. Travelling remains one of the most distinctive features of the Romani community in Britain and annual gatherings at horse fairs in various locations around the country are one of their most important traditions. The Romani language was spoken in Britain until the mid-nineteenth century but English has since taken its place, though Romani Gypsies still maintain a vocabulary of typically several hundred words of Romani origin that they use in conversations among themselves.

Romani clans moved into Scandinavia as early as the fifteenth century and there is evidence to suggest that it was from Norway and Denmark that the Roms first travelled to Britain. Linguistic evidence suggests that the Romani clans that arrived in Scandinavia were related to those that settled in Germany and came from northern Germany, speaking, at first, Low German, the language of commerce used in the towns of the Hanseatic League around the Baltic Sea, alongside their native Romani. Very few traces are left of a Romani population in Denmark, which appears to have assimilated completely by the second half of the twentieth century. In Sweden and Norway, the Roms seem to have integrated and partly assimilated into indigenous travelling populations. Their language was lost, as in Britain, and is kept only in the form of a Romani-derived vocabulary that is used occasionally in conversation within the family. Romani families from Transylvania immigrated into Sweden and Norway in the nineteenth and early twentieth centuries, often via Russia and Poland. Finland has a small Romani community numbering several thousand people. They refer to themselves as *Kaale* or *Romachel*, two terms also found in various other Romani communities in western Europe. They speak a distinct dialect of Romani, strongly influenced by Swedish and Finnish. Much like the *Sinte* and *Polska Roma*, they are very strict in preserving traditional norms and gender and age roles within the family. The Finnish Roms travelled until just one or two generations ago, and although they now have permanent dwellings, seasonal travelling in caravans is still widespread.

Additional References on
Romani Language

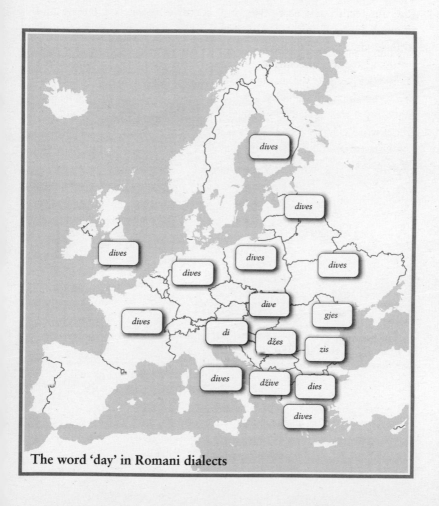

The word 'day' in Romani dialects

jov 'he'
šun- 'hear'
sastipen 'health'
maro 'bread'
gi 'heart'
xačar- 'burn'

ov, vov 'he'
ašun- 'hear'
sastipe 'health'
manro, marno 'bread'
ilo 'heart'
phabar- 'burn'

The Great Divide between northern and southern dialects of Romani

Select Bibliography

HISTORY

Achim, Viorel. 2004. *The Roma in Romanian History*. Budapest: Central European University Press.

Barany, Zoltan. 2002. *The East European Gypsies. Regime Change, Marginality and Ethnopolitics*. Cambridge: Cambridge University Press.

Costi, Natassa. 2010. 'The spectre that haunts Italy: The systematic criminalisation of the Roma and the fears of the *Heartland*'. *Romani Studies* 20:2, 105–36.

Crowe, David. 1995. *A History of the Gypsies of Eastern Europe and Russia*. London/New York: I. B. Tauris.

Ficowski, Jerzy. 1991. *The Gypsies in Poland. History and Customs*. Warsaw: Interpress.

Filhol, Emmanuel and Hubert, Marie-Christine. 2009. *Les Tsiganes en France. Un sort à part (1939–1946)*. Paris: Éditions Perrin.

Fraser, Angus. 1992. *The Gypsies*. Oxford: Blackwell.

Fricke, Thomas. 1996. *Zigeuner im Zeitalter des Absolutismus*. Pfaffenweiler: Centaurus.

Ginio, Eyal. 2004. 'Neither Muslims nor Zimmis: The Gypsies (Roma) in the Ottoman State'. *Romani Studies* 14:2, 117–44.

Lucassen, Leo. 1996. *Zigeuner. Die Geschichte eines polizeilichen Ordnungsbegriffes in Deutschland 1700–1945*. Cologne: Böhlau.

Margalit, Gilad. 2000. 'The uniqueness of the Nazi persecution of the Gypsies'. *Romani Studies* 10:2, 185–210.

———. 2002. *Germany and its Gypsies. A Post-Auschwitz Ordeal*. Madison, WI: The University of Wisconsin Press.

Marushiakova, Elena and Popov, Vesselin. 2001. *Gypsies in the Ottoman Empire*. Hatfield: University of Hertfordshire Press.

Matras, Yaron. 2000. 'Romani migrations in the post-communist era: Their historical and political significance'. *Cambridge Review of International Affairs* 13:2, 32–50.

———. 2004. 'A conflict of paradigms. Review article of Barany, Zoltan, *The East-European Gypsies*; and Hancock, Ian, *We are the Romani people*'. *Romani Studies* 14:2, 193–209.

Montesino, Norma. 2001. 'The "Gypsy Question" and the Gypsy expert in Sweden'. *Romani Studies* 11:1, 1–23.

Mróz, Lech. 2001. *Dzieje Cyganów – Romów w Rzeczypospolitej XV–XVIII*. Warsaw: DIG.

Piasere, Leonardo. 2011. *Roms. Une histoire européenne*. Montrouge: Bayard.

Pym, Richard J. 2007. *The Gypsies of Early Modern Spain, 1425–1783*. Houndmills: Palgrave Macmillan.

Thorne, M. Benjamin. 2011. 'Assimilation, invisibility, and the eugenic turn in the "Gypsy question" in Romanian society, 1938–1942'. *Romani Studies* 21:2, 177–205.

Viaggio, Giorgio. 1997. *Storia degli Zingari in Italia*. Rome: Centro Studi Zingari.

von dem Knesebeck, Julia. 2011. *The Roma Struggle for Compensation in Post-war Germany*. Hatfield: University of Hertfordshire Press.

Zimmermann, Michael. 1996. *Rassenutopie und Genozid. Die nationalsozialistische 'Lösung der Zigeunerfrage'*. Hamburg: Christians Verlag.

———. 2001. 'The Wehrmacht and the National Socialist persecution of the Gypsies'. *Romani Studies* 11:2, 111–35.

CULTURE AND SOCIETY

Cahn, Claude. 2009. 'Romani law in the Timiş County Giambaş community'. *Romani Studies* 19:2, 87–101.

Carrizo-Reimann, Agustina. 2011. 'The forgotten children of Abraham: Iglesia Evangelica Misionera Biblica Rom of Buenos Aires'. *Romani Studies* 21:2, 161–76.

Casa-Nova, Maria José. 2007. 'Gypsies, ethnicity, and the labour market: An introduction'. *Romani Studies* 17:1, 103–23.

Engebrigtsen, Ada. 2007. *Exploring Gypsiness: Power, Exchange and Interdependence in a Transylvanian Village*. Oxford/New York: Berghahn Books.

Gay y Blasco, Paloma. 1999. *Gypsies in Madrid: Sex, Gender and the Performance of Identity*. Oxford: Berg Publishers.

Georgieva, Nadezhda. 2006. '"Bahtalo Te-avel Tumaro Ges!": Contestation and negotiation of Romani identity and nationalism through musical standardisation during the Stara Zagora Romani Festival'. *Romani Studies* 16:1, 1–30.

Gropper, Rena C. and Miller, Carol. 2001. 'Exploring new worlds in American Romani Studies: Social and cultural attitudes among the American Mačvaia'. *Romani Studies* 11:2, 81–110.

Horváth, Kata. 2005. 'Gypsy work–*gadjo* work'. *Romani Studies* 15:1, 31–49.

Jakoubek, Marek and Badilova, Lenka. 2005. 'Ritual impurity and kinship in a Gypsy *osada* in eastern Slovakia'. *Romani Studies* 15:1, 1–29.

Kowarska, Agnieszka J. 2005. *Polska Roma. Tradycja i nowoczesność*. Warsaw: DIG.

Lemon, Alaina. 2000. *Between Two Fires. Gypsy Performance and Romani Memory from Pushkin to Post-Socialism*. Durham, NC: Duke University Press.

Marushiakova, Elena and Popov, Vesselin. 2004. 'Segmentation vs. consolidation: The example of four Gypsy groups in CIS'. *Romani Studies* 14:2, 145–91.

———. 2007. 'The Gypsy Court in Eastern Europe'. *Romani Studies* 17:1, 67–101.

Matras, Yaron. 2011. 'Roma Culture: An Introduction. Fact Sheets on Roma'. Strasbourg: Council of Europe/Graz: Universität Graz. http://romafacts. uni-graz.at/index.php/culture/introduction/roma-culture-an-introduction

Nemeth, David J. 2002. *The Gypsy-American. An Ethnogeographic Study*. Lewiston, NY: Edwin Mellen.

Okely, Judith. 1983. *The Traveller-Gypsies*. Cambridge: Cambridge University Press.

Silverman, Carol. 2012. *Romani Routes. Cultural Politics and Balkan Music in Diaspora*. Oxford: Oxford University Press.

Slavkova, Magdalena. 2007. 'Evangelical Gypsies in Bulgaria: Way of life and performance of identity'. *Romani Studies* 17:2, 205–46.

Stewart, Michael. 1997. *The Time of the Gypsies*. Boulder, CO: Westview Press.

Sutherland, Anne. 1975. *Gypsies. The Hidden Americans*. Prospect Heights, IL: Waveland Press.

Szuhay, Péter and Kőszegi, Edit. 2005. 'Eternal home: A Vlach Roma funeral in Kétegyháza, Hungary'. *Romani Studies* 15:2, 91–124.

Tauber, Elisabeth. 2004. 'Sinti Estraixaria children at school, or, how to preserve "the Sinti way of thinking"'. *Romani Studies* 14:1, 1–23.

———. 2006. *Du wirst keinen Ehemann nehmen! Respekt, die Bedeutung der Toten und Fluchtheirat bei den Sinti Estraixaria*. Berlin: LIT Verlag.

Weyrauch, Walter O. (ed.). 2001. *Gypsy Law. Romani Legal Traditions and Culture*. Berkeley, CA: University of California Press.

IMAGES OF GYPSIES

Bardi, Abby. 2006. 'The Gypsy as trope in Victorian and modern British literature'. *Romani Studies* 16:1, 31–42.

Bogdal, Klaus-Michael. 2011. *Europa erfindet die Zigeuner. Eine Geschichte von Faszination und Verachtung.* Berlin: Suhrkamp Verlag.

Charnon-Deutsch, Lou. 2004. *The Spanish Gypsy. The History of a European Obsession.* University Park, PA: Pennsylvania State University Press.

Dearing, Stewart. 2010. 'Painting the other within: Gypsies according to the Bohemian artist in the nineteenth and early twentieth centuries'. *Romani Studies* 20:2, 161–201.

Douaud, Kristine. 2008. 'The tie that binds: Gypsies, John Clare and English folk culture'. *Romani Studies* 18:1, 1–38.

Glajar, Valentina and Radulescu, Domnica (eds.). 2008. *'Gypsies' in European Literature and Culture.* Houndmills: Palgrave Macmillan.

Houghton-Walker, Sarah. 2009. 'John Clare's Gypsies'. *Romani Studies* 19:2, 125–45.

Malvinni, David. 2004. *The Gypsy Caravan. From Real Roma to Imaginary Gypsies in Western Music and Film.* London: Routledge.

Matthews, Jodie. 2010. 'Back where they belong: Gypsies, kidnapping and assimilation in Victorian children's literature'. *Romani Studies* 20:2, 137–59.

Mayall, David. 2004. *Gypsy Identities 1500–2000. From Egipcyans and Moon-men to the Ethnic Romany.* London: Routledge.

Nord, Deborah Epstein. 2006. *Gypsies and the British Imagination, 1807–1930.* New York: Columbia University Press.

Saul, Nicholas and Tebbutt, Susan (eds.). 2005. *The Role of the Romanies. Images and Counter-images of 'Gypsies'/Romanies in European Cultures.* Liverpool: Liverpool University Press.

LANGUAGE

Bakker, Peter. 2002. 'An early vocabulary of British Romani (1616): A linguistic analysis'. *Romani Studies* 12:2, 75–101.

Friedman, Victor A. 1999. 'The Romani language in the Republic of Macedonia: Status, usage, and sociolinguistic perspectives'. *Acta Linguistica Hungarica* 46:3–4, 317–39.

Granqvist, Kimmo. 2006. '(Un)wanted institutionalization: The case of Finnish Romani'. *Romani Studies* 16:1, 43–62.

Halwachs, Dieter. 2012. 'Functional expansion and language change: The case of Burgenland Romani'. *Romani Studies* 22:1, 49–66.

Hancock, Ian F. 1993. 'The emergence of a union dialect of North American Vlax Romani, and its implications for an international standard'. *International Journal of the Sociology of Language* 99: 91–104.

Hübschmannová, Milena. 1979. 'Bilingualism among the Slovak Rom'. *International Journal of the Sociology of Language* 19: 33–49.

Kenrick, Donald. 1996. 'Romani literacy at the crossroads'. *International Journal of the Sociology of Language* 119: 109–23.

Kovalcsik, Katalin. 1999. 'Aspects of language ideology in a Transylvanian Vlach Gypsy community'. *Acta Linguistica Hungarica* 46:3–4, 269–88.

Matras, Yaron. 2002. *Romani: A Linguistic Introduction*. Cambridge: Cambridge University Press.

———. 2005. 'The future of Romani: Toward a policy of linguistic pluralism'. *Roma Rights Quarterly* 1:31–44.

———. 2005. 'The role of language in mystifying and demystifying Gypsy identity', in Saul, N. and Tebbutt, S. (eds.). *The Role of the Romanies*. Liverpool: University of Liverpool Press. 53–78.

———. 2010. *Romani in Britain. The Afterlife of a Language*. Edinburgh: Edinburgh University Press.

McLane, Merrill. 1977. 'The Caló of Guadix: A surviving Romany lexicon'. *Anthropological Linguistics* 19:7, 303–19.

Réger, Zita. 1999. 'Teasing in the linguistic socialization of Gypsy children in Hungary'. *Acta Linguistica Hungarica* 46:3–4, 289–315.

RomaniNet: Online animated language course for Romani (free access). www.romaninet.com

RomLex. Online Romani dictionary (free access). http://romani.uni-graz.at/romlex/

Tenser, Anton. 2012. 'A report on Romani dialects in Ukraine: Reconciling linguistic and ethnographic data'. *Romani Studies* 22:1, 35–47.

Tong, Diane. 1983. 'Language use and attitudes among the Gypsies of Thessaloniki'. *Anthropological Linguistics* 25:3, 375–85.

POLITICS

Bancroft, Angus. 2005. *Roma and Gypsy-Travellers in Europe. Modernity, Race, Space and Exclusion*. Aldershot: Ashgate.

Guy, Will (ed.). 2001. *Between Past and Future. The Roma of Central and Eastern Europe*. Hatfield: University of Hertfordshire Press.

Klímová, Ilona. 2002. 'Romani political representation in Central Europe. An historical survey'. *Romani Studies* 12:2, 103–47.

Klímová-Alexander, Ilona. 2005. *The Romani Voice in World Politics. The United Nations and Non-state Actors*. Aldershot: Ashgate.

Matras, Yaron. 2012. 'Scholarship and the politics of Romani identity: Strategic and conceptual issues'. *European Yearbook of Minority Issues*, vol. 10 / 2011.

O'Nions, Helen. 2007. *Minority Rights Protection in International Law: The Roma of Europe*. Aldershot: Ashgate.

Sigona, Nando and Trehan, Nidhi (eds.). 2009. *Romani Politics in Contemporary Europe. Poverty, Ethnic Mobilization and the Neo–liberal Order*. Houndmills: Palgrave Macmillan.

Sobotka, Eva. 2003. 'Romani migration in the 1990s: Perspectives on dynamic, interpretation and policy'. *Romani Studies* 13:2, 79–121.

Stauber, Roni and Vago, Raphael (eds.). 2007. *The Roma. A Minority in Europe. Historical, Political and Social Perspectives*. Budapest: Central European University Press.

Stewart, Michael (ed.). 2012. *The Gypsy 'Menace'. Populism and the New Anti-Gypsy Politics*. London: Hurst & Co.

van Baar, Huub. 2011. 'The European Roma. Minority representation, memory, and the limits of transnational governmentality'. PhD dissertation, University of Amsterdam.

Vermeersch, Peter. 2006. *The Romani Movement. Minority Politics and Ethnic Mobilization in Contemporary Central Europe*. Oxford: Berghahn.

Index

absolutism, European 143–8
Achim, Viorel 131
Acingani 130
adultery 80
affluence 56–7
Agoupti 130
Ahnenerbe 179
Albanians 197
Alexander I of Moldavia 137
Alexander the Good 131
Alfonso V of Aragón 136
Ali, Ramadan 171
alphabet, Romani 124, 125, 192, 210
America, North *see* United States of America
Amnesty International 57
Andalusia 141, 239
Andreas, 'Duke of Little Egypt' 135
animals 74
  sacrifice of 85
Anna Ivanovna 154
anthropometric notebooks 172
anti-Romani hatred 107, 196–7, 201–3
  political inflaming in the 1990s 197
  reasons behind 21st-century rise of 202–3
  see a persecution; racial and

ethnic discrimination
Antonescu, Ion 181
apartments 35, 41, 42
Appleby Horse Fair 10, 13, 85
Argentina 64, 98
Armenian language 111–12, 119
assimilation
  enforcement in Norway 169
  Habsburg policy of 152–3, 168
  post-war 191–2
  resistance 22
asylum seekers, Romani 5–6, 8–9, 197–9, 208–9
Athingani 18
Augsburg 134–5, 140
Aurari 132
Auschwitz-Birkenau 176, 177, 179–80, 181–2
Austen, Jane: *Emma* 164
Australia 64, 220
Austria 89, 116, 146, 147, 152, 170, 196–7
  Habsburgs *see* Habsburgs
  Jenische 36
  recognition of Romani minorities 195
Aven Amentza Foundation 210
Aylesbury 142
Äynu 103

ALLEN LANE
an imprint of
PENGUIN BOOKS

Recently Published

Dana Thomas, *Gods and Kings: The Rise and Fall of Alexander McQueen and John Galliano*

Steven Weinberg, *To Explain the World: The Discovery of Modern Science*

Jennifer Jacquet, *Is Shame Necessary?: New Uses for an Old Tool*

Eugene Rogan, *The Fall of the Ottomans: The Great War in the Middle East, 1914-1920*

Norman Doidge, *The Brain's Way of Healing: Stories of Remarkable Recoveries and Discoveries*

John Hooper, *The Italians*

Sven Beckert, *Empire of Cotton: A New History of Global Capitalism*

Mark Kishlansky, *Charles I: An Abbreviated Life*

Philip Ziegler, *George VI: The Dutiful King*

David Cannadine, *George V: The Unexpected King*

Stephen Alford, *Edward VI: The Last Boy King*

John Guy, *Henry VIII: The Quest for Fame*

Robert Tombs, *The English and their History: The First Thirteen Centuries*

Neil MacGregor, *Germany: The Memories of a Nation*

Uwe Tellkamp, *The Tower: A Novel*

Roberto Calasso, *Ardor*

Slavoj Žižek, *Trouble in Paradise: Communism After the End of History*

Francis Pryor, *Home: A Time Traveller's Tales from Britain's Prehistory*

R. F. Foster, *Vivid Faces: The Revolutionary Generation in Ireland, 1890-1923*

Andrew Roberts, *Napoleon the Great*

Shami Chakrabarti, *On Liberty*

Bessel van der Kolk, *The Body Keeps the Score: Mind, Brain and Body in the Transformation of Trauma*

Brendan Simms, *The Longest Afternoon: The 400 Men Who Decided the Battle of Waterloo*

Naomi Klein, *This Changes Everything: Capitalism vs the Climate*

Owen Jones, *The Establishment: And How They Get Away with It*

Caleb Scharf, *The Copernicus Complex: Our Cosmic Significance in a Universe of Planets and Probabilities*

Martin Wolf, *The Shifts and the Shocks: What We've Learned - and Have Still to Learn - from the Financial Crisis*

Steven Pinker, *The Sense of Style: The Thinking Person's Guide to Writing in the 21st Century*

Vincent Deary, *How We Are: Book One of the How to Live Trilogy*

Henry Kissinger, *World Order*

Alexander Watson, *Ring of Steel: Germany and Austria-Hungary at War, 1914-1918*

Richard Vinen, *National Service: Conscription in Britain, 1945-1963*

Paul Dolan, *Happiness by Design: Finding Pleasure and Purpose in Everyday Life*

Mark Greengrass, *Christendom Destroyed: Europe 1517-1650*

Hugh Thomas, *World Without End: The Global Empire of Philip II*

Richard Layard and David M. Clark, *Thrive: The Power of Evidence-Based Psychological Therapies*

Uwe Tellkamp, *The Tower: A Novel*

Zelda la Grange, *Good Morning, Mr Mandela*

Ahron Bregman, *Cursed Victory: A History of Israel and the Occupied Territories*

Tristram Hunt, *Ten Cities that Made an Empire*

Jordan Ellenberg, *How Not to Be Wrong: The Power of Mathematical Thinking*

David Marquand, *Mammon's Kingdom: An Essay on Britain, Now*

Justin Marozzi, *Baghdad: City of Peace, City of Blood*

Adam Tooze, *The Deluge: The Great War and the Remaking of Global Order 1916-1931*

John Micklethwait and Adrian Wooldridge, *The Fourth Revolution: The Global Race to Reinvent the State*

Steven D. Levitt and Stephen J. Dubner, *Think Like a Freak: How to Solve Problems, Win Fights and Be a Slightly Better Person*

Alexander Monro, *The Paper Trail: An Unexpected History of the World's Greatest Invention*

Jacob Soll, *The Reckoning: Financial Accountability and the Making and Breaking of Nations*

Gerd Gigerenzer, *Risk Savvy: How to Make Good Decisions*

James Lovelock, *A Rough Ride to the Future*

Michael Lewis, *Flash Boys*

Hans Ulrich Obrist, *Ways of Curating*

Mai Jia, *Decoded: A Novel*

Richard Mabey, *Dreams of the Good Life: The Life of Flora Thompson and the Creation of* Lark Rise to Candleford

Danny Dorling, *All That Is Solid: The Great Housing Disaster*

Leonard Susskind and Art Friedman, *Quantum Mechanics: The Theoretical Minimum*

Michio Kaku, *The Future of the Mind: The Scientific Quest to Understand, Enhance and Empower the Mind*

Nicholas Epley, *Mindwise: How we Understand what others Think, Believe, Feel and Want*

Geoff Dyer, *Contest of the Century: The New Era of Competition with China*

Yaron Matras, *I Met Lucky People: The Story of the Romani Gypsies*

Larry Siedentop, *Inventing the Individual: The Origins of Western Liberalism*

Dick Swaab, *We Are Our Brains: A Neurobiography of the Brain, from the Womb to Alzheimer's*

Max Tegmark, *Our Mathematical Universe: My Quest for the Ultimate Nature of Reality*

David Pilling, *Bending Adversity: Japan and the Art of Survival*

Hooman Majd, *The Ministry of Guidance Invites You to Not Stay: An American Family in Iran*

Roger Knight, *Britain Against Napoleon: The Organisation of Victory, 1793-1815*

Alan Greenspan, *The Map and the Territory: Risk, Human Nature and the Future of Forecasting*

Daniel Lieberman, *Story of the Human Body: Evolution, Health and Disease*

Malcolm Gladwell, *David and Goliath: Underdogs, Misfits and the Art of Battling Giants*

Paul Collier, *Exodus: Immigration and Multiculturalism in the 21st Century*

John Eliot Gardiner, *Music in the Castle of Heaven: Immigration and Multiculturalism in the 21st Century*

Catherine Merridale, *Red Fortress: The Secret Heart of Russia's History*

Ramachandra Guha, *Gandhi Before India*

Vic Gatrell, *The First Bohemians: Life and Art in London's Golden Age*

Richard Overy, *The Bombing War: Europe 1939-1945*

Charles Townshend, *The Republic: The Fight for Irish Independence, 1918-1923*

Eric Schlosser, *Command and Control*

Sudhir Venkatesh, *Floating City: Hustlers, Strivers, Dealers, Call Girls and Other Lives in Illicit New York*

Sendhil Mullainathan and Eldar Shafir, *Scarcity: Why Having Too Little Means So Much*

John Drury, *Music at Midnight: The Life and Poetry of George Herbert*

Philip Coggan, *The Last Vote: The Threats to Western Democracy*

Richard Barber, *Edward III and the Triumph of England*

Daniel M Davis, *The Compatibility Gene*

John Bradshaw, *Cat Sense: The Feline Enigma Revealed*

Roger Knight, *Britain Against Napoleon: The Organisation of Victory, 1793-1815*

Thurston Clarke, *JFK's Last Hundred Days: An Intimate Portrait of a Great President*

Jean Drèze and Amartya Sen, *An Uncertain Glory: India and its Contradictions*

Rana Mitter, *China's War with Japan, 1937-1945: The Struggle for Survival*

Tom Burns, *Our Necessary Shadow: The Nature and Meaning of Psychiatry*

Sylvain Tesson, *Consolations of the Forest: Alone in a Cabin in the Middle Taiga*

George Monbiot, *Feral: Searching for Enchantment on the Frontiers of Rewilding*

Ken Robinson and Lou Aronica, *Finding Your Element: How to Discover Your Talents and Passions and Transform Your Life*

David Stuckler and Sanjay Basu, *The Body Economic: Why Austerity Kills*

Suzanne Corkin, *Permanent Present Tense: The Man with No Memory, and What He Taught the World*

Daniel C. Dennett, *Intuition Pumps and Other Tools for Thinking*

Adrian Raine, *The Anatomy of Violence: The Biological Roots of Crime*

Eduardo Galeano, *Children of the Days: A Calendar of Human History*

Lee Smolin, *Time Reborn: From the Crisis of Physics to the Future of the Universe*

Michael Pollan, *Cooked: A Natural History of Transformation*

David Graeber, *The Democracy Project: A History, a Crisis, a Movement*